Bass Line ENCYCLOPEDIA

OVER 100 BASS LINES IN ALL STYLES

Alfred Music
P.O. Box 10003
Van Nuys, CA 91410-0003
alfred.com

Copyright © MMX by Alfred Music
All rights reserved. Produced in USA.

No part of this book shall be reproduced, arranged, adapted, recorded, publicly performed, stored in a retrieval system, or transmitted by any means without written permission from the publisher. In order to comply with copyright laws, please apply for such written permission and/or license by contacting the publisher at alfred.com/permissions.

ISBN-10: 0-7390-6985-3
ISBN-13: 978-0-7390-6985-1

Cover photos
Main bass—Schecter Diamond-P bass courtesy of Schecter Guitar Research • Secondary bass—Gibson SG bass courtesy of Gibson USA

Contents

ABOUT THE AUTHOR 4

INTRODUCTION 5

NOTATION AND THEORY REVIEW 7
- Reading Tablature (TAB) 7
- Scale Theory 8
- Chord Theory 10

CHAPTER 1: THE BLUES 13
- A Brief History of the Blues 13
- Delta Blues 14
- Shuffle Blues 15
- Chicago Blues 16
- Slow Blues 17
- Charleston Rhythm Blues 18
- Rock Blues in the Style of Jack Bruce (with Cream) 19
- Texas Blues in the Style of Tommy Shannon
  (with Stevie Ray Vaughan and Double Trouble) 20
- In the Style of Jerry Jemmott (with B.B. King) 21
- 12/8 Stop Time Blues 22

CHAPTER 2: R&B AND SOUL 23
- A Brief History of R&B and Soul 23
- In the Style of Scott Edwards (with Stevie Wonder) 24
- In the Style of James Jamerson (with The Temptations) 27
- In the Style of James Jamerson (with Junior Walker & the All-Stars) 28
- In the Style of James Jamerson (with The Supremes) 29
- In the Style of James Jamerson (with The Four Tops) 31
- In the Style of George Porter, Jr. (with The Meters) 32
- R&B Blues in the Style of Donald "Duck" Dunn (with Booker T. & the MG's) 34

CHAPTER 3: ROCK 35
- A Brief History of Rock 35
- In the Style of Roosevelt Jackson (with Bo Diddley) 36
- In the Style of Willie Dixon (with Chuck Berry) 38
- In the Style of Bill Black (with Elvis Presley) 40
- Doo-Wop 42
- In the Style of Brian Wilson (with The Beach Boys) 43
- In the Style of Jack Bruce (with Cream) 44
- In the Style of Bill Wyman (with The Rolling Stones) 46
- In the Style of Paul McCartney (with The Beatles) 48
- Another Line in the Style of Paul McCartney 50
- In the Style of John Paul Jones (with Led Zeppelin) 52
- In the Style of Noel Redding (with The Jimi Hendrix Experience) 54
- In the Style of John Entwistle (with The Who) 56
- In the Style of Roger Waters (with Pink Floyd) 58
- In the Style of Berry Oakley (with The Allman Brothers Band) 60
- In the Style of Jason Newsted (with Metallica) 62
- In the Style of Cliff Williams (with AC/DC) 64
- In the Style of Mike Dirnt (with Green Day) 67
- In the Style of Krist Novoselic (with Nirvana) 70

CHAPTER 4: FUNK 72
   A Brief History of Funk 72
   In the Style of Bernard Odum (with James Brown) 74
   In the Style of Fred Thomas (with James Brown) 76
   Fingerstyle Funk in the Style of Francis "Rocco" Prestia (with Tower of Power) 77
   Another Line in the Style of Francis "Rocco" Prestia 79
   In the Style of Paul Jackson (with The Headhunters) 80
   Introduction to Larry Graham and Slap & Pop 81
   In the Style of Larry Graham (with Sly & the Family Stone and Graham Central Station) 82
   Disco 84

CHAPTER 5: JAZZ 85
   A Brief History of Jazz 85
   Two Feel in the Style of Ray Brown (with The Oscar Peterson Trio) 86
   Jazz Blues in the Style of Sam Jones (with Cannonball Adderley) 88
   6/8 Blues in the Style of Ron Carter (with The Miles Davis Quintet) 89
   Modal Line in the Style of Paul Chambers (with Miles Davis) 90
   Another Line in the Style of Ron Carter 92
   Minor Jazz Blues 94
   Bird Blues 95
   In the Style of Ahmed Abdul-Malik (with Thelonious Monk) 96
   Ballad 98
   Jazz Waltz 100
   In the Style of Tommy Potter (with Charlie Parker and Dizzy Gillespie) 102
   In the Style of Paul Chambers (with John Coltrane) 104

CHAPTER 6: WORLD MUSIC 105
   A Brief History of World Music 105
   Bossa Nova 106
   Samba 108
   Calypso in the Style of Bob Cranshaw (with Sonny Rollins) 110
   Reggae in the Style of Aston Barrett (with Bob Marley and the Wailers) 111
   Ska in the Style of Joe Gittleman (with The Mighty Mighty Bosstones) 112
   South African/American Pop in the Style of Bakithi Kumalo (with Paul Simon) ... 113

CHAPTER 7: COUNTRY MUSIC 115
   A Brief History of Country Music 115
   Bluegrass in the Style of Amos Garren (with Bill Monroe and His Blue Grass Boys) 116
   Country Waltz 118
   In the Style of Marshall Grant (with Johnny Cash) 120
   In the Style of Herbert "Lum" York (with Hank Williams) 122
   In the Style of Leon Rausch (with Bob Wills and His Texas Playboys) 124

   Conclusion 127

About the Author

Tim Ferguson is a jazz bassist, author, and educator who has performed with many well known artists including Eddie Harris, Tony Scott, Mel Lewis, George Cables, Vanessa Rubin, and Don Friedman. He has appeared at The Village Vanguard, Birdland, Iridium, and other famous New York jazz clubs, and has also performed extensively throughout the United States and Europe. Ferguson can be heard on numerous CDs including *What's Going On?* by The Tom Dempsey/Tim Ferguson Duo, *Perspectives* by The Tom Dempsey/Tim Ferguson Quartet, *My Foolish Heart* by The Don Friedman Quartet (produced by Ferguson for Steeplechase Records), and six CDs by the critically acclaimed piano trio Stevens, Siegel & Ferguson. Ferguson has played on many jingles and in various Broadway pits, acted as musical consultant for the feature film *Ray*, and appeared as a bassist in two episodes of the television series *Spin City*.

Ferguson is the co-author of *The Total Jazz Bassist* and has taught as an adjunct instructor at New York University, The Mannes School of Music, and The State University of New York at New Paltz; he has also been on the faculty of the National Guitar Workshop since 1989. Ferguson is a graduate of the Interlochen Arts Academy and the jazz studies program of William Paterson University. He lives and works in New York City and teaches privately at his studio in Manhattan's Greenwich Village.

Contact Tim and find out more at:

www.timfergusonmusic.com

ACKNOWLEDGEMENTS

I would like to thank everyone at Workshop Arts, particularly Burgess Speed for all the patience, help, and encouragement in writing this book. Thanks to Tom Dempsey for all of his advice, fantastic musicianship, and friendship. Thanks to Michael Sweeney for his suggestions, knowledge, and insight. And a special thanks to my wife Gloria for all of her love and support throughout the years.

Introduction

WHAT IS A BASS LINE?

It would be easy to say that a bass line is the part of a song played by the bassist—but in some pieces of music, it can be a little more complex than that. When the delta blues guitarist, singer, and songwriter Robert Johnson played a song alone, he played a bass line on his guitar, in addition to playing the chords and singing or playing a melody. The same is true of the great stride piano players, whose left hands created some of the strongest bass lines ever played. The Doors, one of the great rock bands of the 1960s, didn't even have a bass player, but their songs still had bass lines (in their case, the bass lines were played on the keyboard). When we listen to Bach's *Goldberg Variations* for solo piano, or his unaccompanied cello suites, there is always a bass line—even if there's no bass player. More recently, with the advent of synthesizers, pop tunes often have a bass line which is played by the synthesizer, either eliminating the bassist (a bad thing!), or freeing the bassist to play other parts. So, when we refer to the "bass line," we're really talking about the lowest voice in the music. Of course, since this is a book for bass players, we'll be focusing on the bass lines played on the bass. But, it's important for a bassist to hear and recognize all of the bass lines in every style of music.

The bass lines in this book cover many of the great bass styles of popular music, starting with music from the early 20th century. However, since the electric bass was invented in the 1950s—and this book concentrates primarily on electric bass styles—the vast majority of the bass lines are from the 1950s to the present.

HOW TO USE THIS BOOK

This is not a standard method book for learning to play the bass (though there is a review of notation and theory starting on page 7). It is highly recommended that beginning bassists start with a good beginning bass method—like *Beginning Electric Bass* or *Beginning Bass for Adults*—and a good private teacher. Learning the technical aspects of bass playing is a necessary first step before this book can be used effectively.

For those who already have a grasp on the basics, this book is intended as a resource for learning the various bass styles that have developed over the years. It can be used in much the same way as a standard encyclopedia: both for studying and for gathering general information. You can learn to play the various lines in order to become more familiar with each style and develop a broader musical vocabulary, or you can look up a particular style in order to become familiar with that specific sound and its musical characteristics. Because today's musical environment is such that a bassist is expected to be familiar with most, if not all, styles, the hope is that this book can be a useful tool for learning a variety of musical genres.

The various bass lines are arranged according to style, and each section includes a short history of that type of music. In most cases, the lines in each section are organized from simpler to more complex, allowing the player to get comfortable with the style before attempting the more challenging lines.

LISTENING TO AND PLAYING WITH RECORDINGS

The material in this book is intended as an introduction to a variety of bass playing styles in popular music. The hope is that these sample bass lines will be useful both for familiarizing the player with different types of music and as a point of departure for a more in-depth study of some or all of the styles represented here. The best way to accomplish this "study" is through playing with a group, but many aspiring bassists either do not have that opportunity or do not feel ready to take that step. Often, for that reason, the most effective and convenient method for this in-depth study is listening to, and playing along with, recordings.

Today, the aspiring bassist has access to a wealth of music. Between CDs, other recorded media, and music available on the internet, both as MP3s and videos, the amount of material is enormous. While it is difficult for a professional musician to function in today's musical environment without the ability to read and write music, learning the styles in this book involves playing by ear as much as—or more than—reading music notation. For that reason, the student of popular music needs to develop her/his ear as finely as possible. This "ear training" can be accomplished by listening to and trying to copy the lines in recordings.

Choose a tune or piece of music and listen to it over and over. If possible, learn to sing the various parts, especially the bass part. Once the music is firmly ingrained in the musical memory, begin learning to play the bass part. Determine the key (or at least the first note), and try to find some of the notes in the line. Listen to the recording many times, with bass in hand, and play whatever notes seem to fit. Listen for the rhythms and the "groove," or "feel," of the music. Gradually, add other notes until the line begins to take shape. It's not so important that all of the notes are correct at the beginning. What is important is the process of listening and playing with the same tune repeatedly. Be patient. With time, the line will become clearer, and the correct notes will become more obvious. After following this process with many tunes, it will become easier, and the ear will become more attuned.

This repetition and targeted listening will eventually help you develop the skills necessary for playing by ear, which are also many of the same skills needed for improvisation. In addition, this will help familiarize you with a variety of tunes, thereby creating the beginning of a musical repertoire and helping you feel more confident in actual playing situations.

Notation and Theory Review

Reading Tablature (TAB)

Tablature, often referred to as TAB, is a system of notation for fretted, stringed instruments. It is a graphic illustration that depicts the string on which each note is played, together with a number, which corresponds to the fret number where the note is found.

The TAB staff used in this book consists of four lines. Each line represents a string on the bass, with the highest line being the 1st, or G, string; the 2nd highest, the 2nd, or D, string; the 3rd highest, the 3rd, or A, string; and the lowest, the 4th, or E, string. So, if for example you see a "3" on the bottom line, the note is to be played on the 3rd fret of the E string. This note corresponds to the G on the lowest line of the bass clef in standard bass notation. (See example below.)

TAB is a useful system for quickly communicating the location of notes on a fretted instrument, but it has drawbacks. If a bassist or guitarist wants to play a piece of music together with players of non-string, or even non-fretted instruments (i.e., piano, horns, vocalists, violins, etc.), TAB would be useless for the purpose of communication, since it does not show the location of notes on other instruments. So, while it is valuable for purposes of communication among guitarists and bassists, as is the case in this book, it is strongly recommended that the student also learn to read and write standard music notation in order to be a fully literate musician. Another drawback is that TAB does not indicate rhythm; you will have to refer to the standard music notation for that.

In addition, left-hand finger numbers are included under the TAB staff. (The fingers of the left hand are numbered 1–4, starting with the index finger.) So, in the example below, you would be playing the 3rd fret of the 4th string with your 3rd finger.

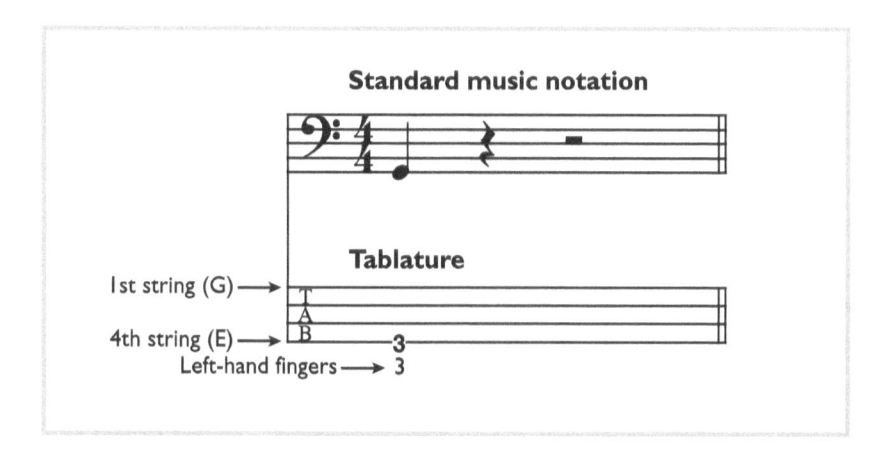

Scale Theory

A *scale* is a series of notes organized in a specific pattern of intervals, usually *whole steps* (two frets) and *half steps* (one fret). While there are many types of scales, some with more notes and some with fewer, most of the scales we use regularly in Western music have seven notes. The most important of these is the *major* scale, which can be used as a point of reference for understanding many other scales and musical concepts.

THE MAJOR SCALE

Below is a C Major scale. Look carefully at the pattern, or formula, of whole steps (W) and half steps (H). This formula (whole step–whole step–half step–whole step–whole step–whole step–half step) is the formula for every major scale. Another way to think of it is that all of the intervals between the notes are whole steps except for those between the 3rd and 4th notes and the 7th and 8th notes.

Each tone of the major scale can be referred to by its *degree*, or number, for easy reference. So, the first note is the 1, the second note is the 2, etc. Notice that the last note in the scale is an *octave* (12 half steps) above the *root*, or *tonic* (the 1). We can define a scale using scale degrees. For instance, the formula for a major scale is 1–2–3–4–5–6–7.

The C Major scale below is written using a *universal fingering*, one that can be used for every major scale. Simply start the fingering on the root of the scale, on either the E or A string (or B string for 5-string basses), and play the fingering: 24–124–134. (In other words, play the 2nd finger and then the 4th finger on the string with the root, then play the 1st finger, 2nd finger, and 4th finger on the next string, etc.). For instance, if you start on the 5th fret of the A string, you get a D Major scale, and if you start on the 3rd fret of the E string, you get a G Major scale.

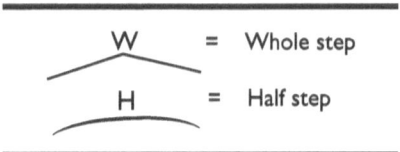

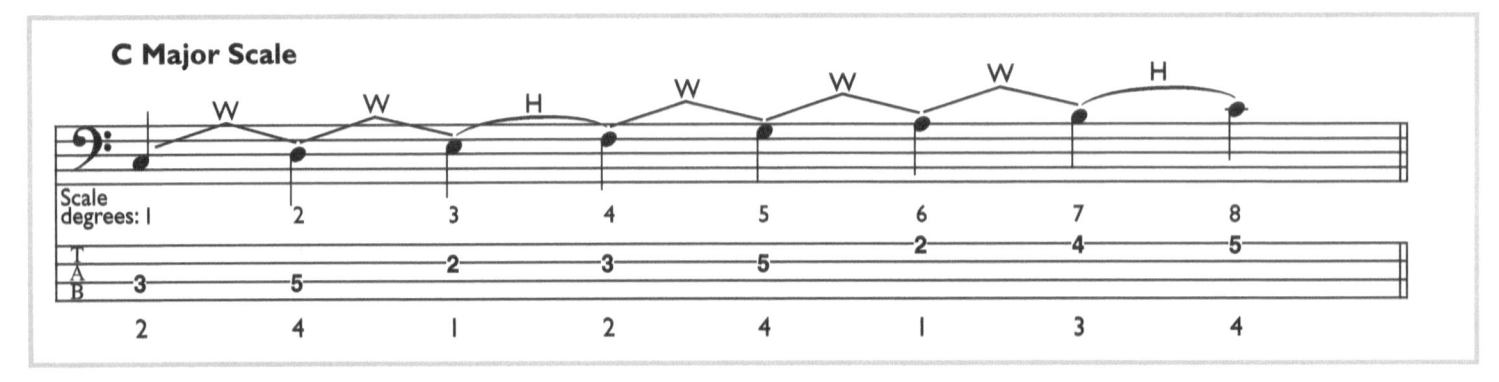

W = Whole step
H = Half step

C Major Scale

THE MINOR SCALE

Minor scales are different from major scales in one important way: they have a lowered, or flatted, 3rd degree (♭3). This creates an interval of a *minor 3rd* (three half steps) between the root and the 3, while the major scale has an interval of a *major 3rd* (four half steps, or two whole steps) between those notes. There are three types of minor scales: the *natural minor scale* (1–2–♭3–4–5–♭6–♭7), the *harmonic minor scale* (1–2–♭3–4–5–♭6–7), and the *melodic minor scale* (1–2–♭3–4–5–6–7). The one that is used most frequently in this book is the natural minor scale. Following is a C Natural Minor scale with a common fingering pattern (134–134–13). This fingering can be used for every natural minor scale in the same way that the fingering above can be used for every major scale.

C Natural Minor Scale

THE MIXOLYDIAN MODE

While this book will not go into an in-depth study of mode theory and the modes of the major scale, it is important for us to look at one mode that is used extensively in all popular music, particularly in the blues and blues-related styles. That mode is the *Mixolydian* mode and its most important characteristic, and the only thing that separates it from a major scale, is that it has a lowered, or flatted, 7th degree (♭7). This ♭7 allows the scale to fit with the dominant 7th chords that are so prevalent in the blues. The formula for the Mixolydian mode is 1–2–3–4–5–6–♭7. Below is a universal fingering for the Mixolydian mode: 24–124–124.

C Mixolydian Mode

THE BLUES SCALE

The last scale we will look at is the *blues* scale, which is extremely useful for playing the blues and blues-related styles. The blues scale is considered a minor scale because it has a ♭3. It also has a ♭5 and a ♭7. These three "flatted" notes (♭3, ♭5, and ♭7) are known as *blue notes* and create the scale's signature "bluesy" sound. The blues scale is the only scale covered here that does not have seven tones; it has six, and its formula is 1–♭3–4–♭5–5–♭7. Though this scale is a minor scale (due to its minor 3rd), it is often used over dominant 7th chords (which have major 3rds). The dissonance created by the major and minor 3rds is one of the most recognizable sounds of the blues. Once again, here is a universal fingering that will allow you to play the blues scale in every key: 14–123–13.

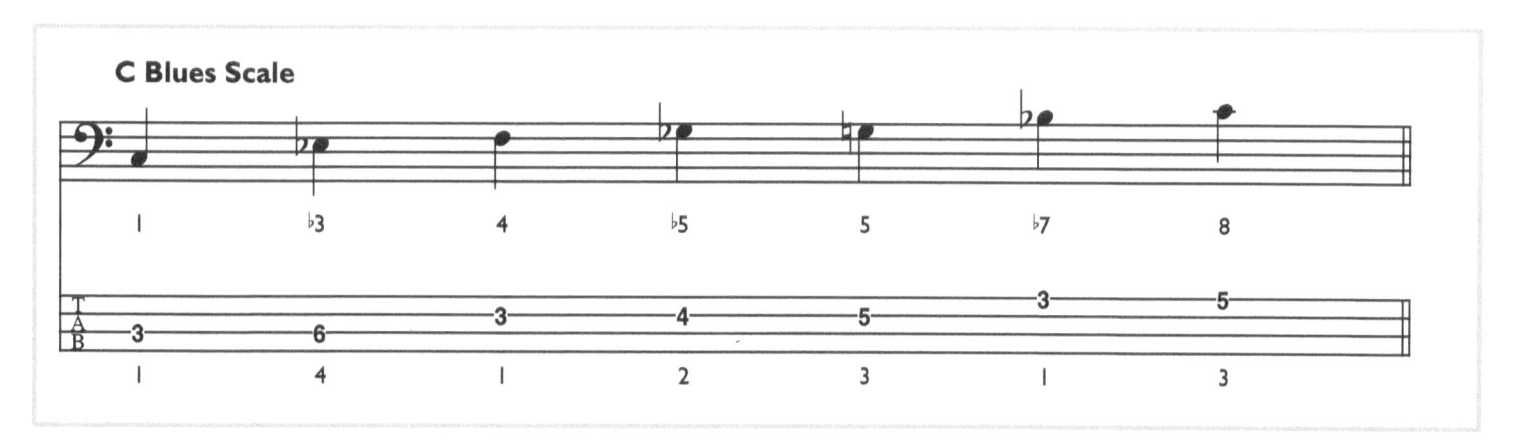

C Blues Scale

Chord Theory

To understand how bass lines are constructed, it is necessary for bassists to have at least a basic understanding of *harmonic*, or chord, theory. We'll start by looking at three of the basic building blocks of harmony: *intervals*, *triads*, and *7th chords*.

INTERVALS

In order to begin building chords, we have to start with the smallest harmonic unit: two notes. The distance between two notes is referred to as an *interval*. Intervals are the smallest of the melodic and harmonic structures used to make scales and chords. We call each interval by a name that reflects the number of notes between and including the two notes. So, if the notes are C and E, we call the interval a 3rd because there are three notes total: C, D, and E. We use the numeric names 2nds, 3rds, 4ths, 5ths, etc. when referring to intervals. However, there are two exceptions to this numeric nomenclature: we do not refer to two notes that are the same as a "1st," but as a *unison*; and we do not use the name "eighth," but instead use the term *octave* for the interval with eight notes in it.

There are five types of intervals: *major, minor, perfect, augmented,* and *diminished*. 2nds, 3rds, 6ths, and 7ths can be either major or minor; and 4ths, 5ths, octaves, and unisons are perfect.

Major, minor, and perfect intervals can be altered to become either augmented or diminished. If the top note of a major or perfect interval is raised by a half step, increasing the distance between the two notes, it becomes augmented; and if the top note of a minor or perfect interval is lowered, decreasing the distance between the two notes, it becomes diminished.

A good source of reference for intervals is the major scale. All of the intervals in the major scale are either major or perfect (unison–major 2nd–major 3rd–perfect 4th–perfect 5th–major 6th–major 7th). Increasing their size by raising the top note will make them augmented. Decreasing them by lowering the top note will make the major intervals minor, and the perfect intervals diminished.

Following are all the intervals in an octave.

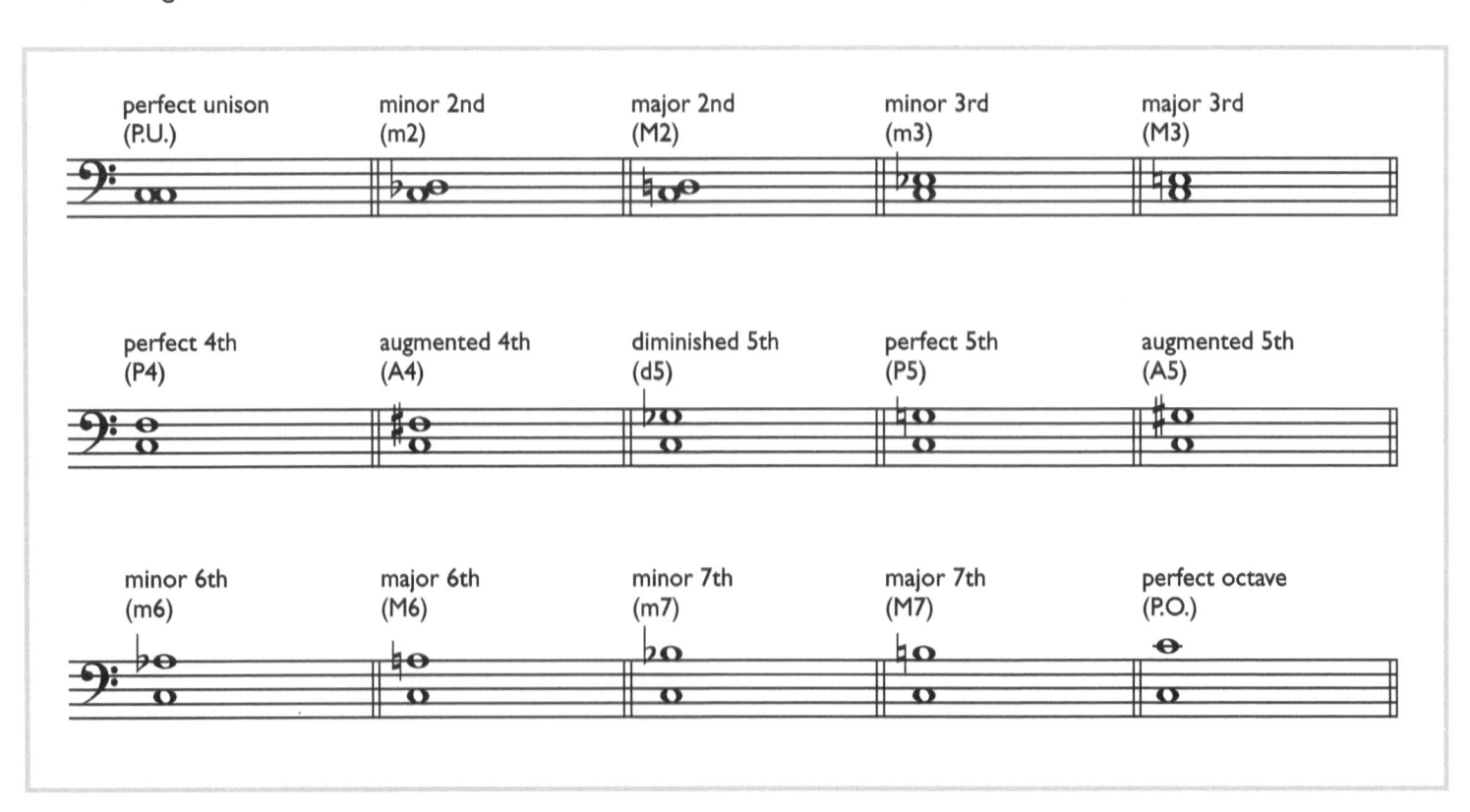

TRIADS

The next step in building harmony is the *triad*. Triads are three-note chords and are built by a process called *stacking 3rds*, which just means to stack every other note from a scale to form a chord. In other words, to form a triad, you would play the first note, skip the second, play the third, skip the fourth, and play the fifth. Depending on the type of scale (major, minor, etc.), or which scale degree we start on, we will get different triads.

There are four basic types of triads from which most chords are built: *major, minor, diminished,* and *augmented*. Each triad has a root, 3rd, and 5th. Major triads have a root, major 3rd, and perfect 5th (or 1–3–5); minor triads have a root, minor 3rd, and perfect 5th (or 1–♭3–5); diminished triads have a root, minor 3rd, and diminished 5th (or 1–♭3–♭5); and augmented triads have a root, major 3rd, and augmented 5th (or 1–3–♯5). Below are these four types of triads built on the root C. Take some time and get to know the triads well because they are the foundation on which all chords are built. Knowing how to construct, play, and recognize the sound of these four triads is a requirement for understanding and developing a good ear for harmony.

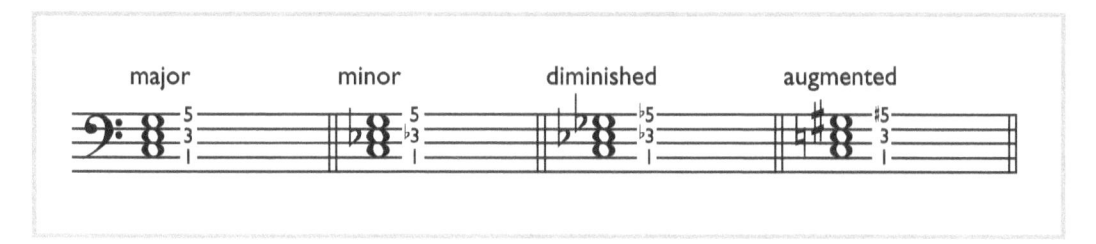

7TH CHORDS

The next step in building chords is to stack another 3rd on top of the triad. We know that triads contain a root, 3rd, and 5th, so if we skip the 6th degree and add the next note, we are adding a 7th. For that reason, these four-note chords are referred to as 7th chords. 7th chords are richer in harmonic texture than triads, and there are a few more of them to get familiar with.

Most 7th chords are built on one of the four triads we have already covered, and their names are similar. Below are some 7th chords you will encounter in the harmony throughout this book. They are *major 7th* (1–3–5–7), *minor 7th* (1–♭3–5–♭7), *diminished 7th* (1–♭3–♭5–♭♭7), *augmented 7th* (1–3–♯5–♭7), *minor 7th flat five,* or *half-diminished 7th* (1–♭3–♭5–♭7), and *dominant 7th* (1–3–5–♭7). Notice that almost all of these 7th chords have names that are related to the triad names: major, minor, diminished, and augmented. But there is one exception: the dominant 7th. The dominant 7th is a chord built on a major triad but with a minor 7th (♭7) on top. It is arguably the most important chord in Western harmony. The dominant 7th is the chord that gives the blues much of its distinct sound, and that blues sound has been incorporated into much of our popular music. Learn all of these 7th chords. Play their *arpeggios* (notes of the chords played separately) and listen to how they sound. Pay special attention to the sound of the dominant chord, as you will being seeing a lot of these throughout this book.

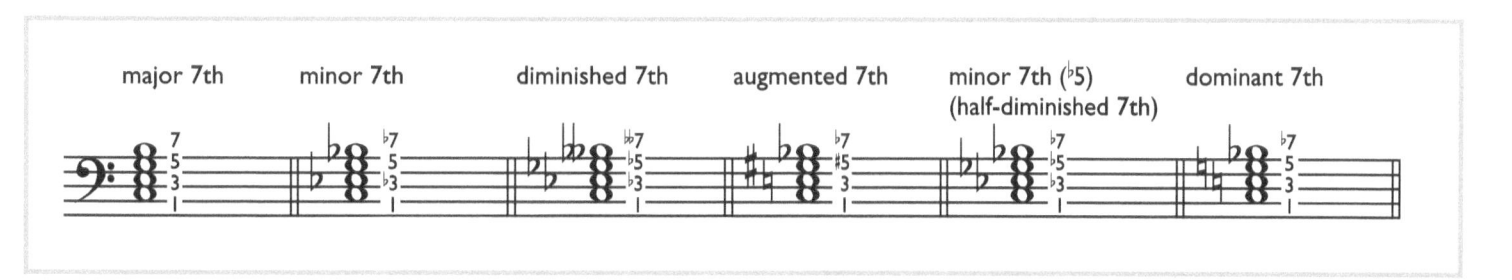

DIATONIC HARMONY

Diatonic is a word of Greek origin meaning "through a tonality" or "across a key." When we refer to a piece of music as being in a particular *key*, we are saying that all of the notes are derived from one scale. The term *harmony* refers to chords, so *diatonic harmony* means that we use only the chords that can be made from the notes of one scale. The most common form of diatonic harmony is major scale diatonic harmony, or chords derived from a major scale.

Diatonic Triads

If we take the C Major scale and build a triad in exactly the way we discussed on page 11—starting on C and using every other note in the scale—we get a triad of C, E, and G. This is a major triad and we refer to it as the *one chord* of the key because it is built on the 1st degree of the scale. If we build a triad starting on the 2nd degree of the scale (D) and using every other note, we get the triad D, F, and A. This is a minor triad and is referred to as the *two chord* because it is built on the 2nd degree of the scale, etc. We assign a Roman numeral to each chord built on a scale degree: upper case for the major triads and lower case for minor or diminished triads. So the one chord is indicated with the Roman numeral I, the two chord ii, and so on.

Below are all the triads built on the major scale. Notice the pattern: I (major)–ii (minor)–iii (minor)–IV (major)–V (major)–vi (minor)–vii (diminished). Every major scale will have the same pattern of triads. When a piece of music is composed using these chords, we call it diatonic. If a song used only the chords below, we would say it is in the key of C Major.

Roman Numeral Review	
I or i 1	V or v 5
II or ii 2	VI or vi 6
III or iii 3	VII or vii 7
IV or iv 4	

Diatonic Triads in the Key of C Major

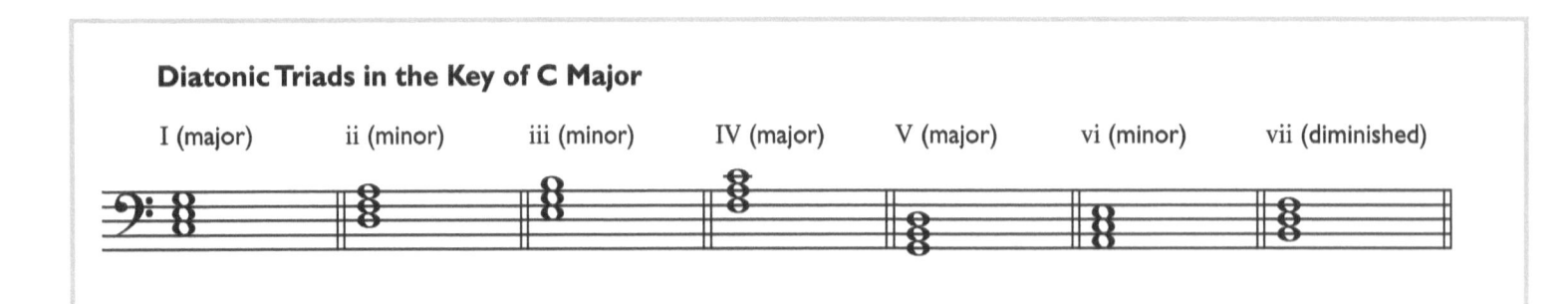

I (major) ii (minor) iii (minor) IV (major) V (major) vi (minor) vii (diminished)

Diatonic 7th Chords

As mentioned earlier, we often use 7th chords as well as triads. To figure out what 7th chords belong to a key, we can go through the same process as above, but this time adding another 3rd on top of each chord. This gives us the diatonic series of 7th chords in the following pattern: I (major 7th)–ii (minor 7th)–iii (minor 7th)–IV (major 7th)–V (dominant 7th)–vi (minor 7th)–vii (minor 7th flat five). Following are the 7th chords in the key of C Major.

Diatonic 7th Chords in the Key of C Major

I (major 7th) ii (minor 7th) iii (minor 7th) IV (major 7th) V (dominant 7th) vi (minor 7th) vii (minor 7th flat five)

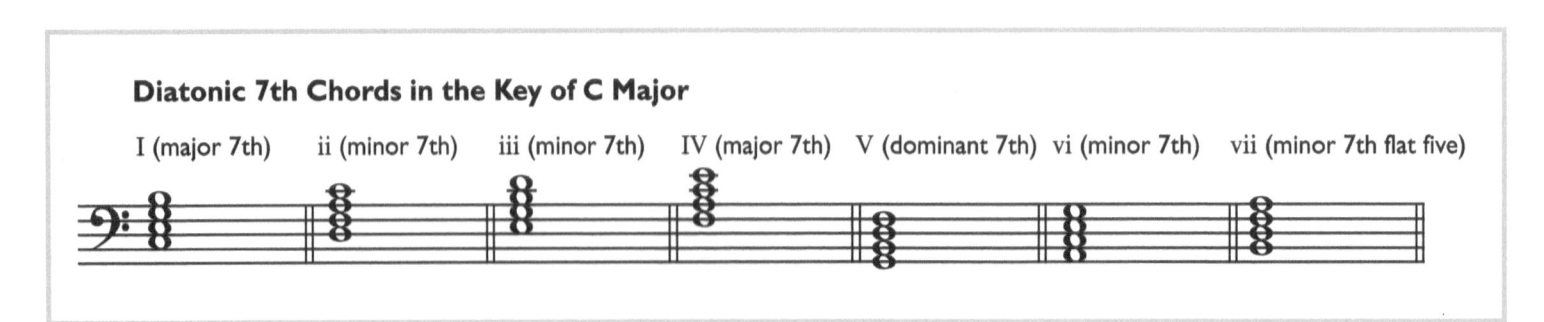

Chapter 1: The Blues

A Brief History of the Blues

Without a doubt, the single style that has had the most influence in American popular music is the blues. Most historians agree that the blues originated in the Mississippi Delta region and was the result of a combination of influences, including work songs, gospel music, African music, and European musical instruments. The blues grew out of the cultural intersection of the African slaves and the new country and culture in which they found themselves. Most early blues was played and sung by one person playing a guitar, with the possible addition of a harmonica. Musicians like Son House, Bukka White, and the great Robert Johnson are examples of early blues musicians.

Starting in the 1920s, the African-American community began to migrate north, following the employment opportunities of the Industrial Revolution. As new recording and broadcasting technologies began to emerge, the blues started to reach a wider audience. When the electric guitar rose to prominence in the 1950s, the music took on a new and exciting character, and cities like Detroit, Cleveland, Houston, and especially Memphis and Chicago became new centers of the blues. With the sound of the electric blues, a new group of bands and players emerged. The new electric blues bands featured the addition of the electric bass and often included drums and sometimes saxophones. Guitarists like Muddy Waters, Son Seals, Buddy Guy, and B. B. King became blues stars, and their music influenced countless musicians in other musical styles. The sound of the blues is present (in some form) in almost all of American music and much of the music in the world. Its influence is clearly seen in rock, jazz, soul, funk, country, and even modern American classical music.

Every good blues band is anchored by a bassist who understands the importance and function of the bass line. Blues bass playing is deceptively simple, but the art of bass playing is personified in the great blues bassists playing behind the blues stars. Many of the most famous rock bassists like John Paul Jones of Led Zeppelin, Bill Wyman of The Rolling Stones, and Jack Bruce of Cream were deeply influenced by their careful study of the great bass playing on classic blues recordings.

In recent years there has been a wave of younger blues musicians who have carried the musical torch. Musicians like Stevie Ray Vaughan, Jimmy Vaughan, Robert Cray, Keb Mo, and Shemekia Copeland (among many others) are continuing to carry the traditions of the past into the future.

To the right is a suggested listening list for all of the styles in this chapter. The bass players are indicated with an asterisk (*). In the chapters that follow, only bass players will be listed, unless otherwise noted.

Suggested Listening
- Delta, or country, blues: Robert Johnson, John Lee Hooker
- Shuffle blues: Albert Collins, Freddie King
- Chicago blues: Buddy Guy
- Slow blues: Jerry Jemmott* with B. B. King
- Charleston rhythm blues: James P. Johnson, Duke Ellington
- Rock blues: Jack Bruce* (Cream)
- Texas blues: Tommy Shannon* (Stevie Ray Vaughan and Double Trouble)
- $\frac{12}{8}$ stop-time blues: Muddy Waters

Delta Blues

Early blues players like Robert Johnson and John Lee Hooker generally played solo guitar. When their style of Delta, or country, blues is played by a band with a bass player, the bass line tends to be very simple with a strong beat. The following line is deceptively simple, but playing the right groove or feel takes real concentration. Try to give it a *backbeat*, which means to accent beats 2 and 4.

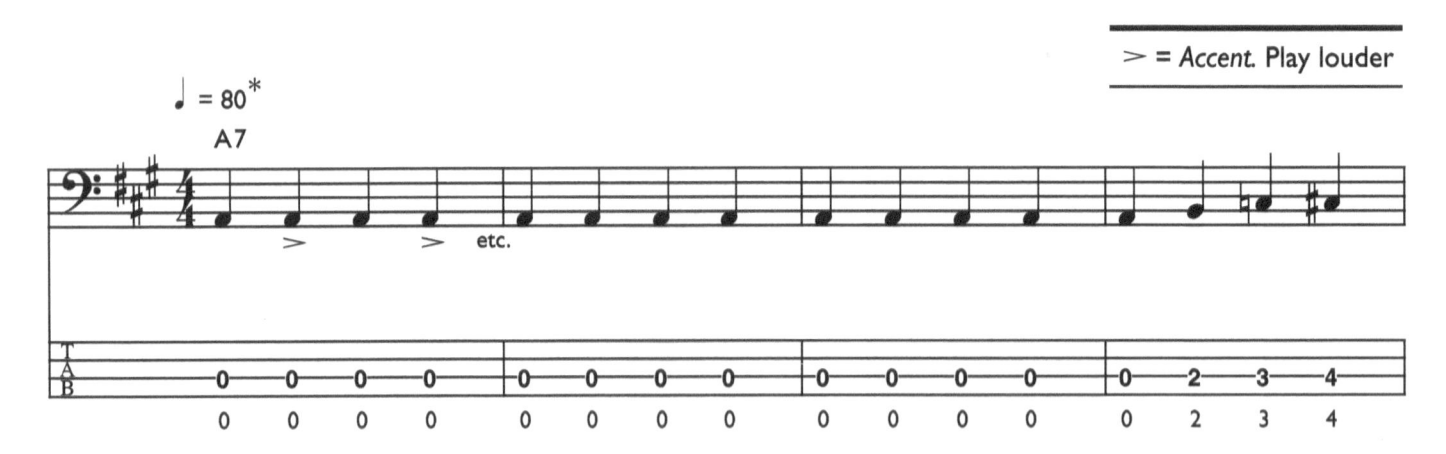

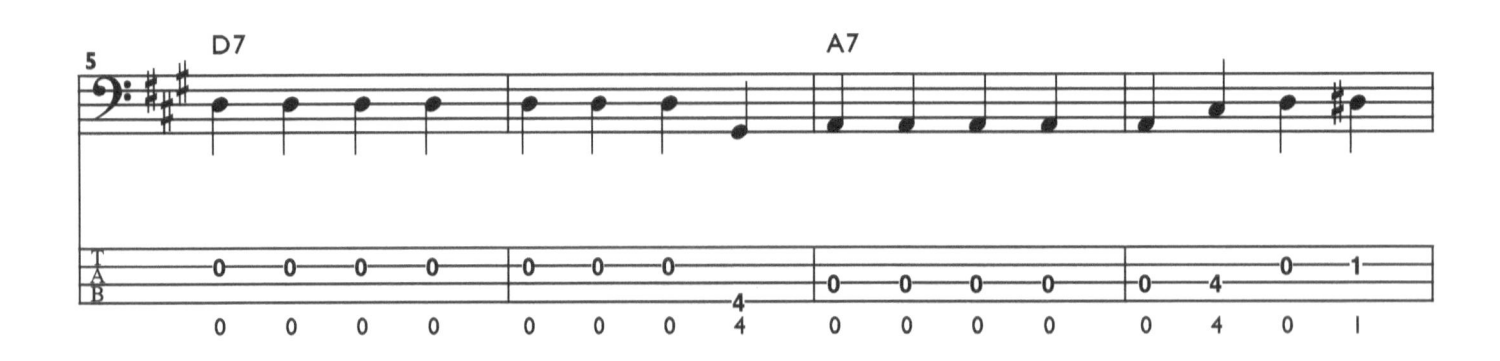

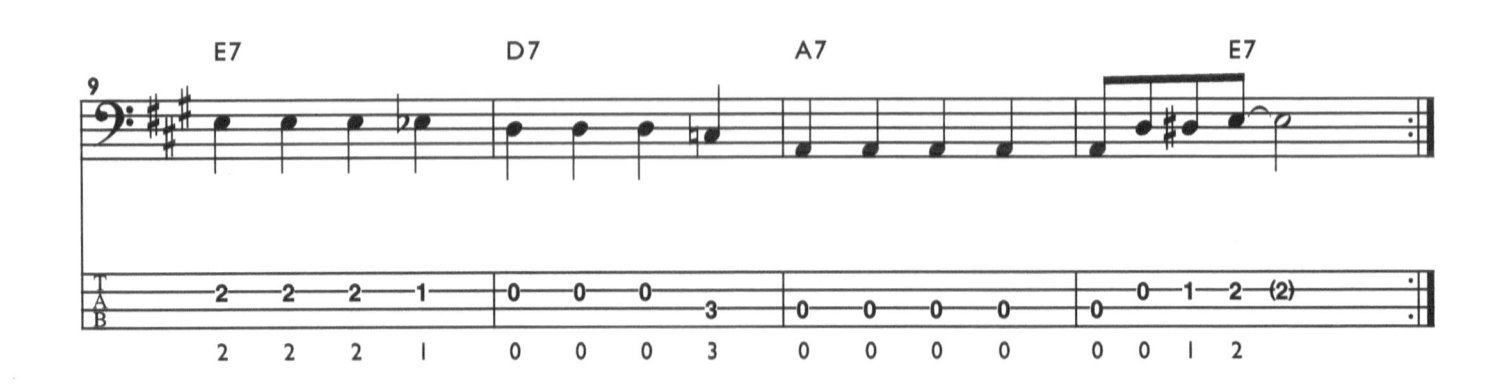

> = *Accent.* Play louder

* This is a *tempo marking* and indicates the speed at which the music should be played.
  In this case, the music should be played at a rate of 80 quarter notes per minute.

Shuffle Blues

The *shuffle* (characterized by the recurring dotted eighth/sixteenth-note pattern) is one of the most important grooves in the blues. Chicago blues giants like Buddy Guy and Freddie King are masters of this style. Don't rush the tempo, and be sure to emphasize beats 2 and 4.

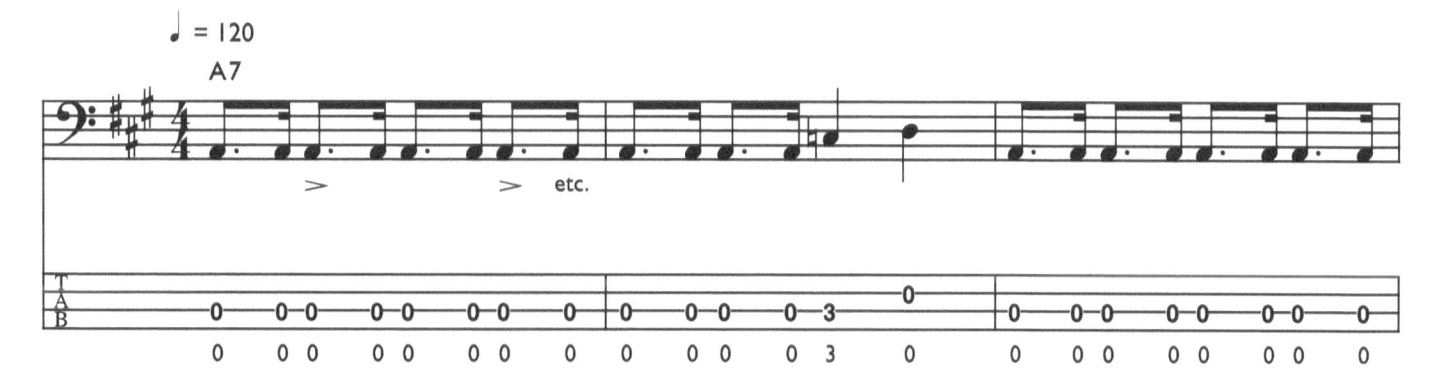

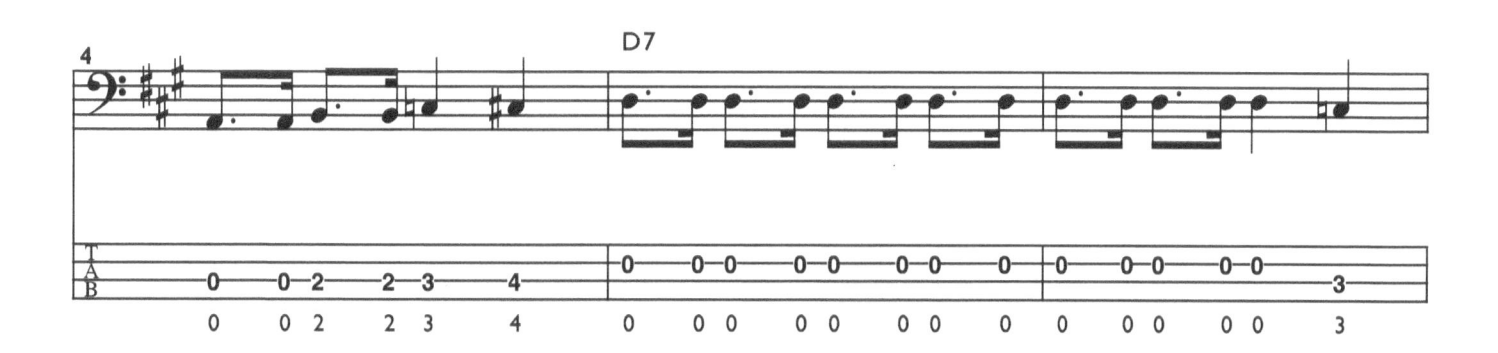

Chicago Blues

Here's a variation on the shuffle that is very common in Chicago blues. Notice the triplet figure on beat 4.

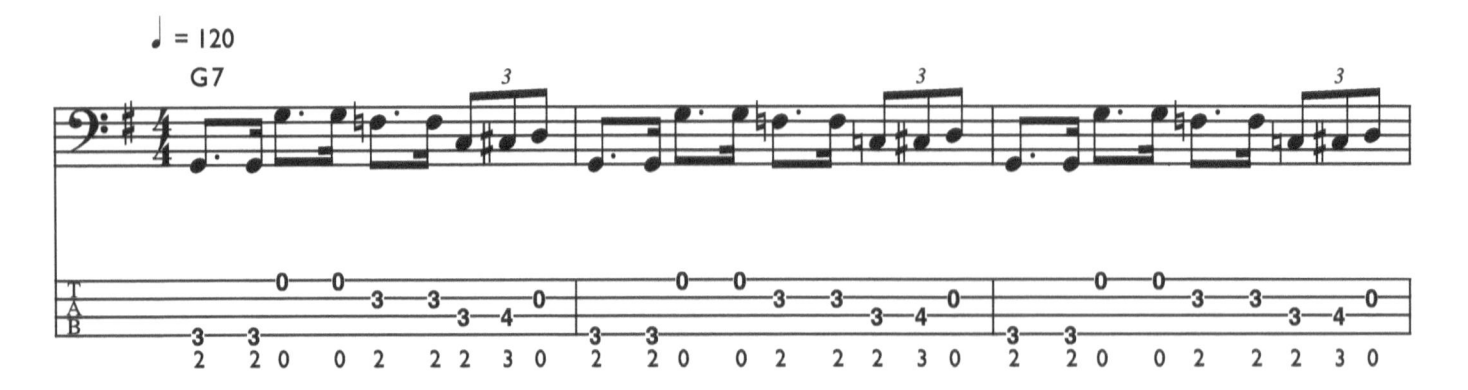

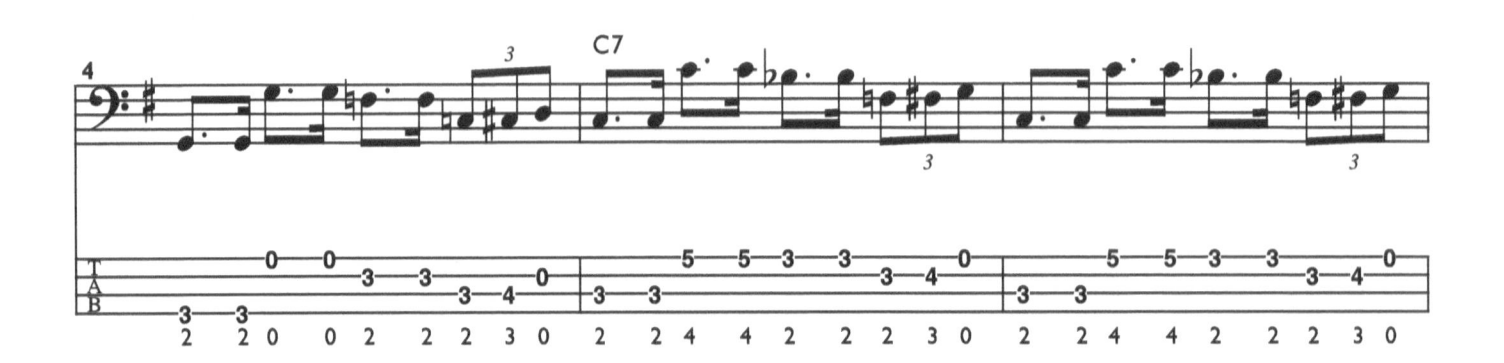

Slow Blues

This blues is similar to the preceding shuffle blues but played much slower.

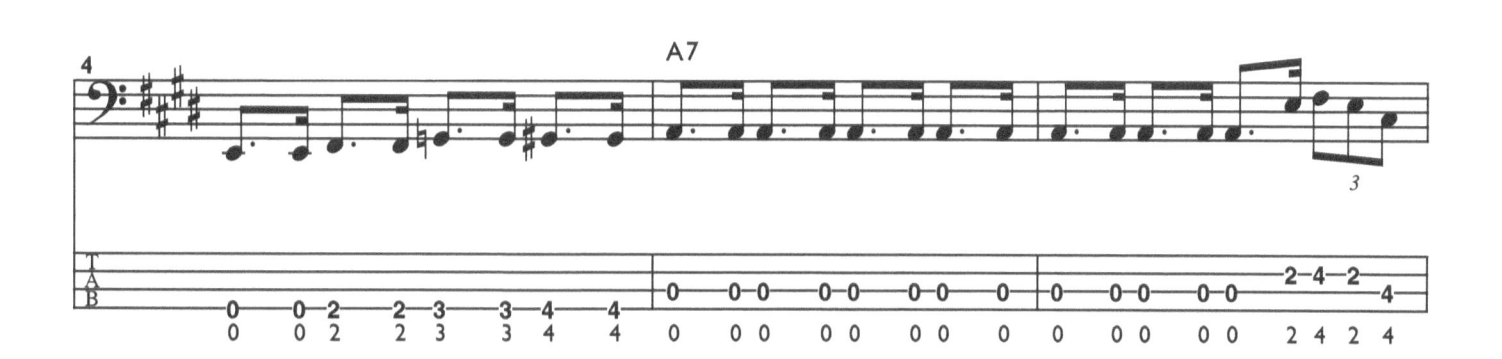

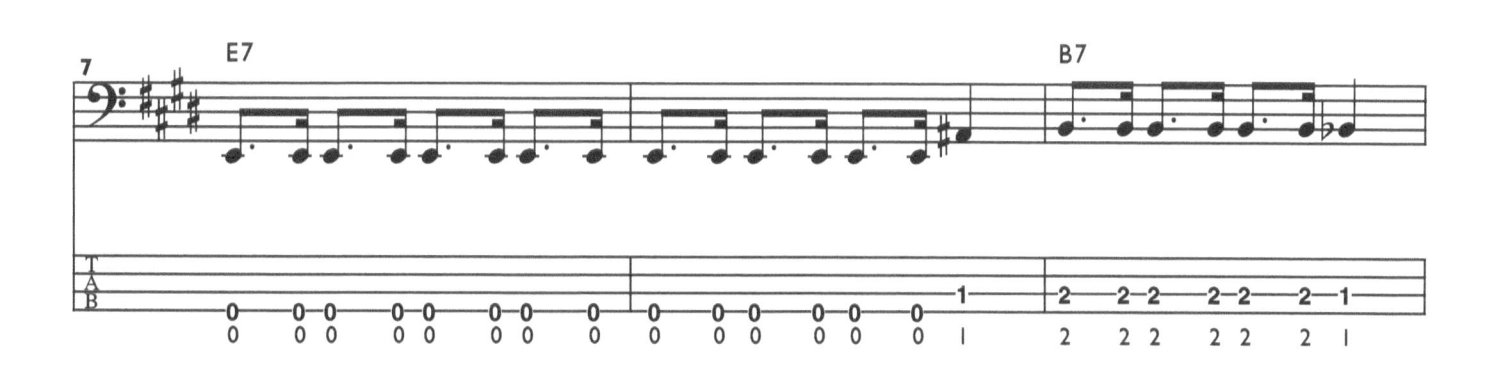

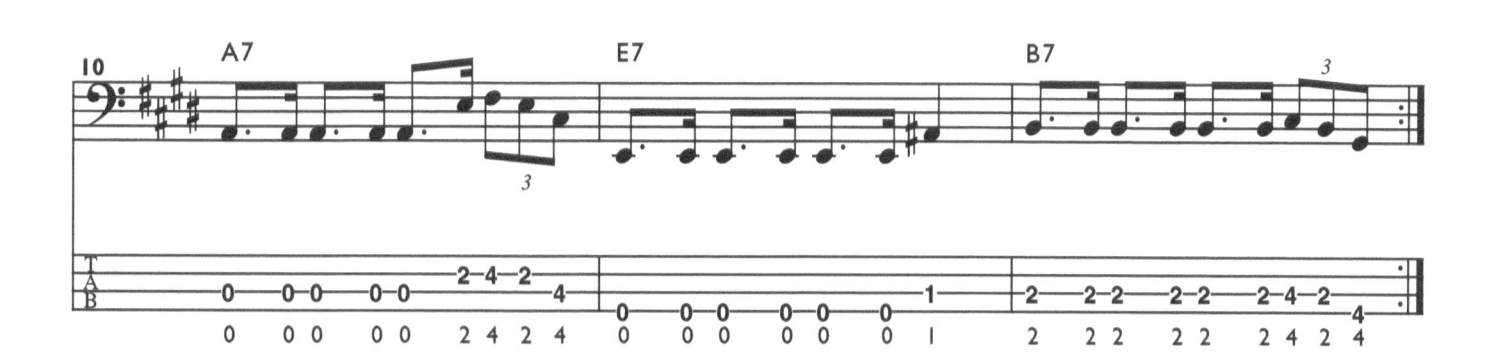

Charleston Rhythm Blues

The "Charleston" was an enormously popular tune and dance in the 1920s. Since then, its rhythmic motif has been used in many ways in popular music. The Charleston rhythm, which is another variation commonly used in blues, is the *syncopated* two-note riff (see right) repeated in the first eight bars of the following example. Syncopation occurs when emphasis is placed on weaker beats, or weaker parts of the beat.

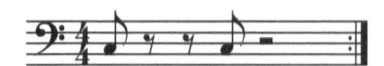

Swing 8ths *

♩ = 124

---

* *Swing 8ths* indicates that eighth notes are to be played with a *swing feel* (long-short, long-short). In other words, they should sound like triplets with the first two notes tied.

Rock Blues in the Style of Jack Bruce (with Cream)

Guitarist Eric Clapton, bassist Jack Bruce, and drummer Ginger Baker of the British band Cream were heavily influenced by early blues musicians like Robert Johnson. Cream's recordings had a lot to do with the direction the blues took after the 1960s. The following line is in the style of Jack Bruce.

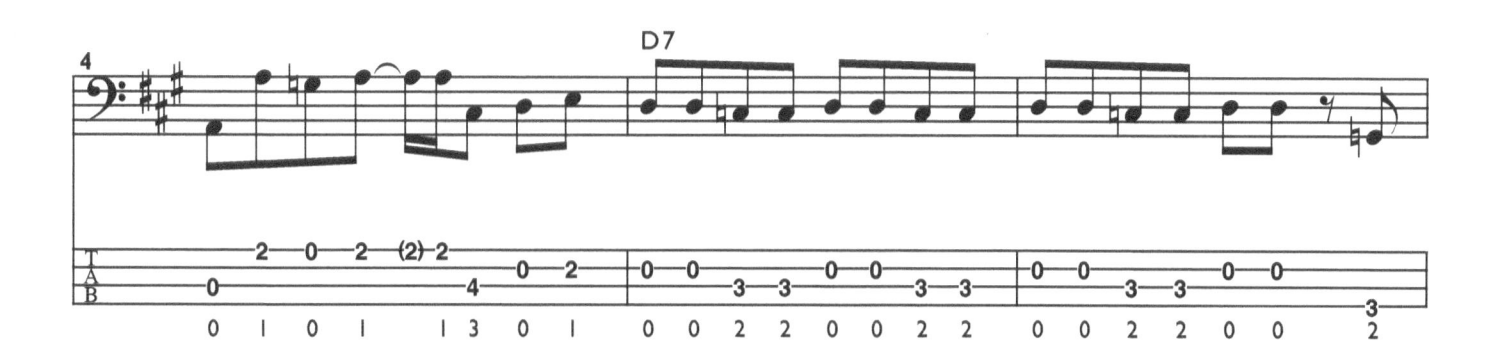

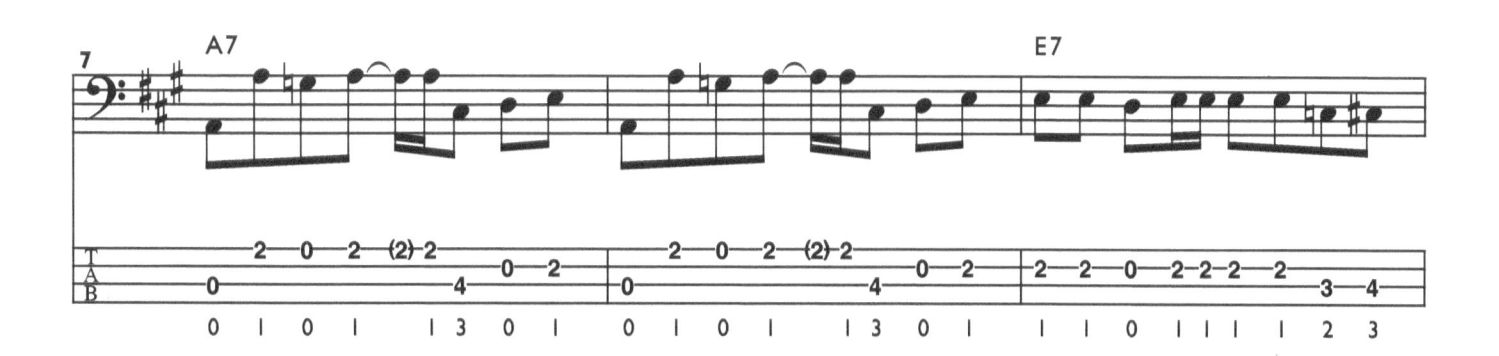

Texas Blues in the Style of Tommy Shannon (with Stevie Ray Vaughan and Double Trouble)

Below is a blues line in the style of Tommy Shannon, who played bass with the late, great Texas blues guitarist Stevie Ray Vaughan in his band Double Trouble. Texas blues is similar to Chicago blues, but the guitar sounds and arranging styles are slightly different. Listen to Stevie Ray and his brother Jimmy Vaughan, Johnny Copeland, Albert "The Ice Man" Collins, and Johnny Winter to hear a sample of what Texas blues is all about.

In the Style of Jerry Jemmott (with B. B. King)

The great blues guitarist B. B. King is in a class by himself. His singing and guitar playing has influenced countless blues musicians over his long career. Bassist and educator Jerry Jemmott played on some of King's most important recordings. Here is an example of a slow blues bass line in Jemmott's style with B. B. King.

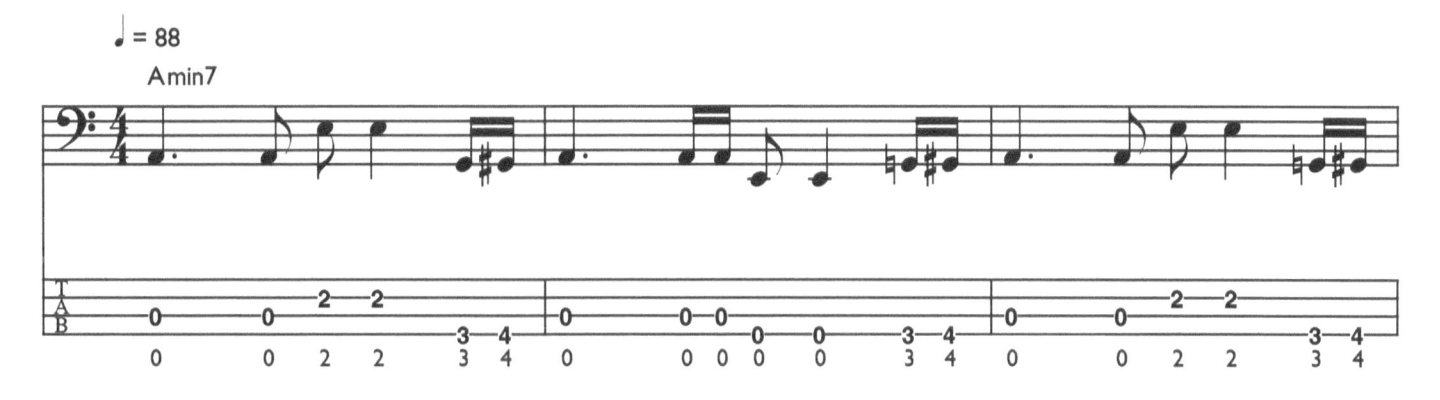

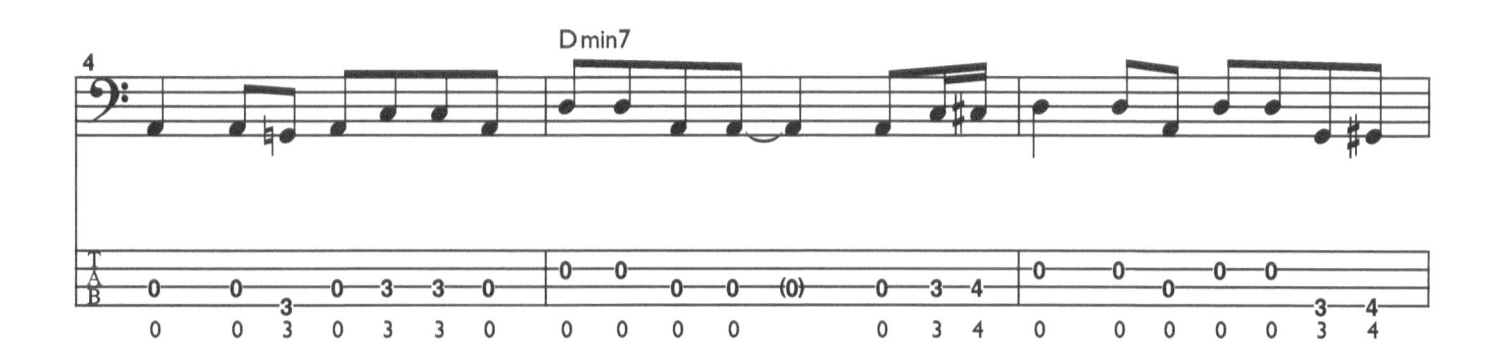

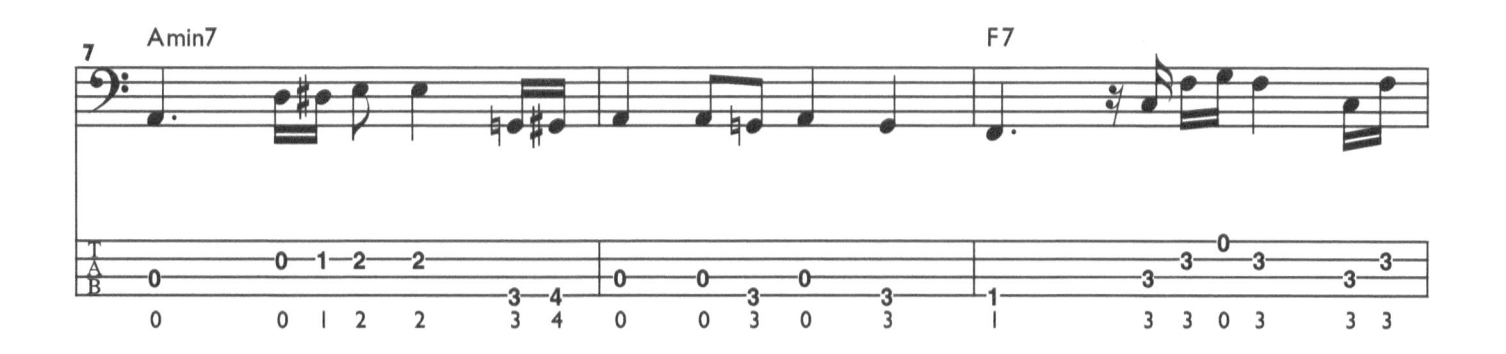

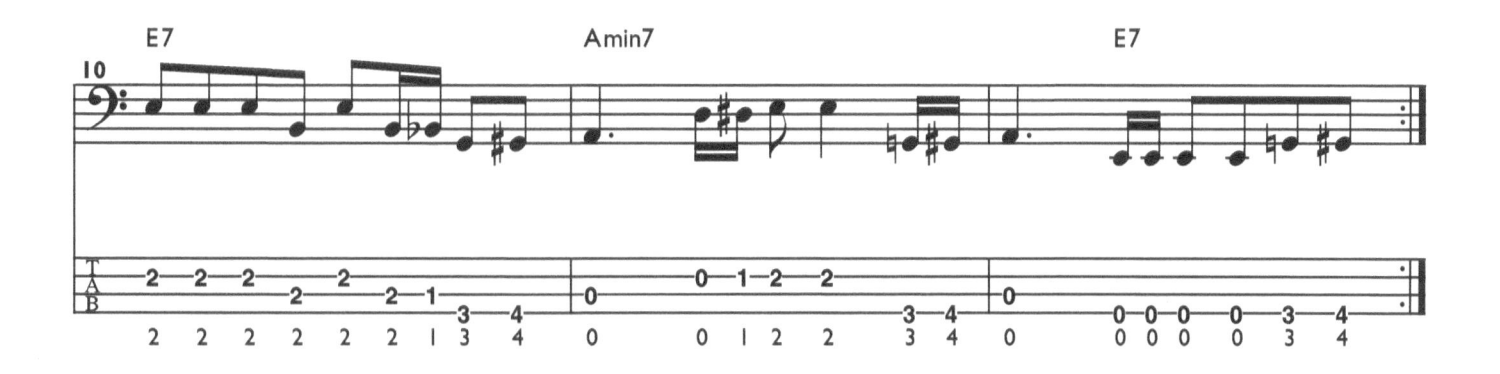

12/8 Stop Time Blues

Another common rhythmic variation in the blues is called *stop time*. Stop time generally features a repeated rhythmic riff, played in unison by the band, which stops abruptly, leaving space for a singer or soloist. The stop time figure is usually played on the melody chorus, and sometimes the first chorus of solos, and then changes to a normal blues groove. Following is a stop time bass line in 12/8 time, which has 12 eighth-note beats per measure, with the pulse on beats 1, 4, 7, and 10. Notice the underlying triplet feel in 12/8 time.

Chapter 2: R&B and Soul

A Brief History of R&B and Soul

Rhythm and blues, otherwise known as R&B, is a style of African-American music that first came to prominence in the 1930s. It is a style, rooted in the blues, that has grown to incorporate elements of jazz, gospel, and soul music. In the 1930s and '40s, artists like Cab Calloway and Louis Jordan played a swing/big-band style similar to Count Basie and Duke Ellington, but favoring more animated vocals and a more energetic backbeat. Their music also featured comical "novelty" songs like Jordan's "Saturday Night Fish Fry" and Calloway's "Minnie the Moocher." This music was originally categorized by the music industry, along with nearly all music by African-American musicians, as "race" music, but that name was changed by the record companies in the 1940s to rhythm and blues. In the 1950s, R&B became more and more popular and radio stations began to give it air time. As R&B artists like Fats Domino, Little Richard, and Chuck Berry started to have national hits, the music was renamed "rock and roll" by a radio disc jockey, and many of the R&B artists of the time went on to be known as pioneers of the music. At the same time, R&B artists like Ray Charles began to incorporate more gospel influence along with blues and jazz elements into their styles, resulting in a new variation which became known as soul music.

While the East and West coasts were the most important centers of the music business, the soul music of the 1960s originated from other geographical sources. The most notable were Detroit (with its Motown Records) and Memphis (with its Sun Studio and Stax Records). Soul recordings from both Memphis and Detroit were notable for their bass lines. The playing of Donald "Duck" Dunn, bassist on most of the Stax hits, was an important element of the Memphis sound. His driving, funky bass lines were featured in the music of Stax vocalists like Otis Redding, as well as the instrumental sounds of the Memphis soul band Booker T. & the MG's. During the same period, Detroit's Motown Records featured the playing of bassist James Jamerson, who appeared on countless hits by stars like The Supremes, The Temptations, Marvin Gaye, Stevie Wonder, and Aretha Franklin. Many consider Jamerson to have been the single most influential bassist of his time. His syncopated, jazz-influenced bass lines were an essential element of the Motown sound; they had a lasting influence on not only the sound of soul music, but all electric bass playing from that time on. For anyone who is serious about studying the electric bass, the work of James Jamerson is some of the most important in the history of the instrument.

In recent years, the term R&B has come to refer to a general category that includes a fairly wide range of funky pop music and modern soul singers. It can include artists as varied as Prince, Mariah Carey, and hip-hop-influenced artists like The Black Eyed Peas. R&B has influenced music and musicians all over the world. Jamaican ska and reggae and countless British rock musicians have acknowledged R&B artists as inspirations for their work. Rock and roll would not exist if it were not for R&B, and funk and jazz fusion are also direct offshoots of the style. As a direct descendant of the blues, R&B is at the very heart of American pop music.

Suggested Listening
- Scott Edwards (Stevie Wonder)
- James Jamerson (The Temptations, Junior Walker & the All-Stars, The Supremes, The Four Tops)
- George Porter, Jr. (The Meters)
- Donald "Duck" Dunn (Booker T. and the MG's)

In the Style of Scott Edwards (with Stevie Wonder)

Stevie Wonder is one of the most important and prolific R&B/soul artists ever. As a child prodigy, Wonder stunned the listening public when he burst onto the scene in the 1960s with his virtuoso singing, and piano and harmonica playing. Following is an example of a line in the style of bassist Scott Edwards, who played with Stevie Wonder on his 1972 album *Talking Book*.

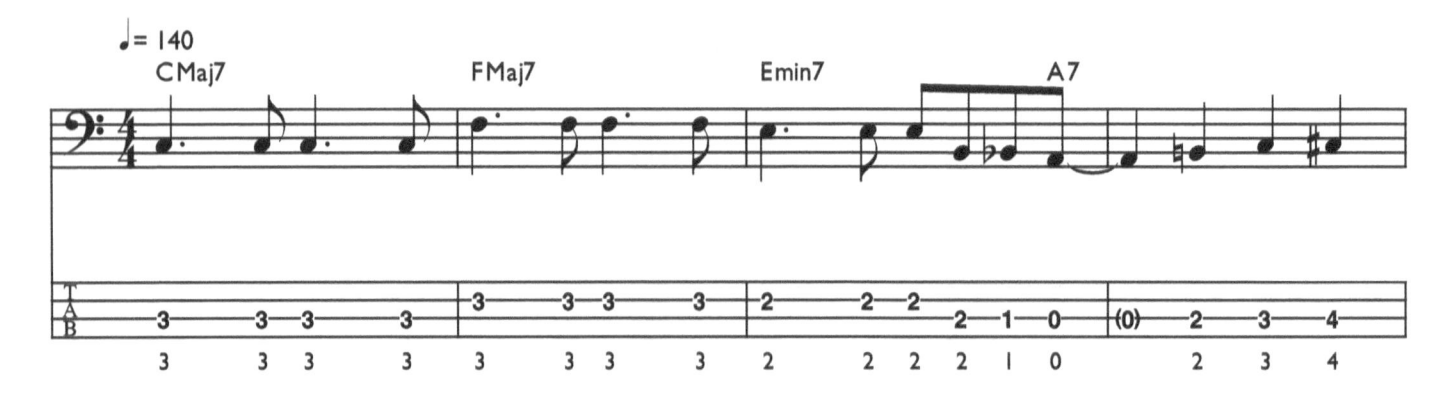

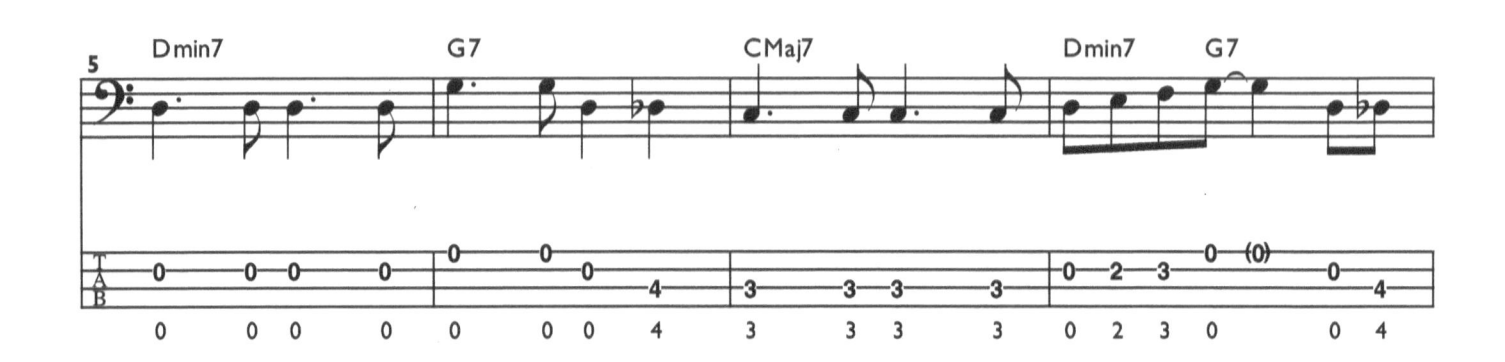

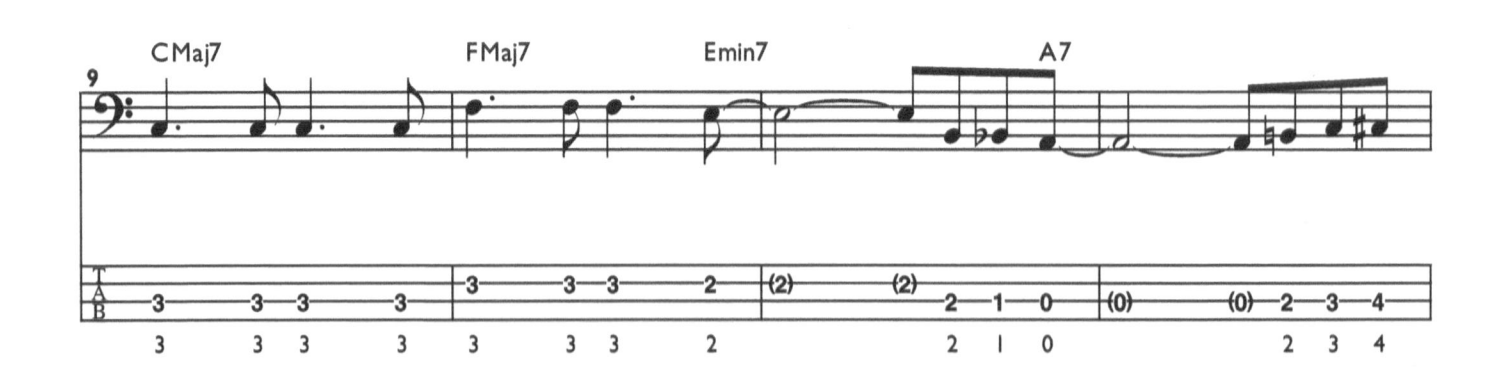

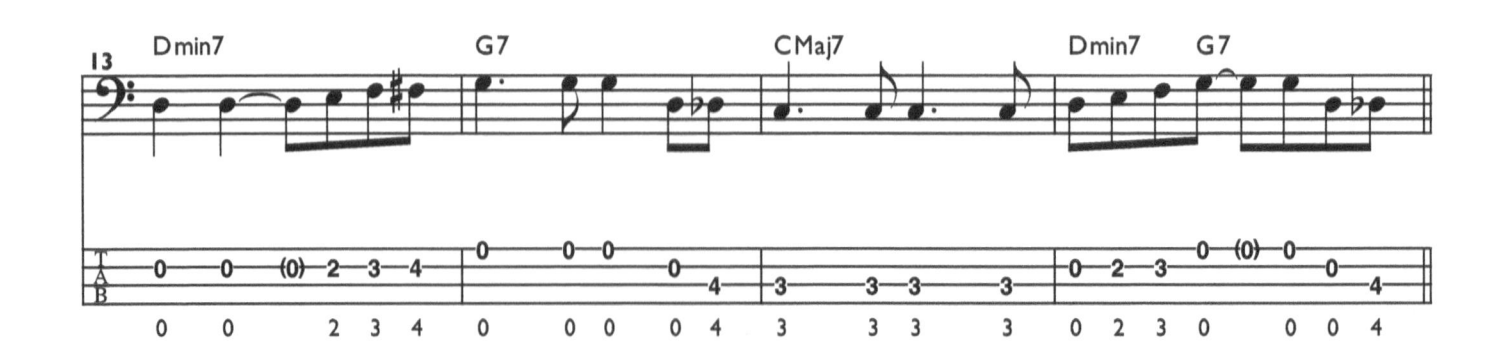

25

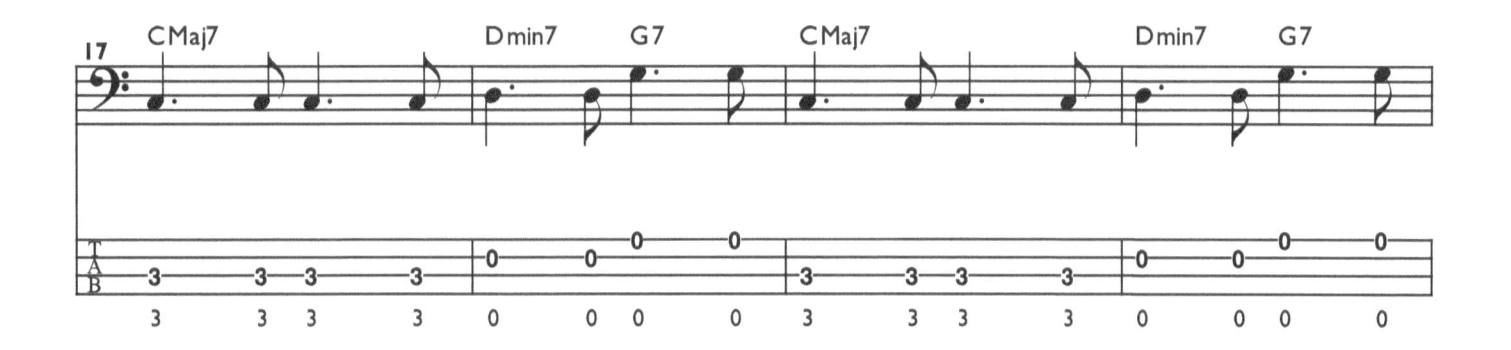

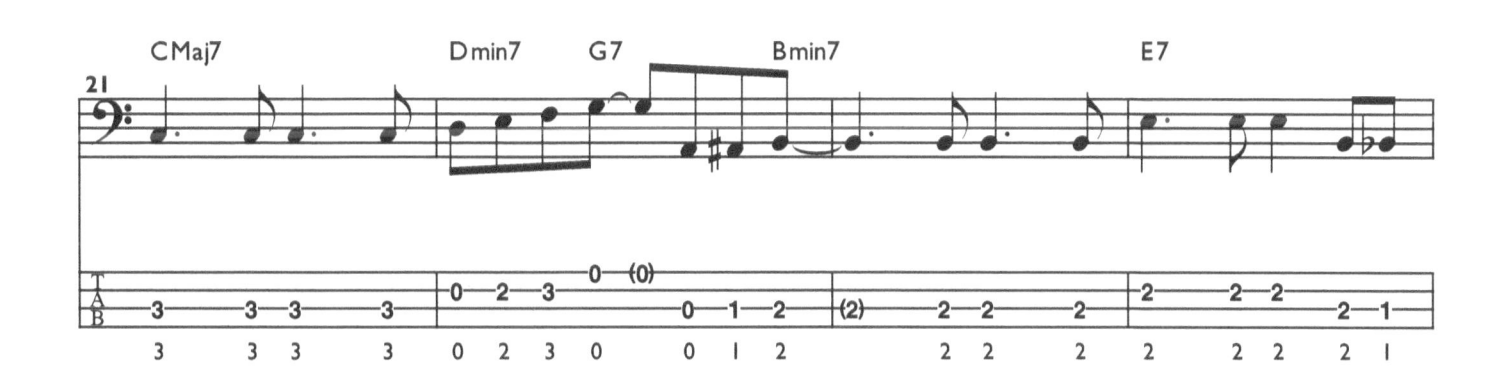

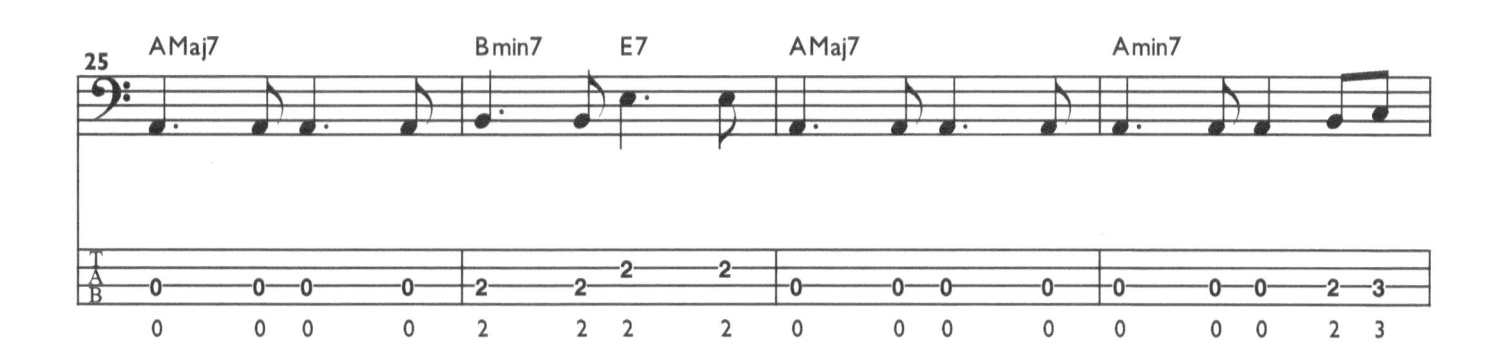

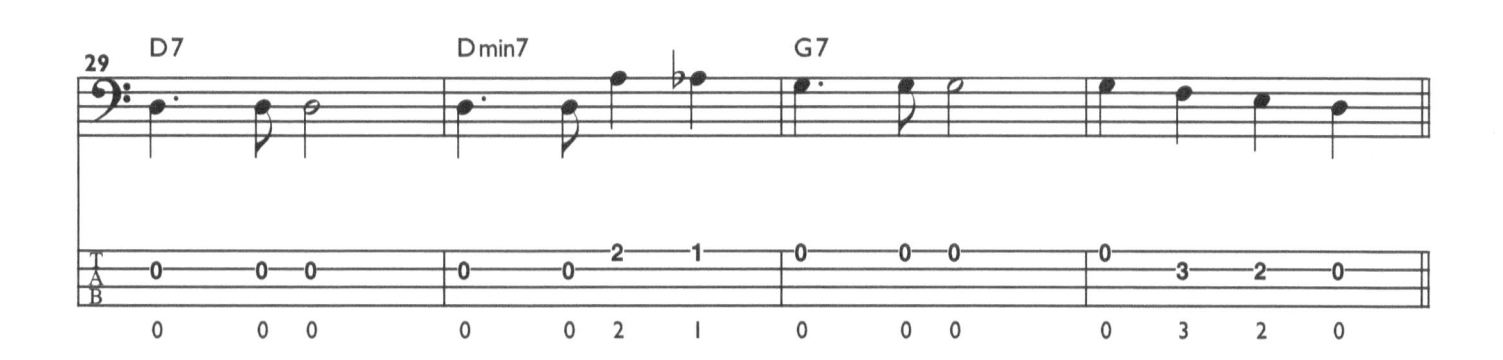

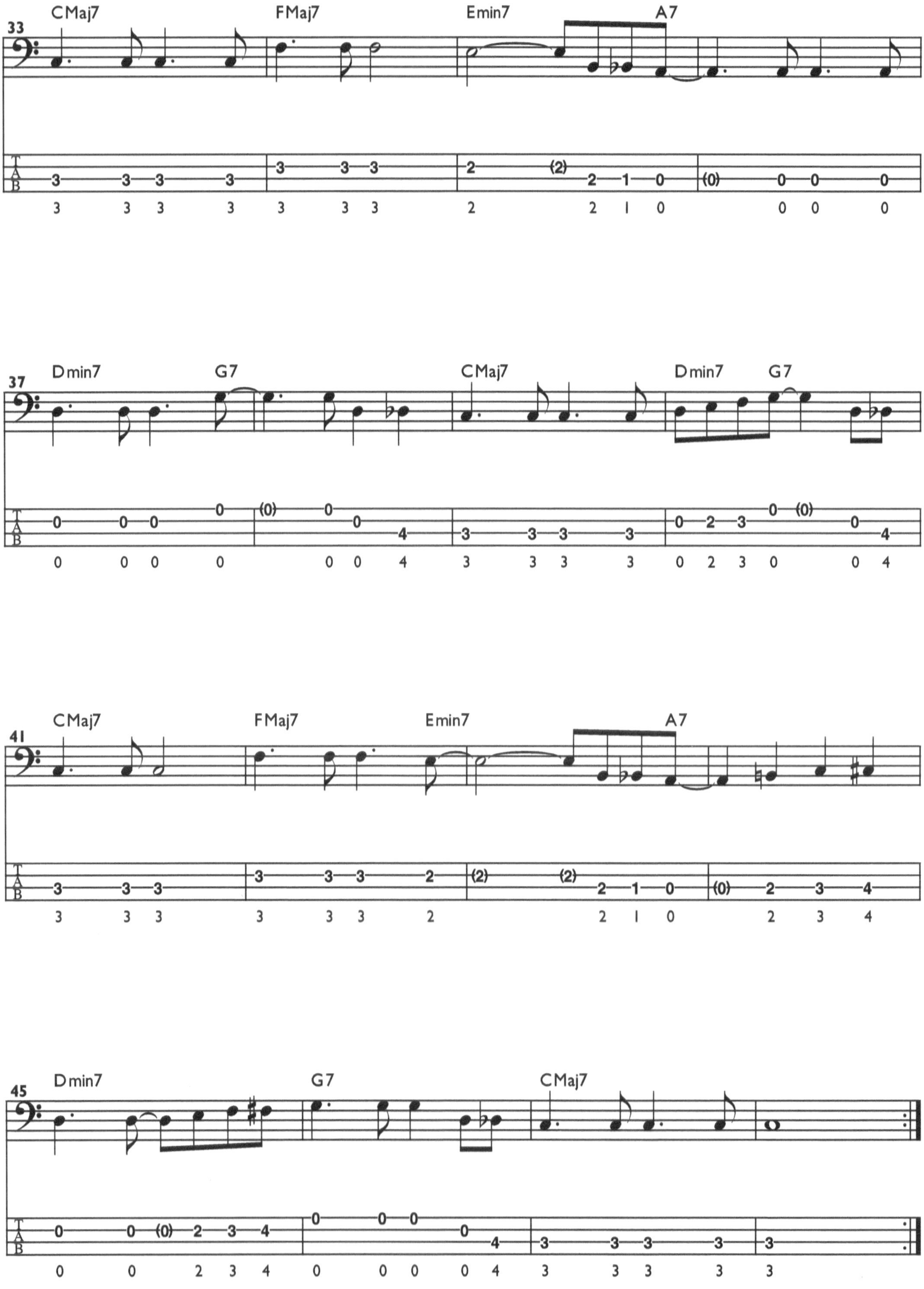
33
CMaj7
FMaj7
Emin7
A7
37
Dmin7
G7
CMaj7
Dmin7
G7
41
CMaj7
FMaj7
Emin7
A7
45
Dmin7
G7
CMaj7

James Jamerson is one of the most important musicians to ever play the electric bass. Over the more than 15 years that he recorded for Motown, he provided the bass lines for an incredible number of hit records by an equally impressive number of stars. Although he was never listed on the credits of the majority of his Motown recordings, Jamerson appeared on hits by artists like Stevie Wonder, The Supremes, The Temptations, Marvin Gaye, Junior Walker & the All-Stars, The Four Tops, and many others. Because of his historical significance and the influence he has had on so many bass players that followed him, a number of lines in his style have been included in this book. Jamerson played with so many different artists in such a wide variety of musical situations that, while his signature sound remained unchanged, the lines he played varied notably depending on the artist and song. Following are some examples.

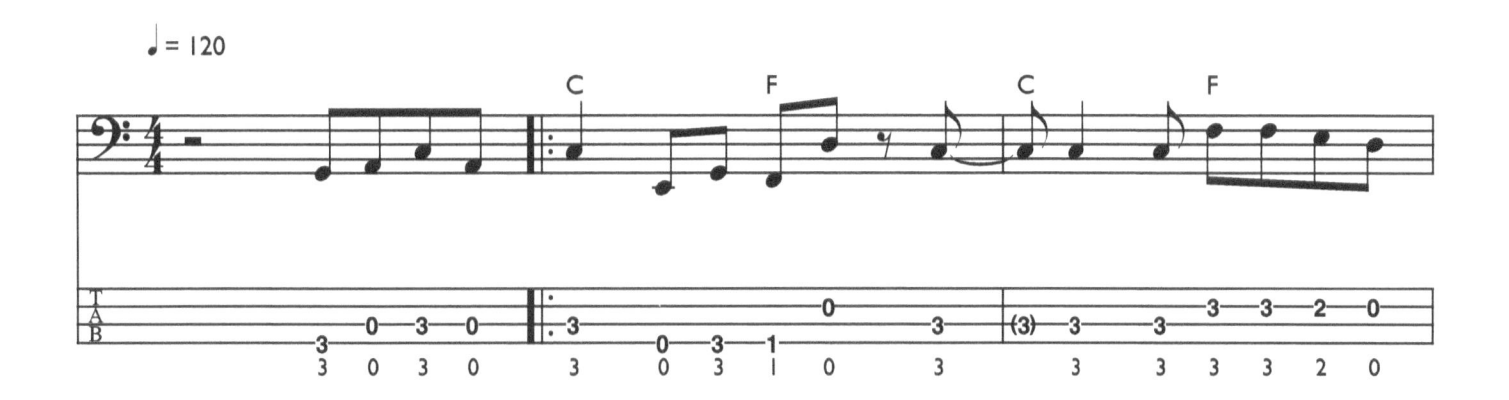

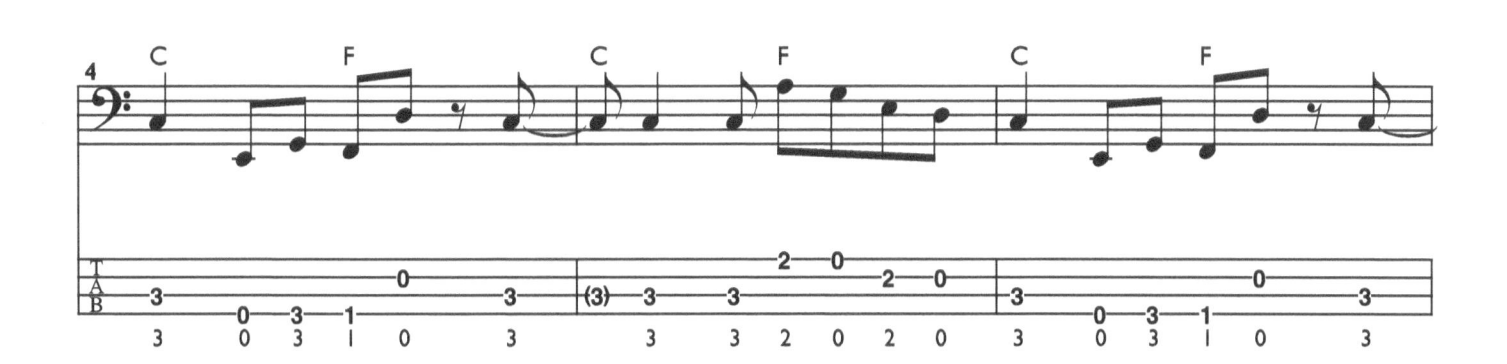

In the Style of James Jamerson (with The Temptations)

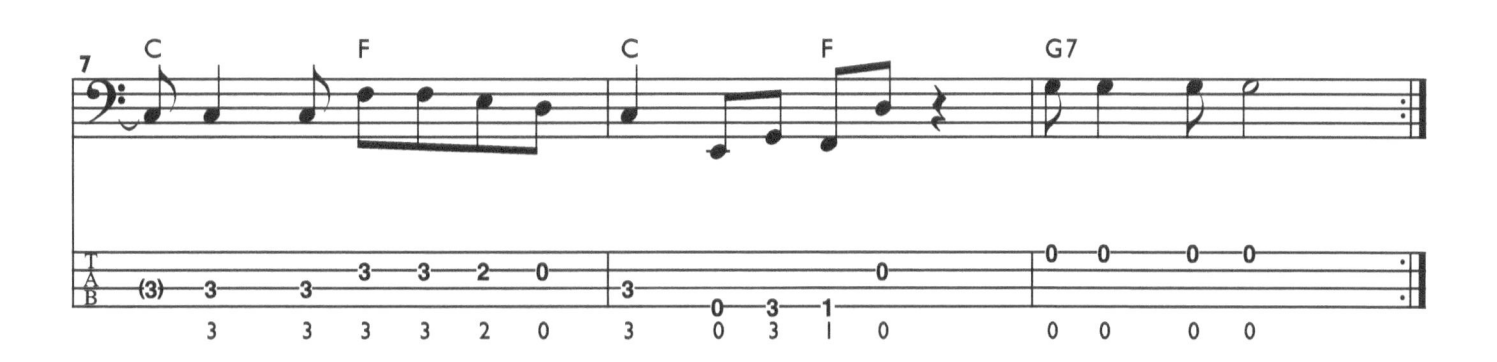

In the Style of James Jamerson (with Junior Walker & the All-Stars)

In the Style of James Jamerson (with The Supremes)

Note: See next page for an explanation of the musical terms and symbols used in this chart.

(Continued on next page)

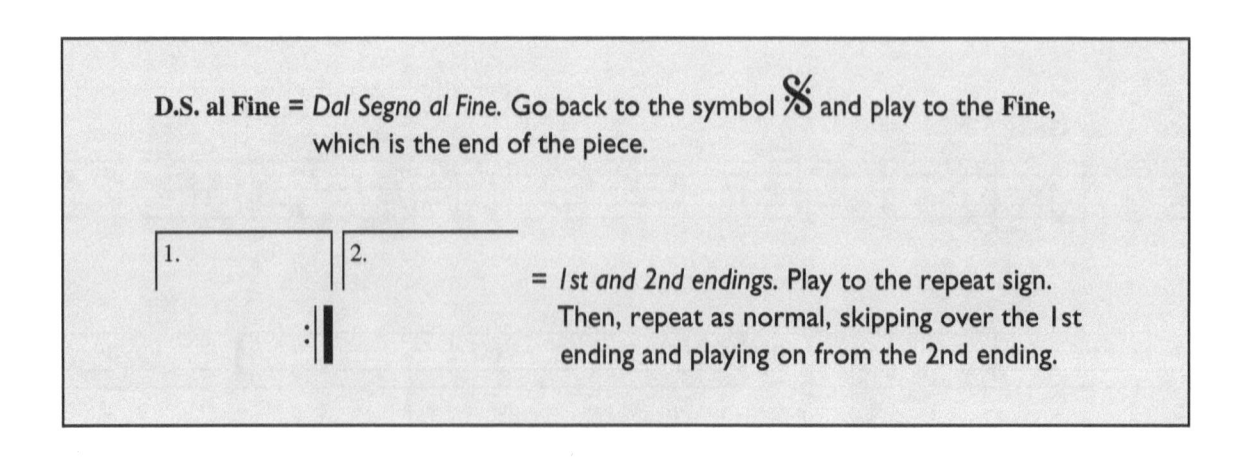

D.S. al Fine = *Dal Segno al Fine*. Go back to the symbol 𝄋 and play to the **Fine**, which is the end of the piece.

= 1st and 2nd endings. Play to the repeat sign. Then, repeat as normal, skipping over the 1st ending and playing on from the 2nd ending.

In the Style of James Jamerson (with The Four Tops)

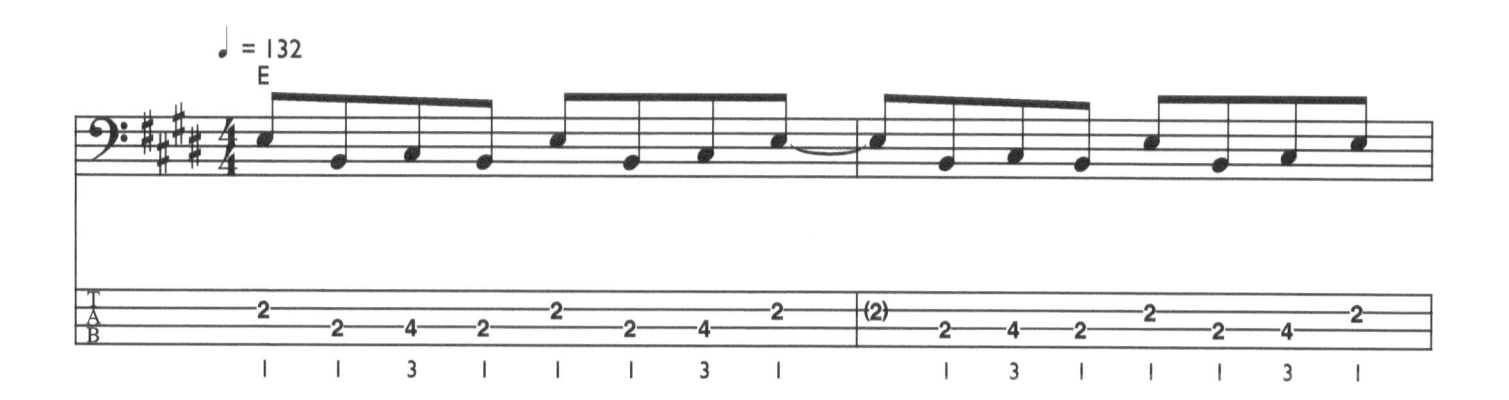

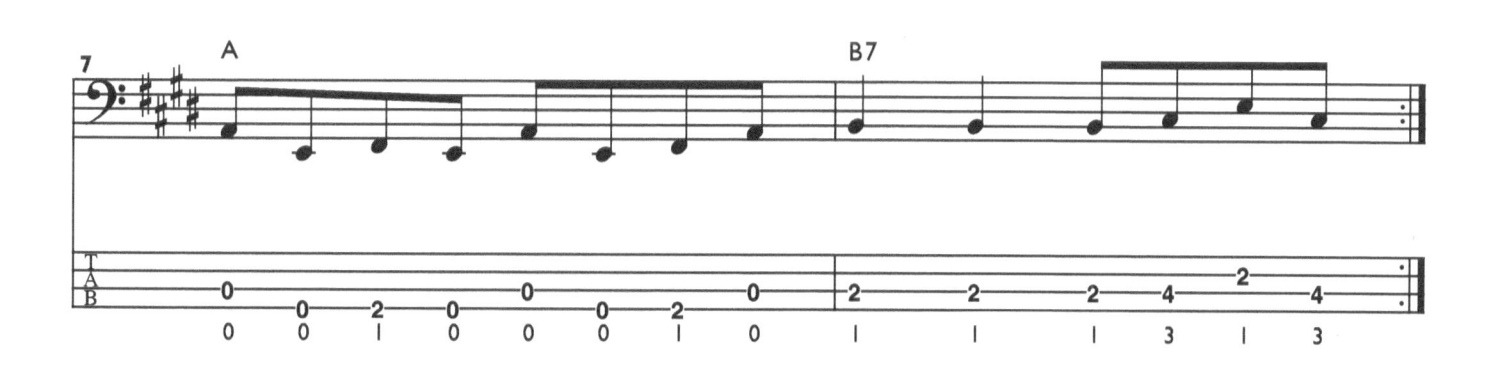

In the Style of George Porter, Jr. (with The Meters)

New Orleans has a long tradition of wonderfully creative bands who play fantastic dance music, and no modern band illustrates this better than The Meters. Meters bassist George Porter, Jr. plays with a dark, warm sound and deep, funky groove that are essential elements in The Meters' signature sound.

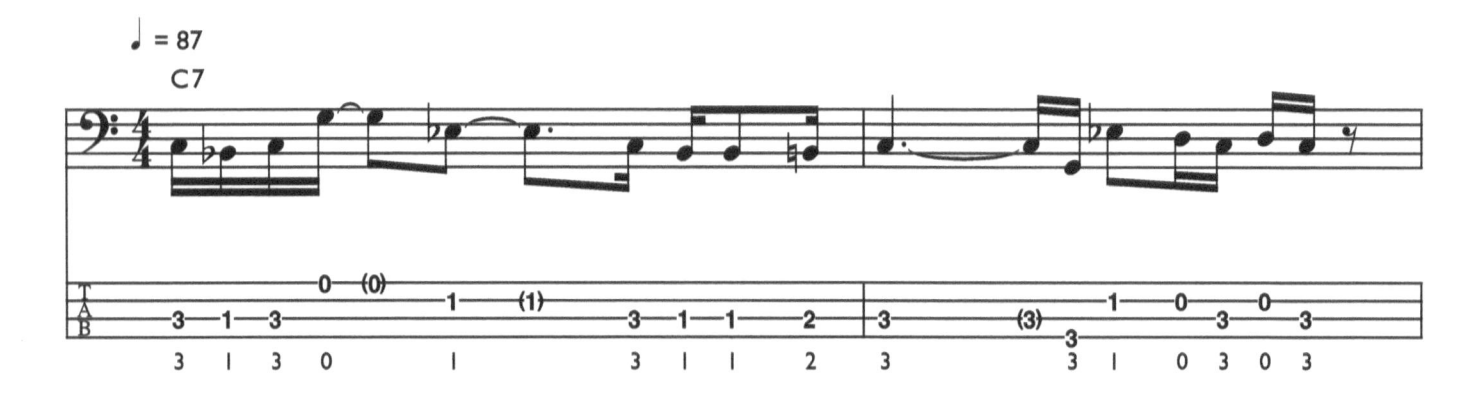

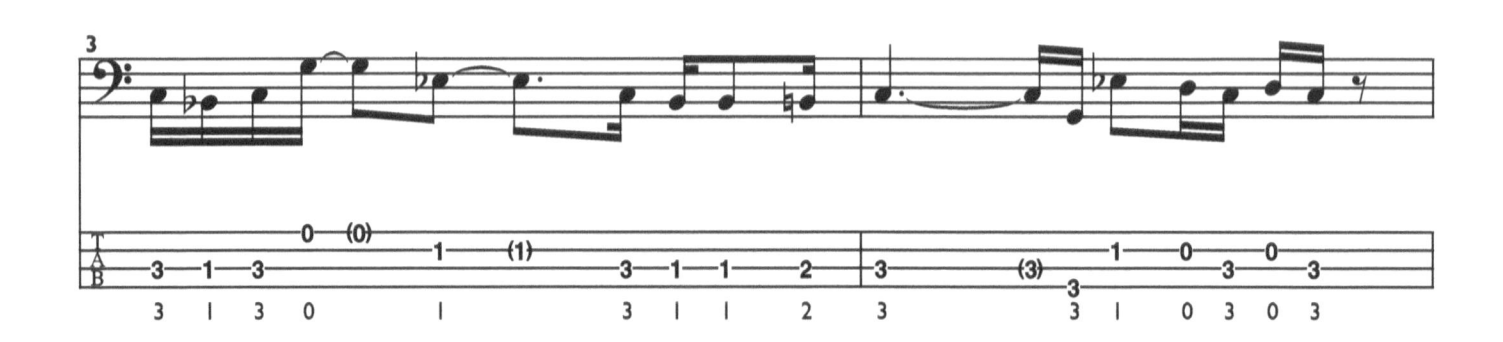

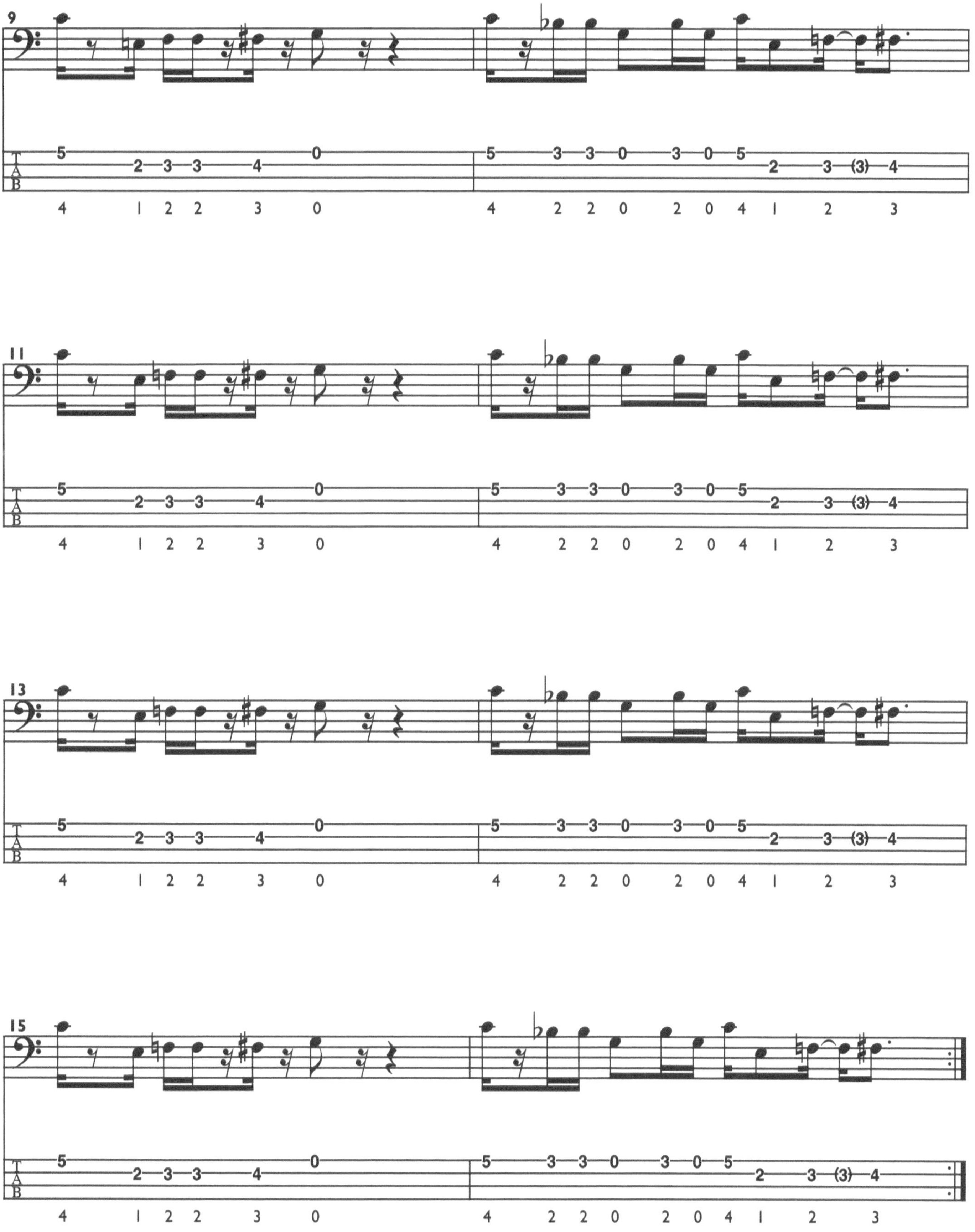

R&B Blues in the Style of Donald "Duck" Dunn (with Booker T. & the MG's)

Donald "Duck" Dunn is one of the most influential bassists in the R&B style. His playing with Booker T. & the MG's, and as house bassist for Stax Records, helped create the Memphis soul sound that made the city famous. In addition, Dunn has performed with and produced countless stars, contributing to many hit recordings. Following is an R&B blues bass line in the style of "Duck" Dunn.

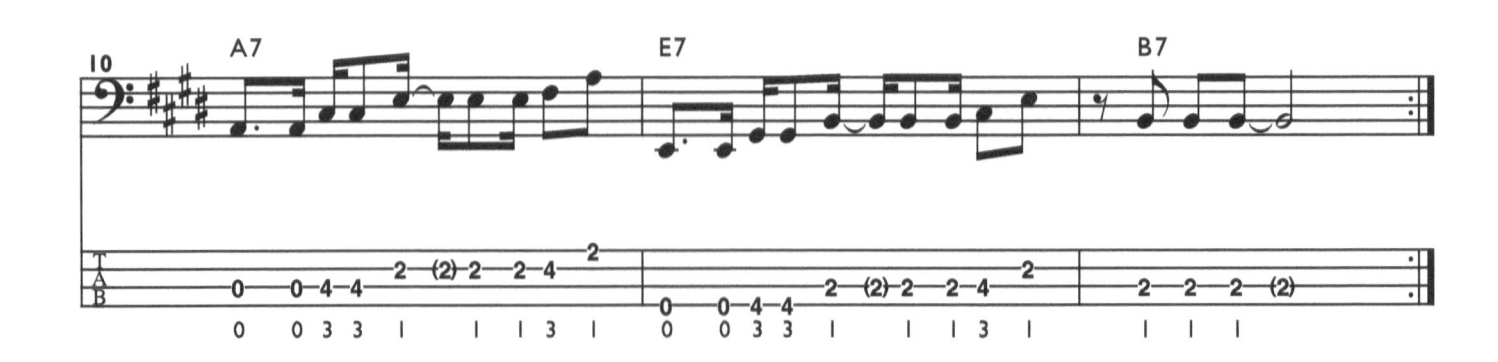

Chapter 3: Rock

A Brief History of Rock

Most everyone alive knows what rock and roll is, but like so many things we take for granted, we probably don't know some of the basic facts about this multi-faceted style. For example, why is it called "rock and roll?" A disc jockey is often credited with popularizing the name in the early 1950s to refer to the music that was known up until then as "rhythm and blues." But there is evidence that musicians used the phrase "rock and roll" long before that in lyrics and song titles. While it's difficult to pinpoint the actual origin of the name, one possible source of the term is a reference to a type of bass line. The great virtuoso boogie woogie piano players of the 1930s and '40s, like Pete Johnson, Albert Ammons, and Meade Lux Lewis, were known for their exciting and powerful left-hand bass lines. Two of the most common variations were the "rocking" and "rolling" left hand—rocking being a style that used large intervals (octaves, 5ths, 10ths, etc.), and rolling being an arpeggiated style of running through the chord tones. At some point, Ammons claimed to have developed a hybrid of the two that he called the "rock and roll." It seems clear that this "rock and roll" left-hand style became the genesis for the standard bass lines heard in the piano styles of rock and roll pioneers like Little Richard, Fats Domino, and Jerry Lee Lewis—as well as the bass lines of early rock and roll tunes by musicians like Chuck Berry, Elvis Presley, and Bill Haley. In view of this, it's safe to say that the bass line has been one of the key elements of rock and roll since its inception.

Early rock and roll, and blues, were played on urban radio stations that had primarily black audiences and were part of a category created by the radio and record industry known as "race" music. Young white listeners became aware of the music through these radio stations and the popularity of rock and roll among white youth took off from there. Following the earliest rock and roll in the 1950s, the music began to emerge in various regional styles. The doo-wop styles of the East Coast singing groups like The Coasters, The Drifters and The Four Seasons, and the surf style from California vocal groups like The Beach Boys, and Jan and Dean, and instrumental bands like The Ventures, are examples of this regional development. In addition, around this time, the same "race" music that was influencing young listeners in the U.S. was also being heard by young people in England and, as a result, young English musicians began playing their own interpretations of the blues, and rock and roll. The resulting "British Invasion" of rock bands from England in the 1960s—including The Rolling Stones, The Yardbirds, Cream, and maybe most notably, The Beatles—changed rock and roll forever.

In the early 1950s, rock and roll bands used double basses. The first hits—from artists like Little Richard, Bill Haley, and Elvis Presley—featured bass lines played by a double bassist (sometimes while spinning or standing on their instruments). Later in the decade, bassists began switching to the newly invented electric bass. As the electric bass became the instrument of choice, amplification improved, and rock styles evolved and diversified, bass players became more and more visible as featured members of rock bands. With the British Invasion of the 1960s, a new group of bassists arrived with a different vision of the role for the instrument. Singing bassists like Paul McCartney of The Beatles and Jack Bruce of Cream drew attention to the bass, and because they were such strong bassists and composers, bass lines took on a new prominence in rock. Other British groups had bassists with strong musical personalities, and players like John Paul Jones of Led Zeppelin and John Entwistle of The Who took rock bass playing to new technical heights.

While the British bands were creating their version of rock and roll, bands in the U.S. were doing the same, and once again, regional influences were of key importance. Detroit's rock scene (with bands like Iggy & the Stooges and The MC5), San Francisco's Grateful Dead (with bassist Phil Lesh) and Jefferson Airplane (with bassist Jack Cassidy), southern rock from the deep south with groups like The Allman Brothers Band (with bassist Berry Oakley), and the countless bands from New York and Los Angeles—were all contributing to an exciting musical mix.

Since that time, rock music has enjoyed enormous popularity and constant development. While there have not been any "seismic" events like the changes of the '50s and '60s, rock music has seen technical growth, stylistic development, and virtuoso players in great numbers. Many subcategories have developed, inspiring new and different bands and styles. The 1970s saw the development of progressive rock, with bands like Yes, Gentle Giant, Brand X, and Rush. These bands featured bass virtuosos like Chris Squire, Percy Jones, and Geddy Lee. New musical styles were explored, like the jazz-influenced rock of Steely Dan and the psychedelic rock-fusion of Pink Floyd. Disco became a craze with the music of the Bee Gees (featured in the 1977 film *Saturday Night Fever*), and bands like Van Halen and AC/DC played their own brands of hard rock. The '80s brought the genius of Prince and Michael Jackson, as well as the rise in popularity of heavy metal with bands like Metallica and Megadeth. The Red Hot Chili Peppers also came to prominence in the '80s, and with them the virtuosity of their bassist Flea. The '90s was the decade of indie rock, and more and more rock bands gave up or refused major label contracts for the freedom of being independent. The Seattle sound became popular with Nirvana, and bands like Soundgarden and Pearl Jam adding their unique takes. Guitar virtuosos like Steve Vai and Joe Satriani stunned listeners with their technique, while their bass counterparts, Stuart Hamm and Billy Sheehan, became widely known, setting new technical standards for rock bassists.

The first decade of the 21st century has brought a wide variety of specialized musicians. The rock spectrum is even more varied, and the level of technical proficiency is higher than ever. Players have more and more information and tools at their fingertips and the music is constantly growing and changing.

Suggested Listening
- Early rock and roll: Roosevelt Jackson (Bo Diddley), Willie Dixon (Chuck Berry), Bill Black (Elvis Presley)
- Doo-wop: Little Anthony & the Imperials
- Surf rock: Brian Wilson (The Beach Boys)
- Classic rock: Jack Bruce (Cream), Bill Wyman (Rolling Stones), Paul McCartney (The Beatles), John Paul Jones (Led Zeppelin), Noel Redding (The Jimi Hendrix Experience), John Entwistle (The Who)
- Progressive rock: Roger Waters (Pink Floyd)
- Southern rock: Berry Oakley (The Allman Brothers Band)
- Heavy metal: Jason Newsted (Metallica)
- Hard rock: Cliff Williams (AC/DC)
- Pop punk: Mike Dirnt (Green Day)
- Grunge: Krist Novoselic (Nirvana)

In the Style of Roosevelt Jackson (with Bo Diddley)

Bo Diddley was one of the early rock and roll stars, and his sound is totally unique. Bassist Roosevelt Jackson played with him for many years. The following example features the *Bo Diddley beat*, a syncopated, two-bar pattern based on the Latin clave rhythm. In the first measure, there are three pulses, and in the second, there are two (see right).

Count: 1 (2) & (3) 4 | (1) 2 3 (4)

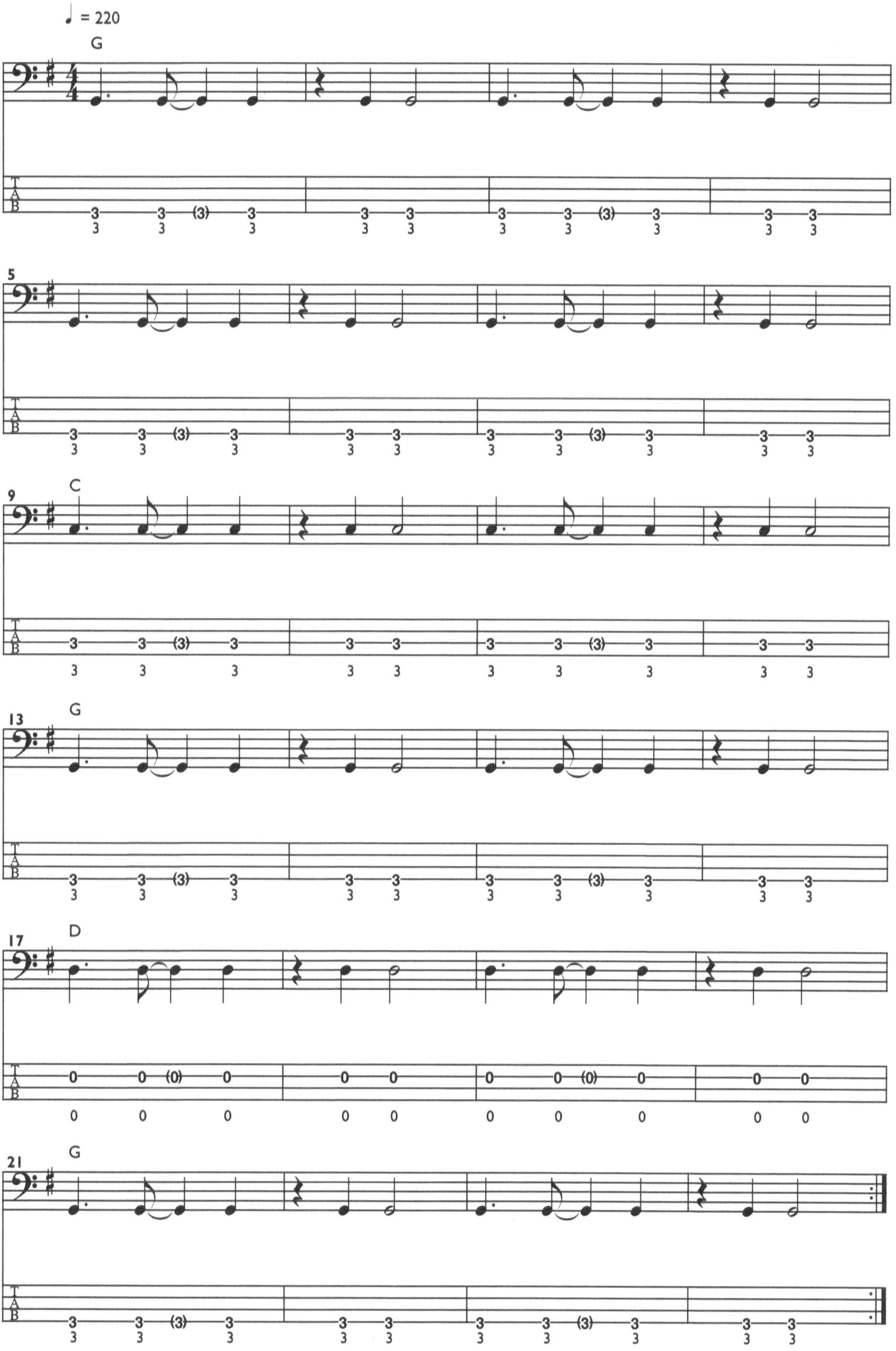
♩ = 220
G
5
9
C
13
G
17
D
21
G

In the Style of Willie Dixon (with Chuck Berry)

Chuck Berry's contributions to R&B and rock and roll are enormous. Double bassist Willie Dixon played on Berry's hits in the early 1950s. Here's a bass line in Dixon's pioneering rock and roll bass style.

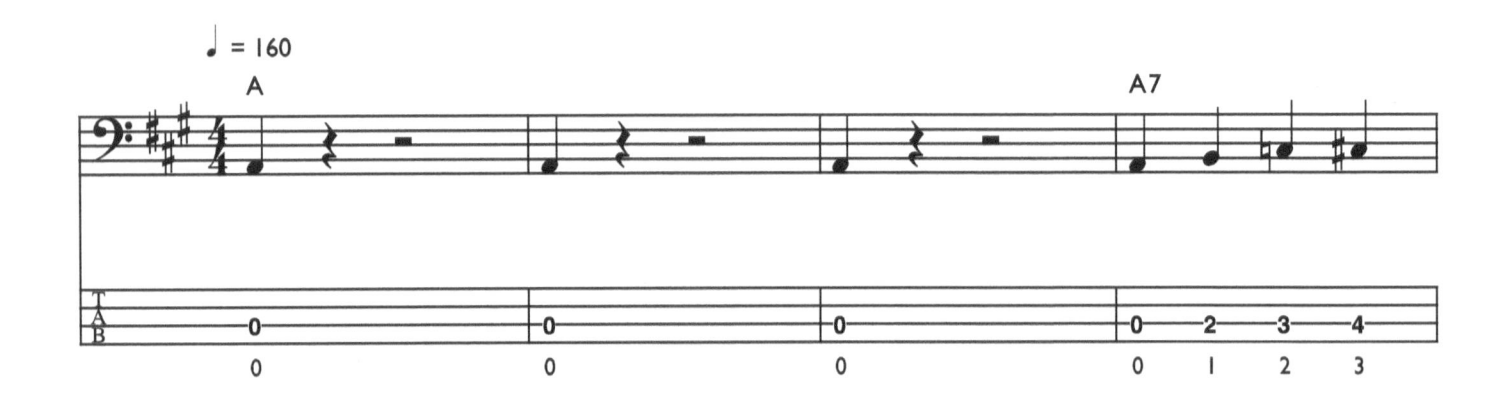

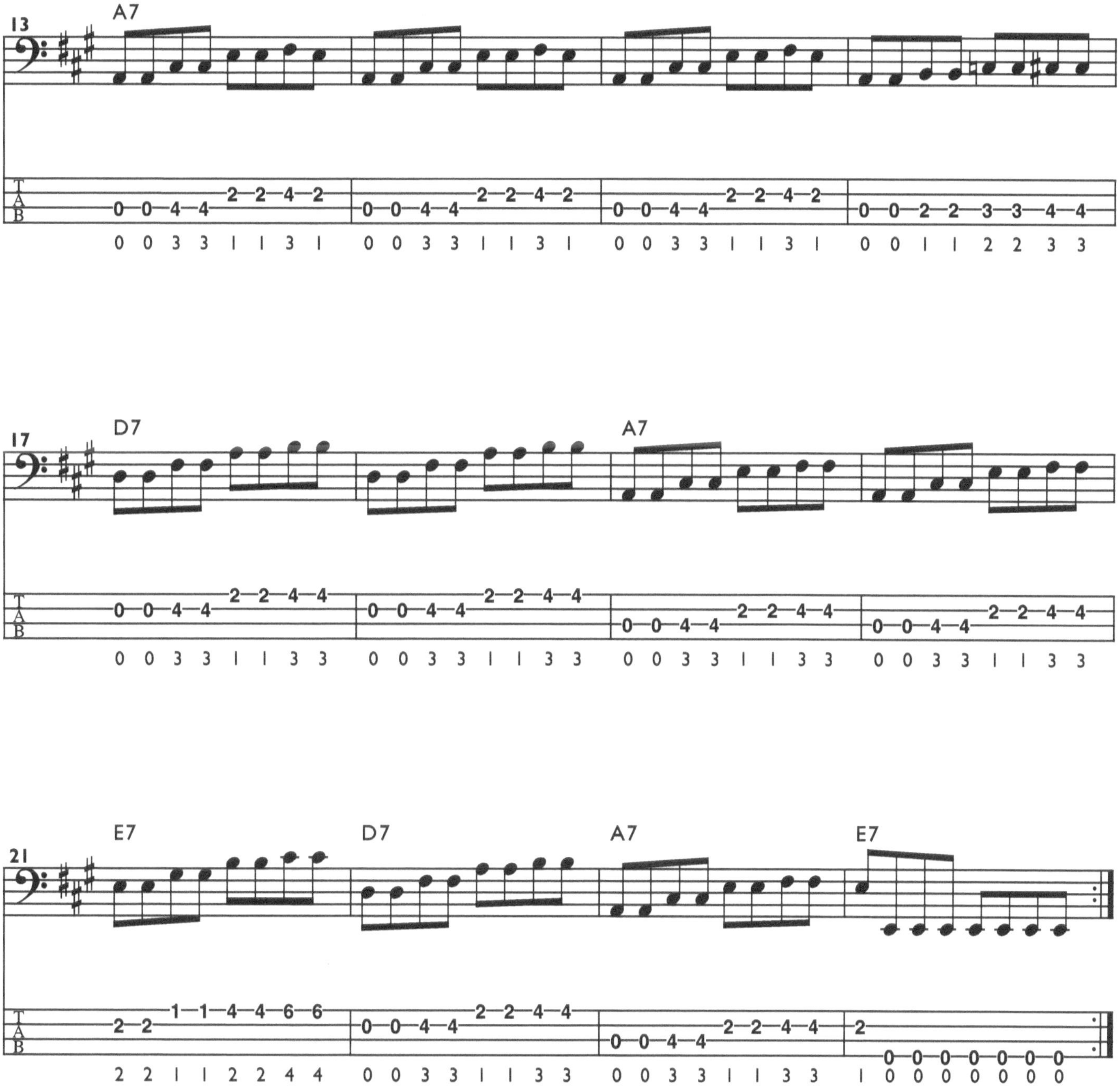
13
A7
TAB
17
D7
A7
TAB
21
E7
D7
A7
E7
TAB

In the Style of Bill Black (with Elvis Presley)

Few musicians have had the impact on popular music that Elvis Presley had. Originally considered a "hillbilly" singer, Elvis was greatly influenced by African-American singers, and his style shocked the public and set a standard for rock and roll. Following is a bass line in the style of Bill Black, who played on Presley's early rock and roll hits.

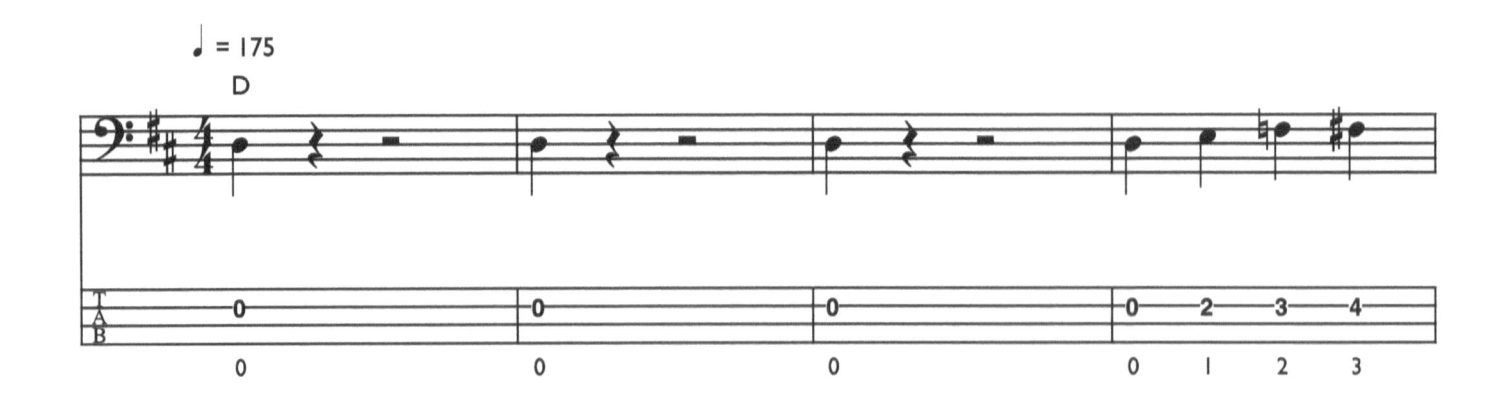

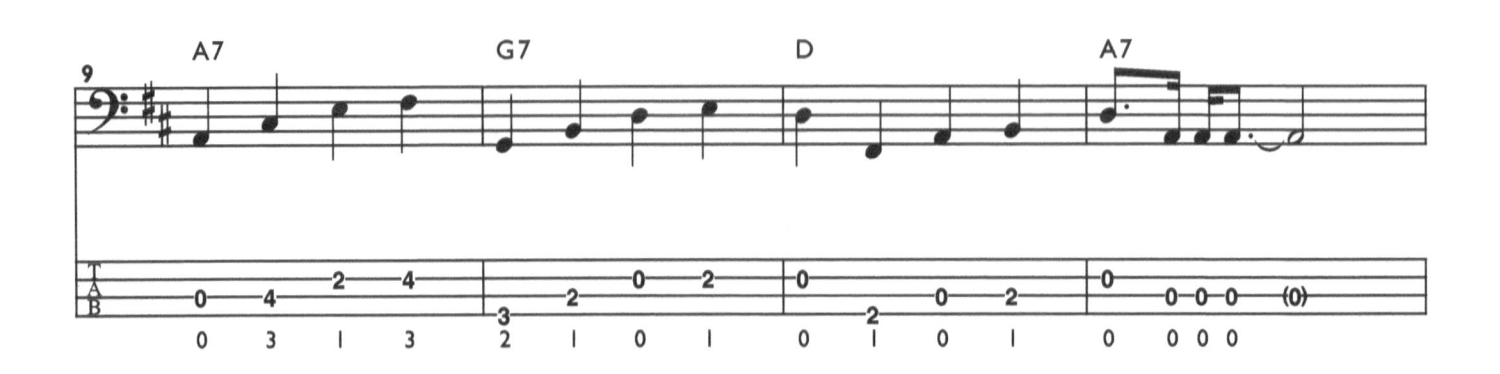

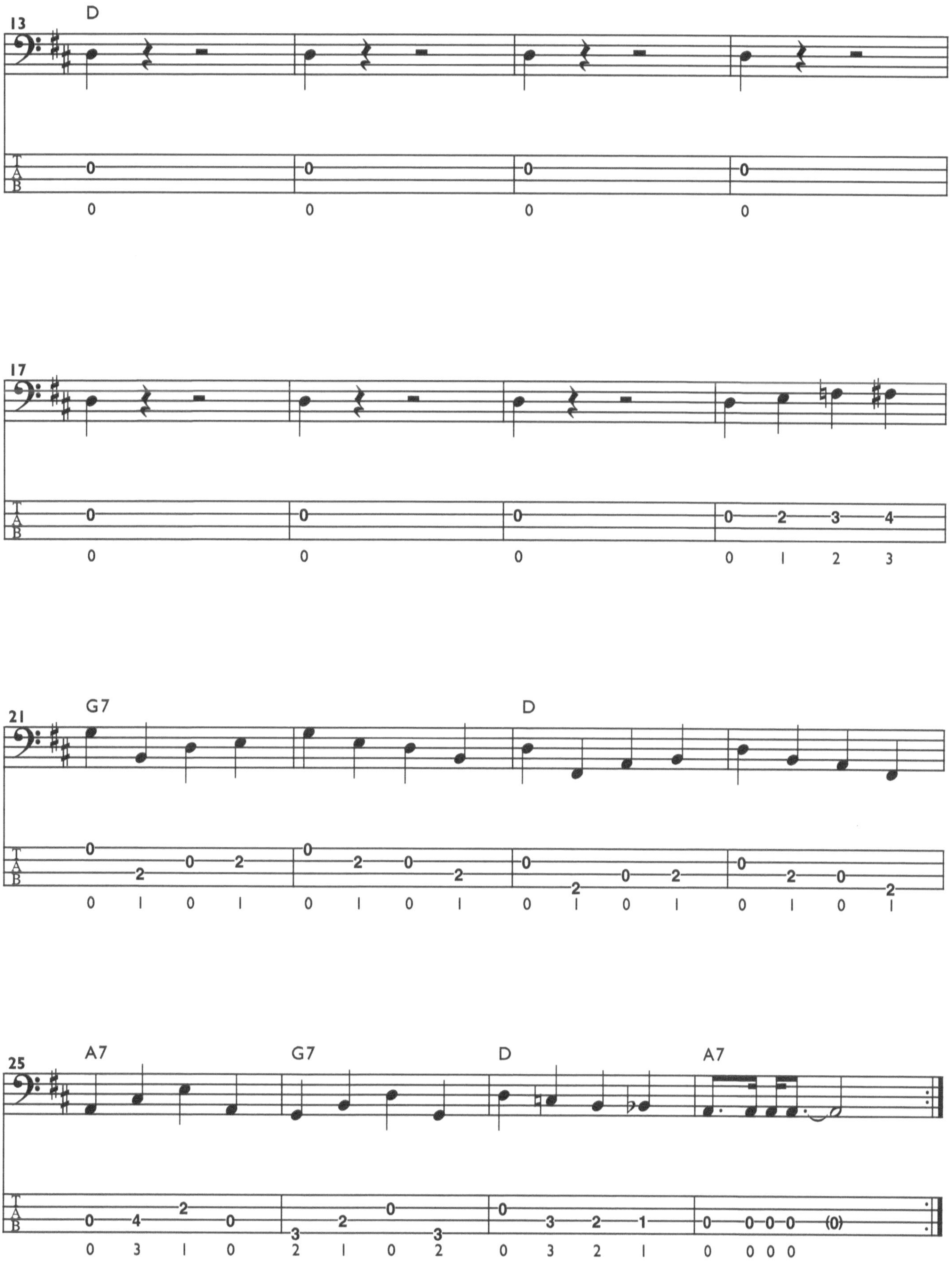
13
D
17
21
G7
D
25
A7
G7
D
A7

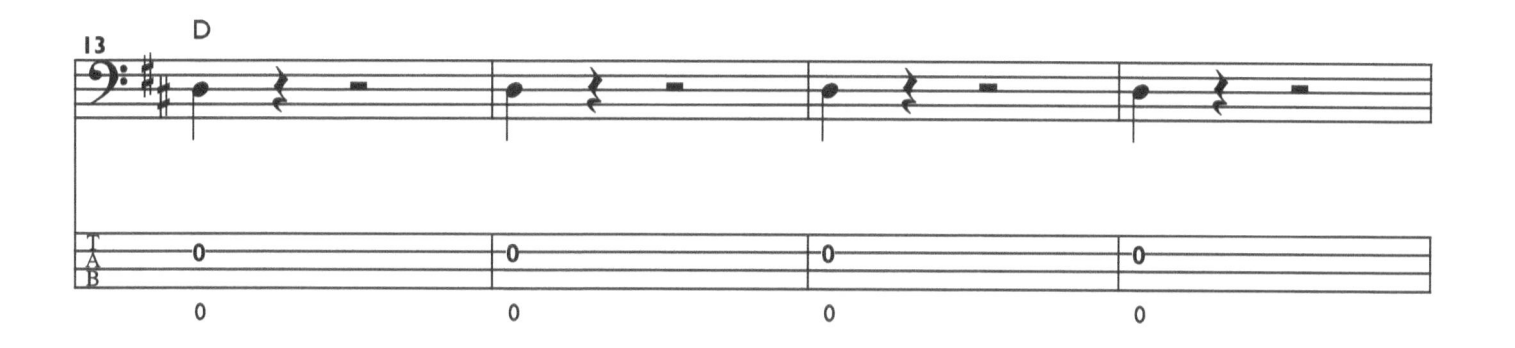

Doo-Wop

The doo-wop sound was primarily created on East Coast city streets by *a cappella* (all-vocal) quartets. Groups like The Drifters, The Coasters, and Little Anthony & the Imperials had huge hits with doo-wop songs in the 1950s. Here's a bass line in the style of a doo-wop ballad in 6/8 time (which has six eighth-note beats per measure, with the dotted quarter note getting the pulse).

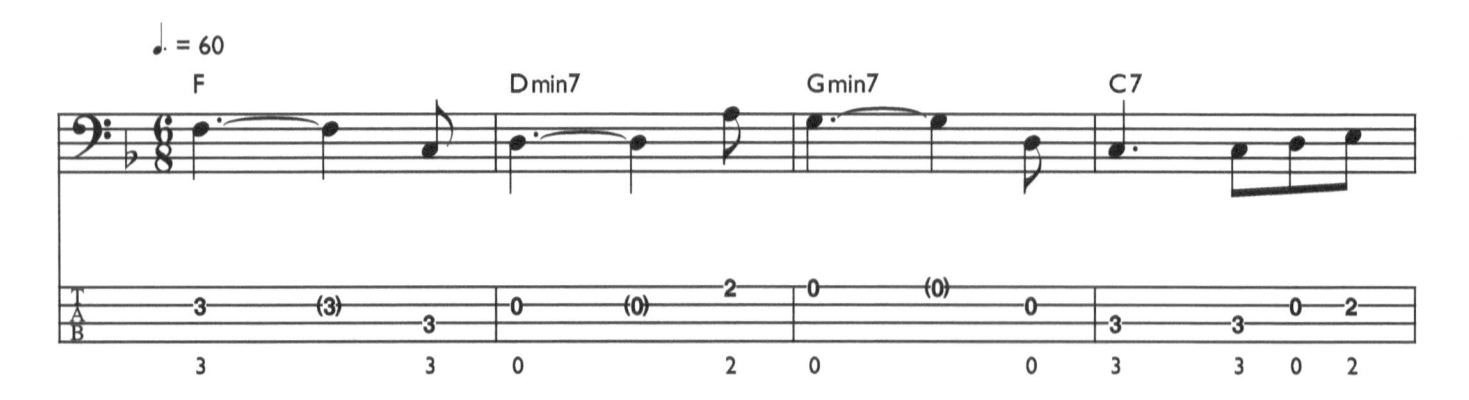

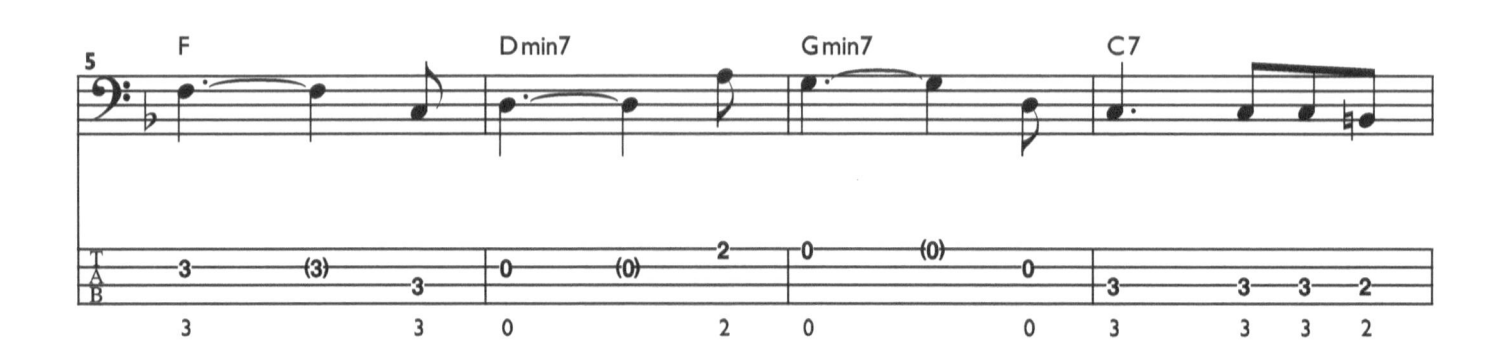

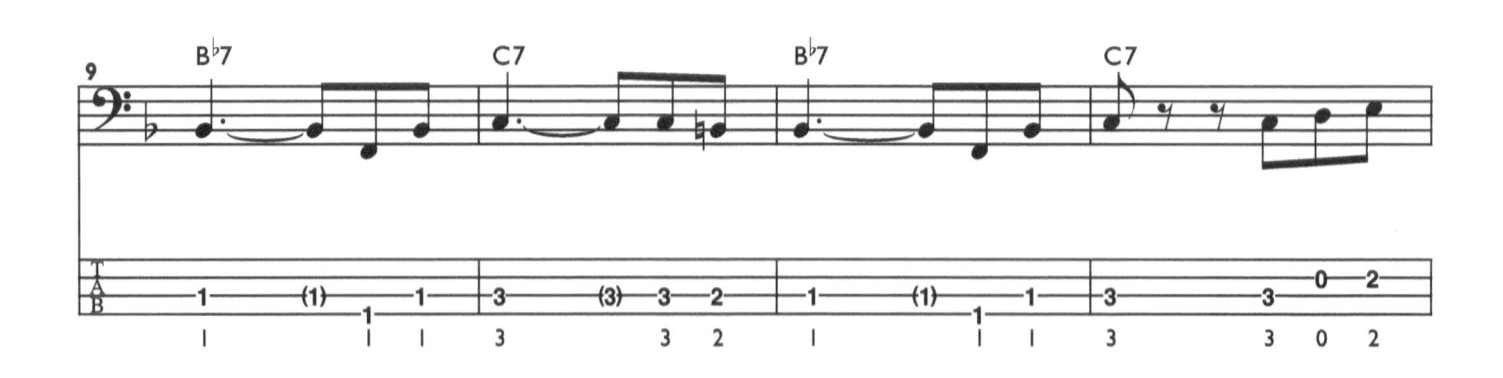

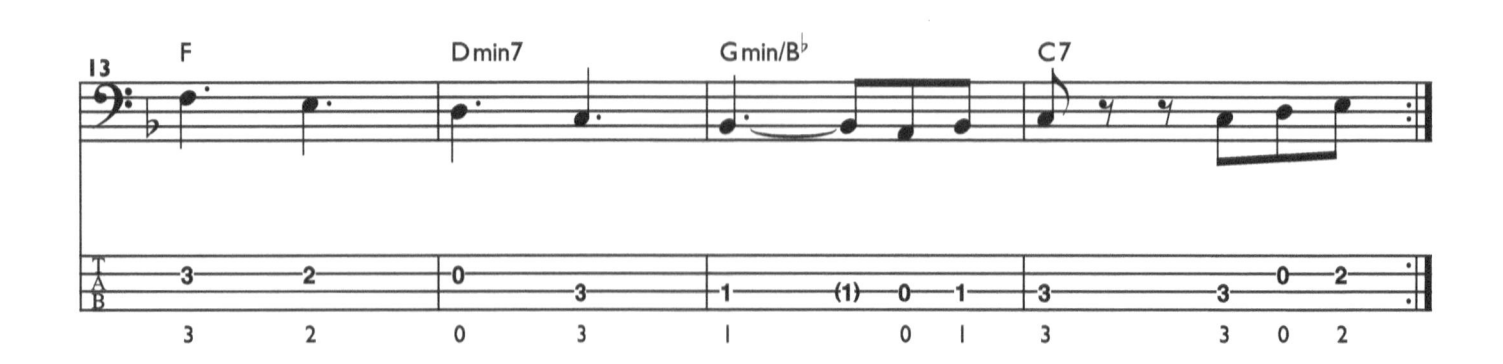

In the Style of Brian Wilson (with The Beach Boys)

In the 1950s and '60s, rock and roll bands in California—like The Ventures, Jan and Dean, and The Beach Boys—created a unique sound that became known as surf rock. Brian Wilson, who was the driving force behind The Beach Boys, wrote many of their songs and played almost all of the instruments, including the bass, on their early albums.

In the Style of Jack Bruce (with Cream)

An important part of the British Invasion movement, the seminal blues-based power trio Cream had an enormous influence on the rock sound of the 1960s. Cream's bassist Jack Bruce is one of the most important and influential bassists in rock. His unique bass style and powerful vocals were an essential part of Cream's sound.

45

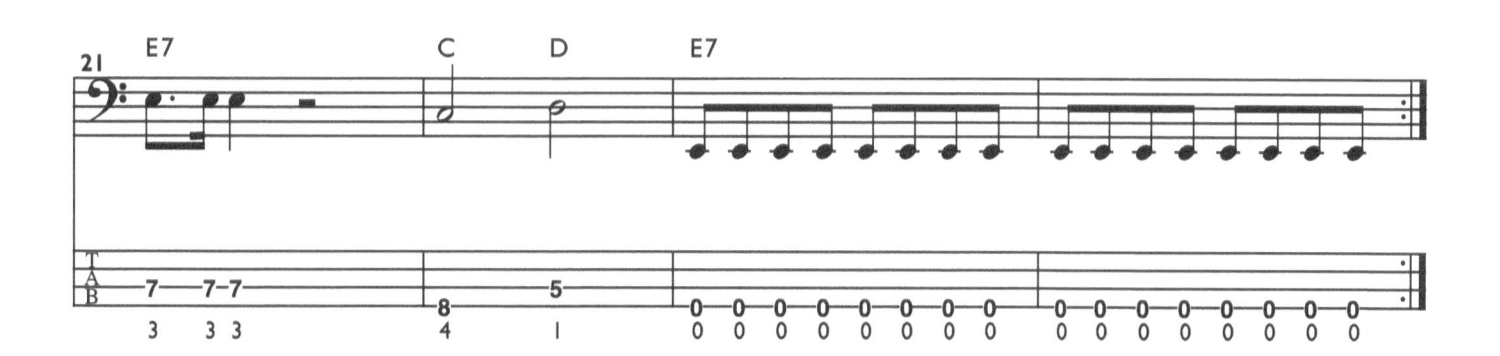

In the Style of Bill Wyman (with The Rolling Stones)

As the bassist for The Rolling Stones, Bill Wyman has been at the center of rock music for half a century. His unique style of playing, inspired by the earlier walking bass style of Willie Dixon and others, has had a huge impact on rock bass playing.

47

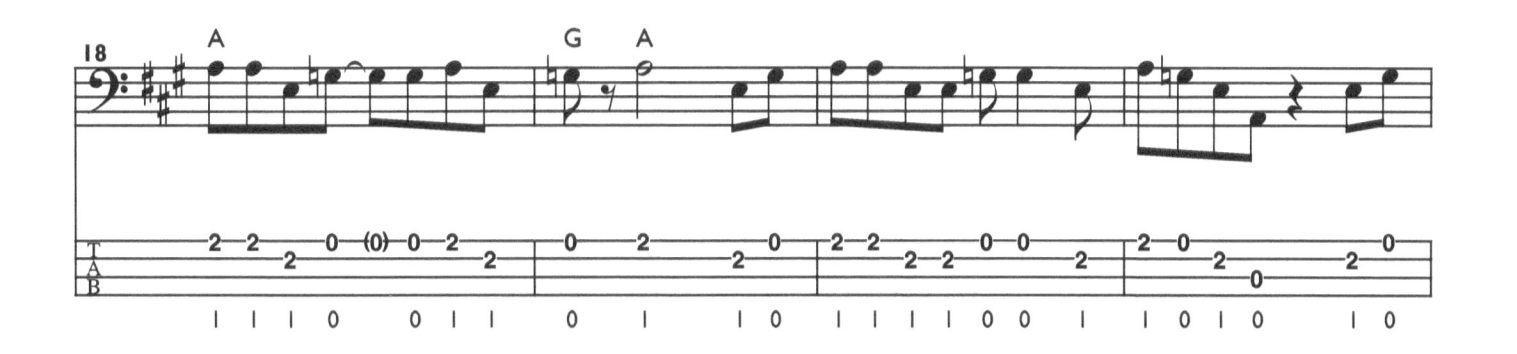

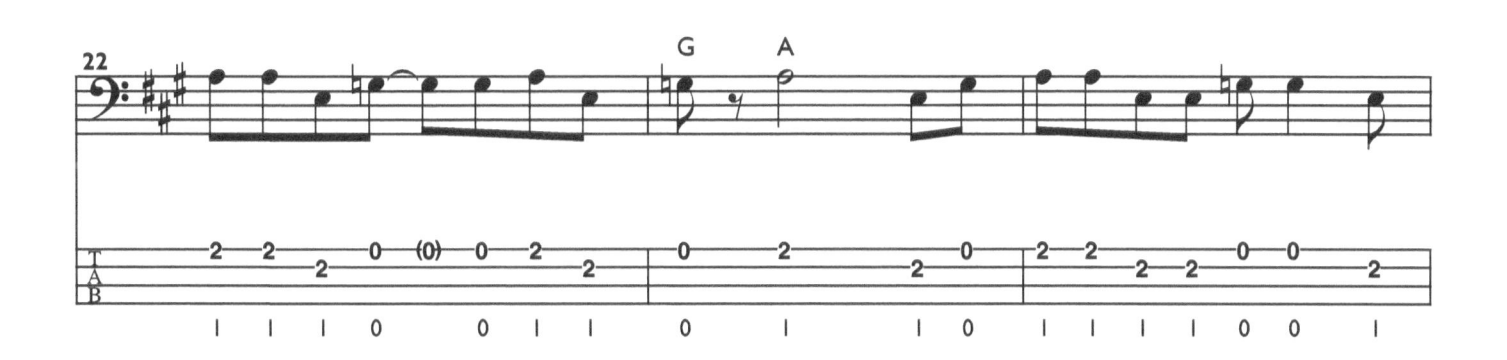

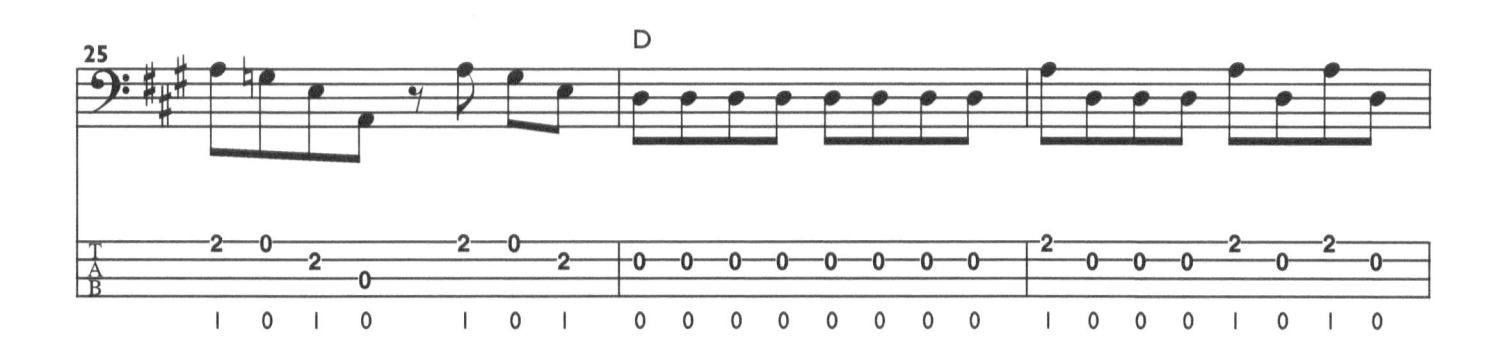

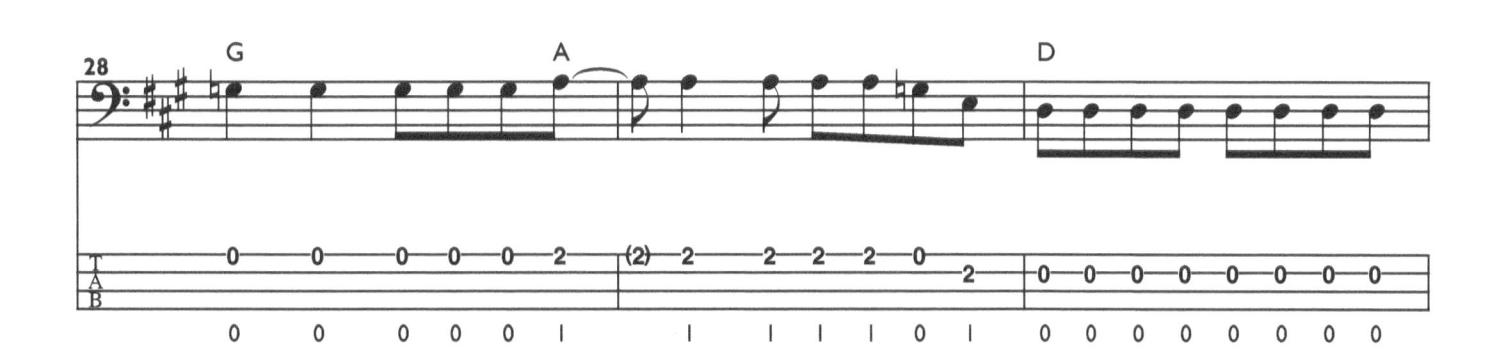

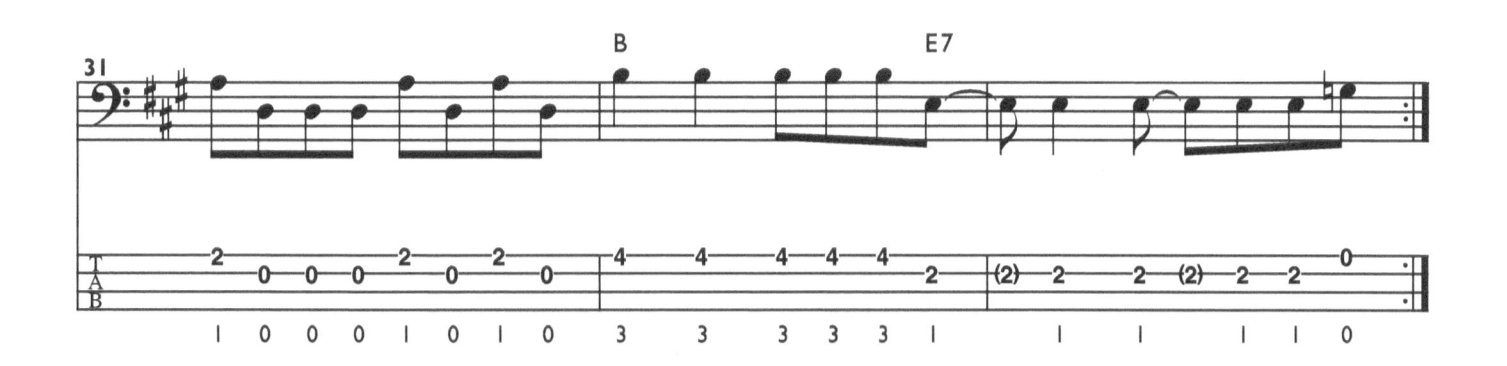

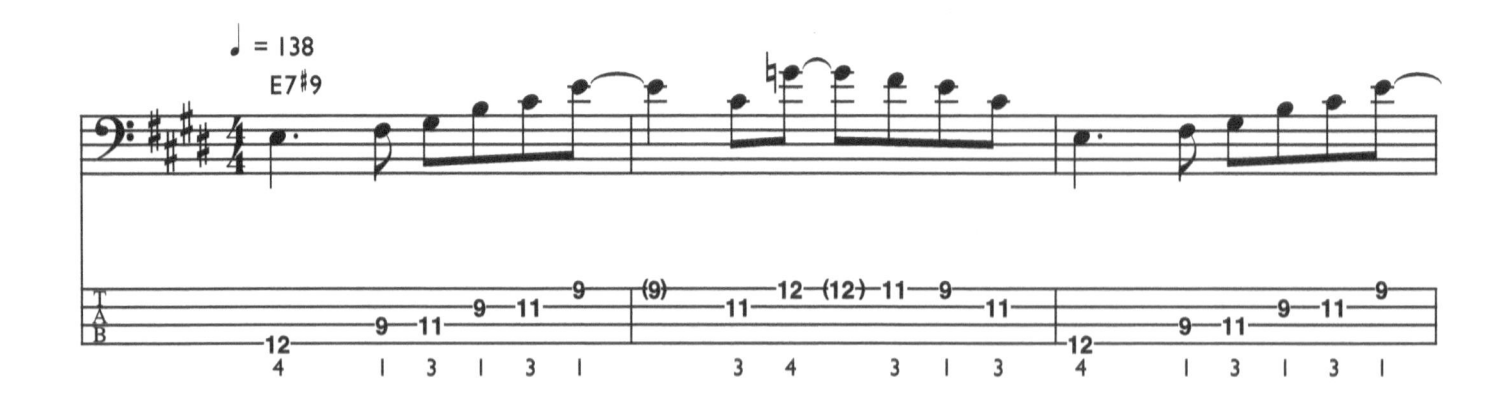

In the Style of Paul McCartney (with The Beatles)

Paul McCartney almost needs no introduction. As a founding member and co-songwriter for The Beatles (along with John Lennon), he helped to create the rock style that we know today. With the magnitude of those accomplishments, it's easy to overlook his unmistakable bass sound. McCartney's melodic bass playing is truly distinctive and was a key element to the sound of The Beatles.

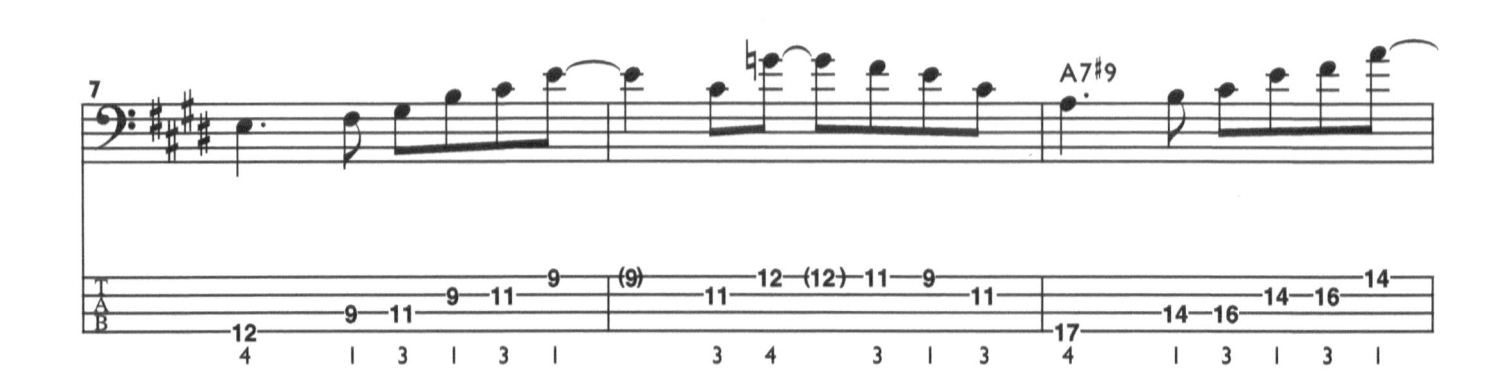

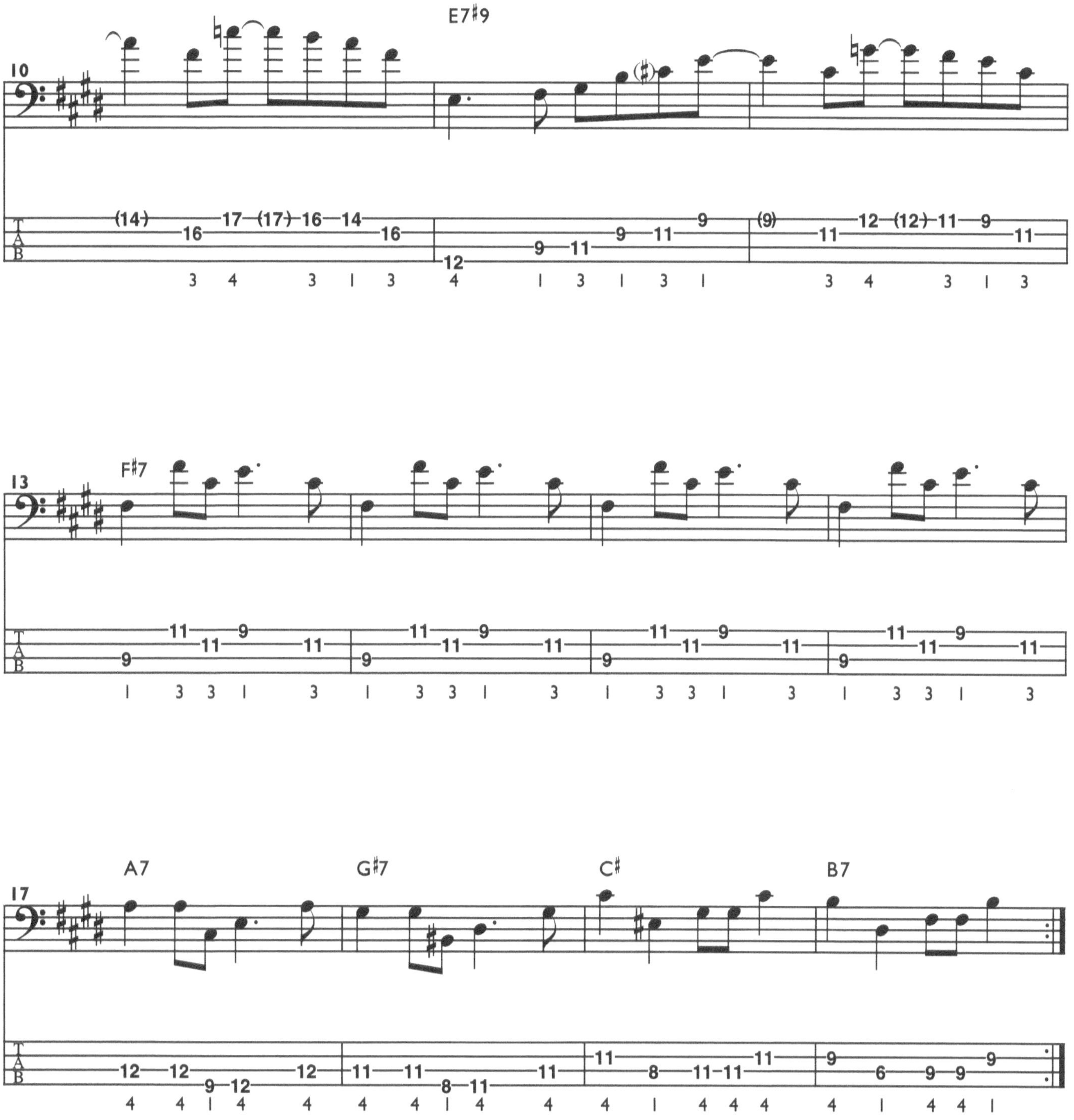
10
E7♯9
13
F♯7
17
A7
G♯7
C♯
B7

Another Line in the Style of Paul McCartney

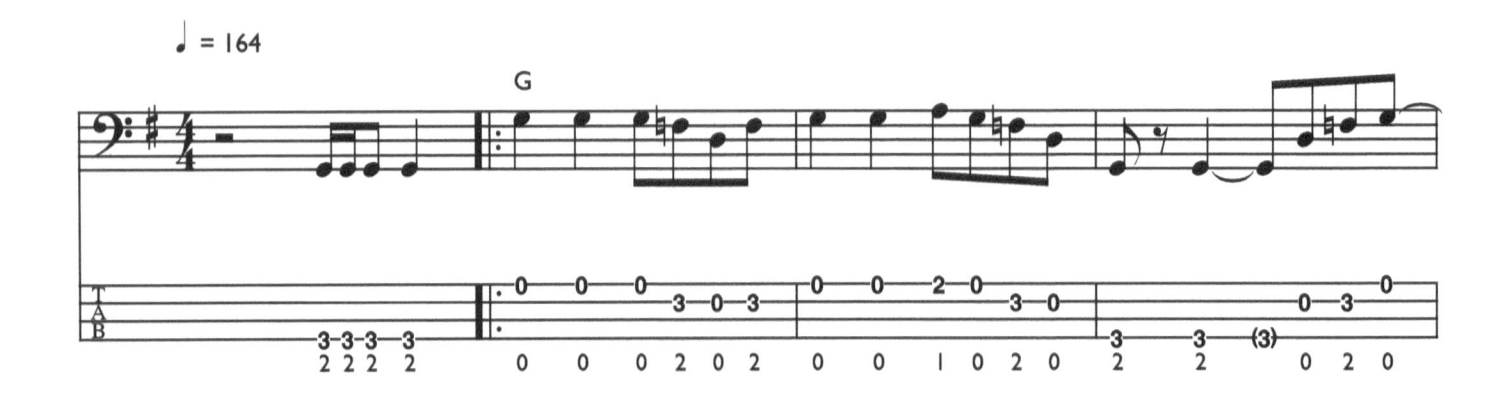

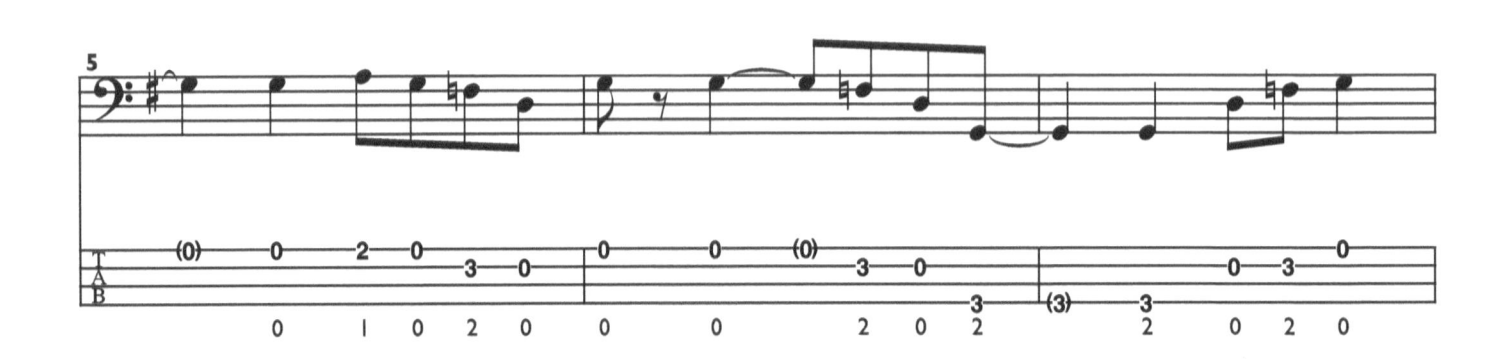

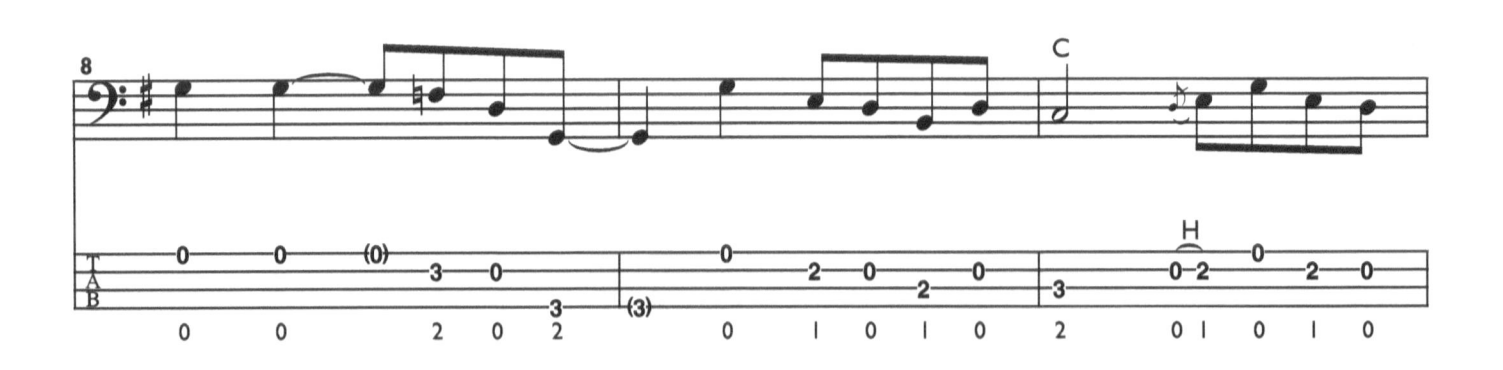

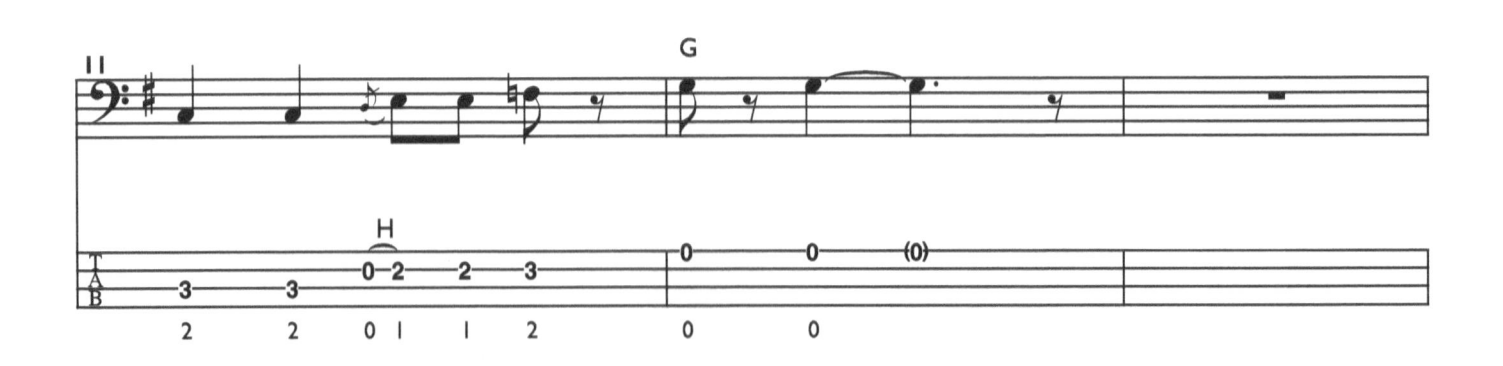

51

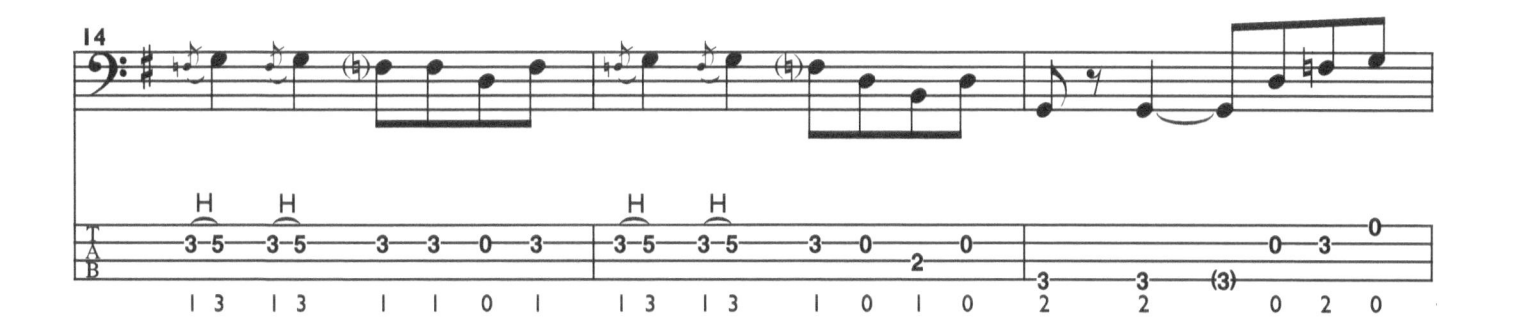

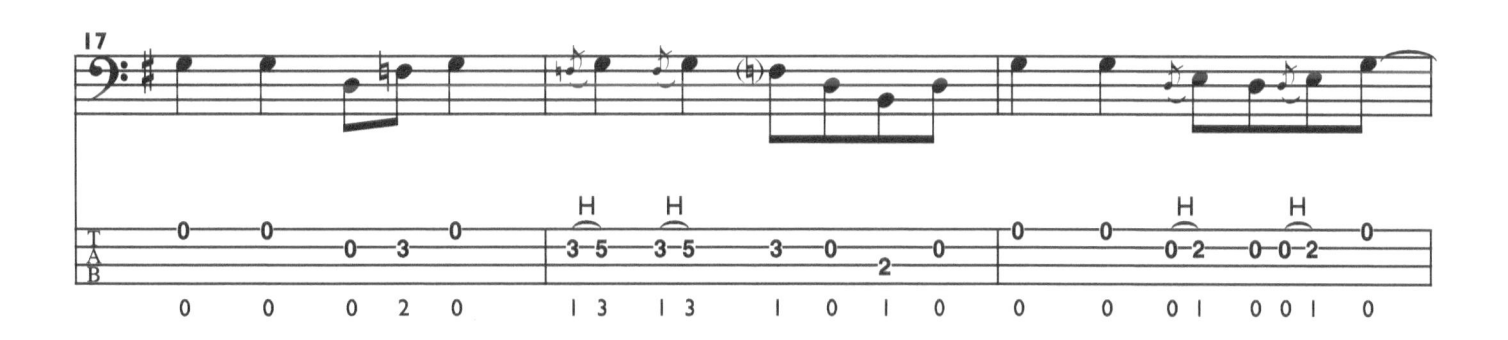

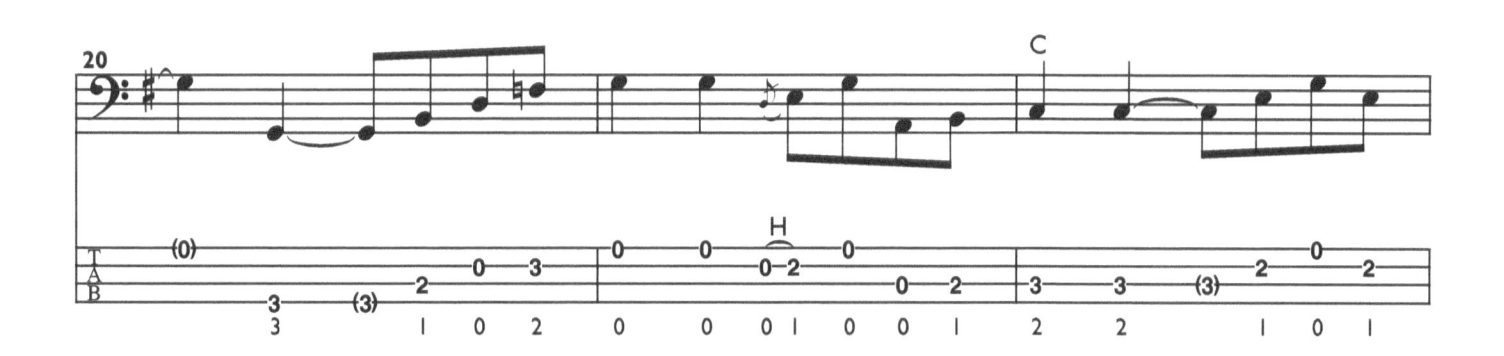

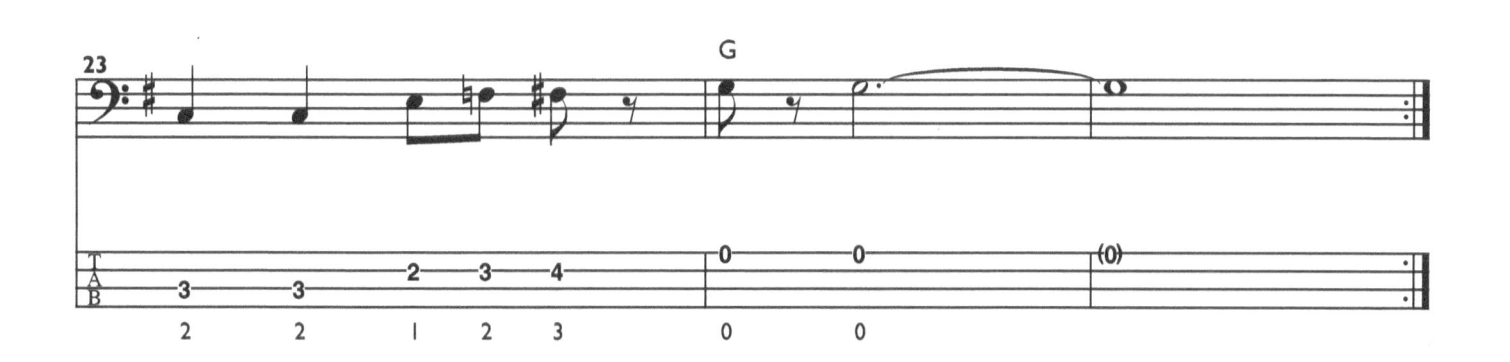

In the Style of John Paul Jones (with Led Zeppelin)

As the bassist for Led Zeppelin, John Paul Jones has had as much influence on the rock bass style as any bassist alive. His solid playing in Zeppelin's "power trio" format is the benchmark for all rock bassists that have come after him.

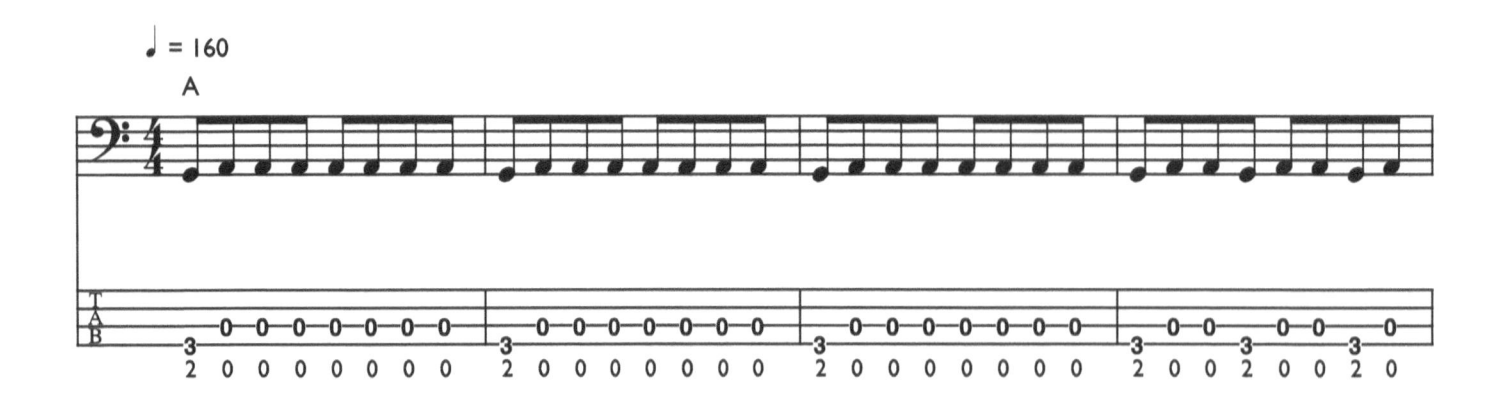

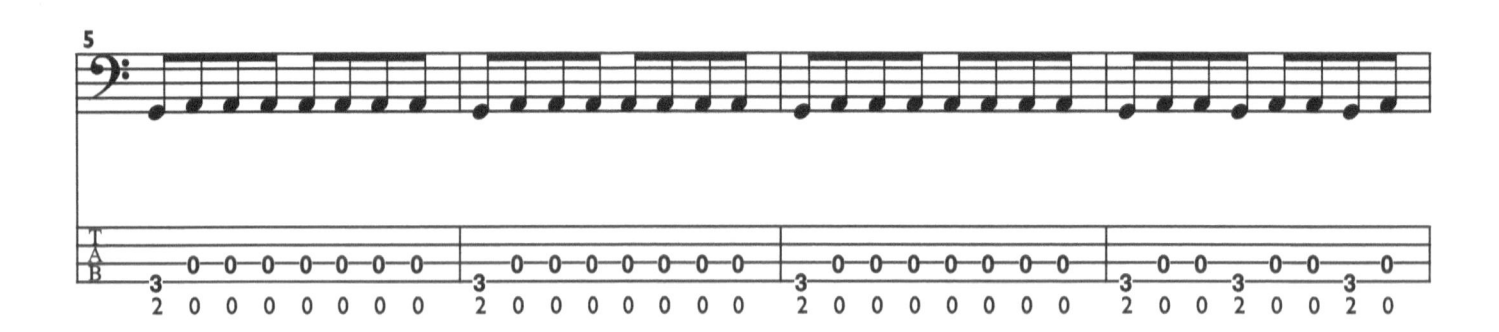

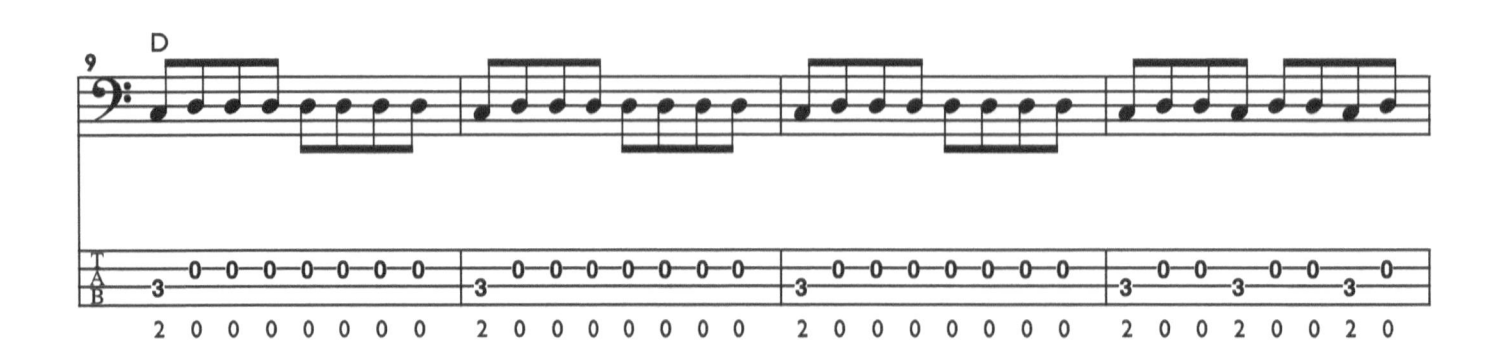

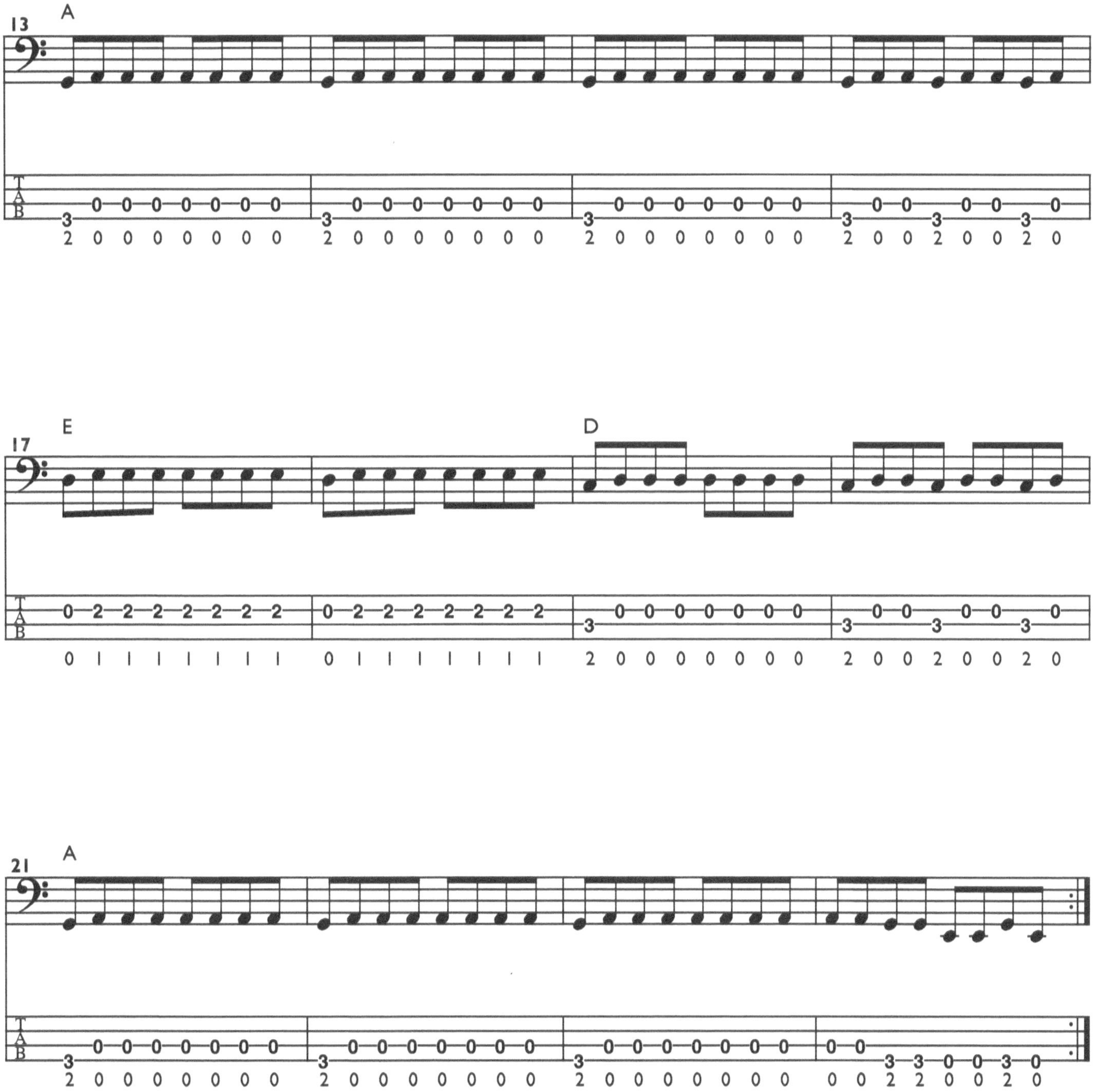
13
A
17
E
D
21
A

In the Style of Noel Redding (with The Jimi Hendrix Experience)

Noel Redding, bassist for the Jimi Hendrix Experience, was originally a guitarist; possibly for that reason, he played the bass with a pick. Redding was an extremely important part of the Hendrix trio because his solid bass playing served to anchor the time, leaving Hendrix and drummer Mitch Mitchell free to play more loosely, which contributed to the signature sound of the trio.

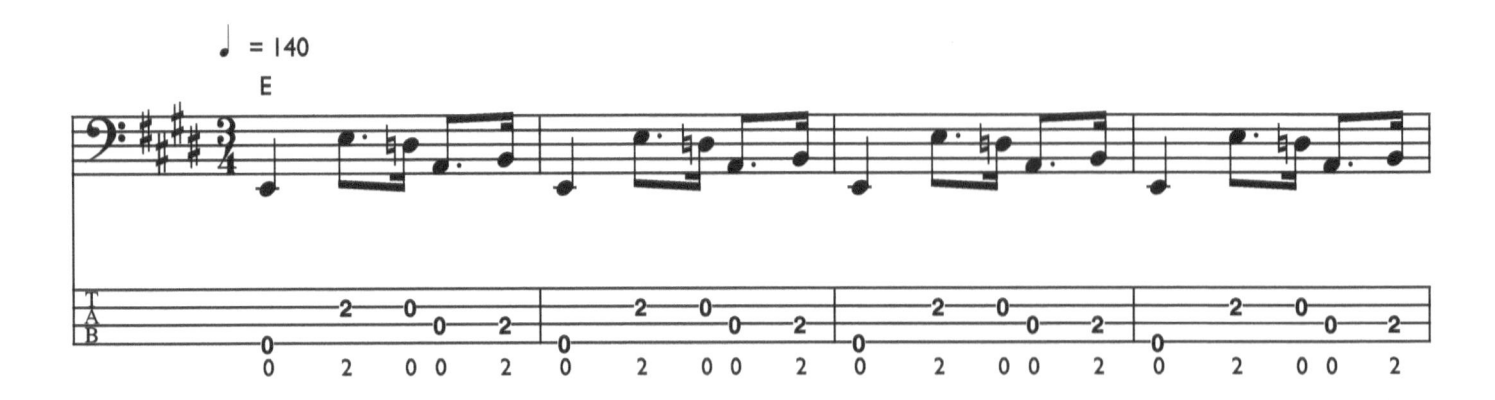

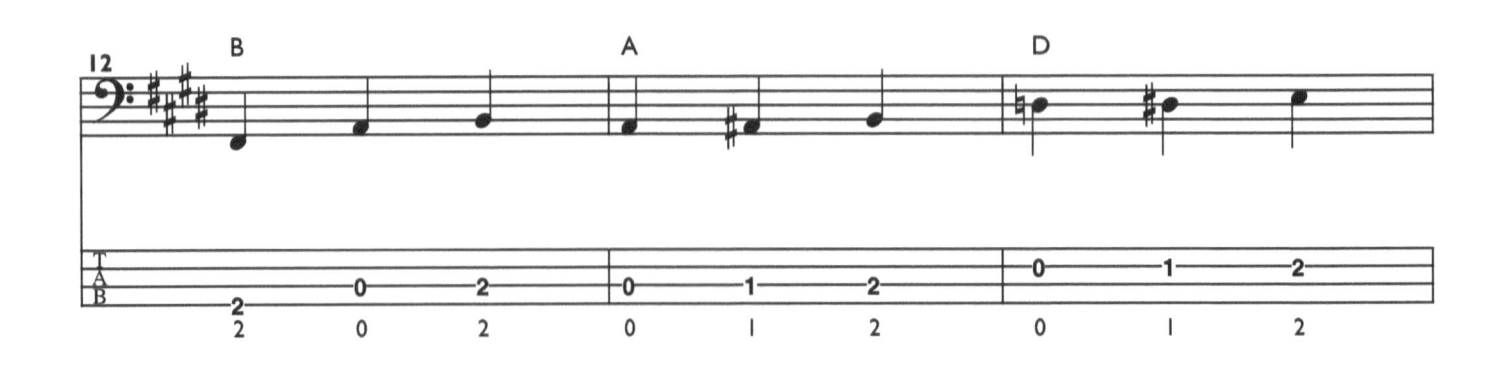

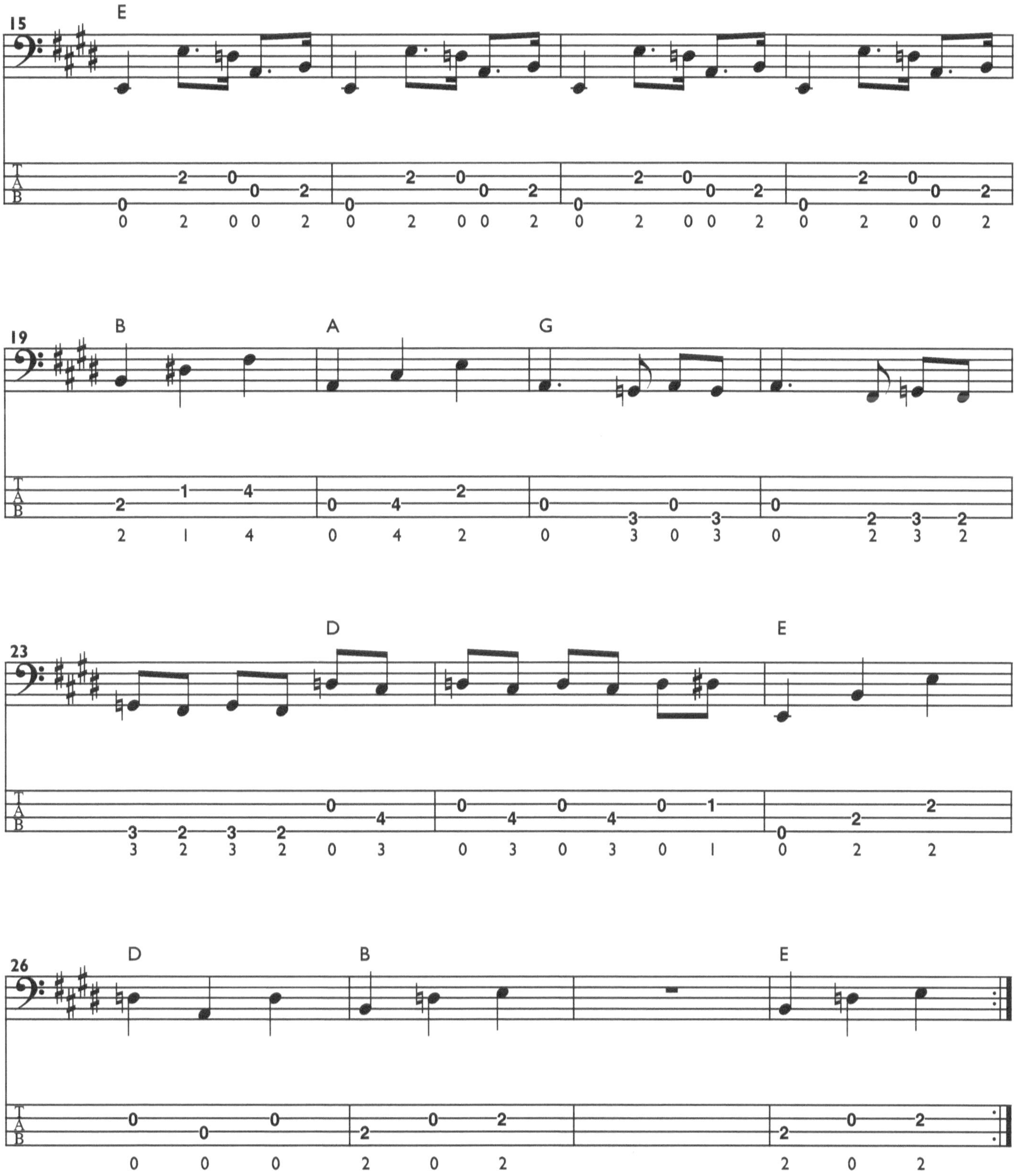
15
E
19
B
A
G
23
D
E
26
D
B
E

In the Style of John Entwistle (with The Who)

John Entwistle is one of the most technically skilled bassists in rock. His virtuosic playing as bassist for The Who has been inspirational to countless rock bassists.

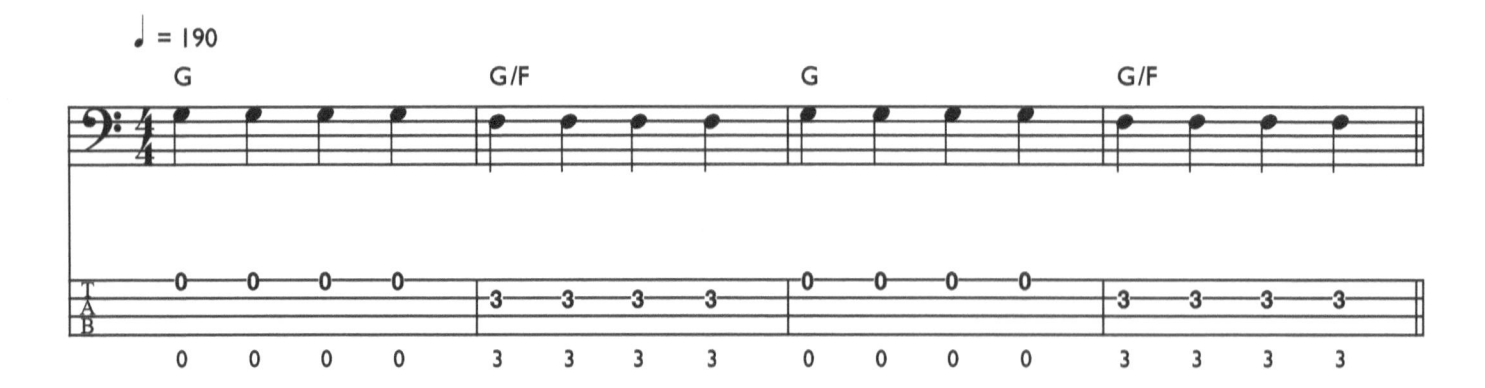

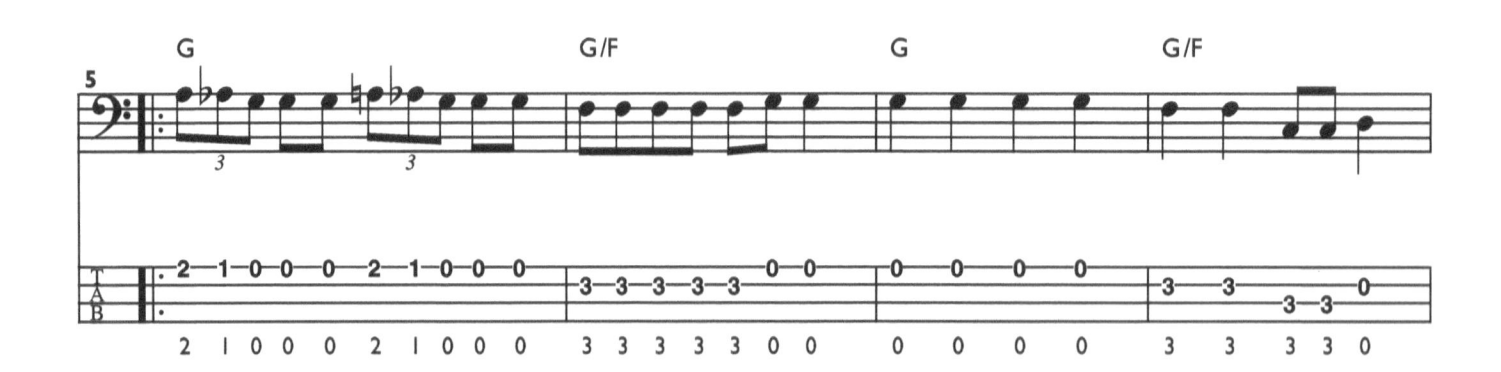

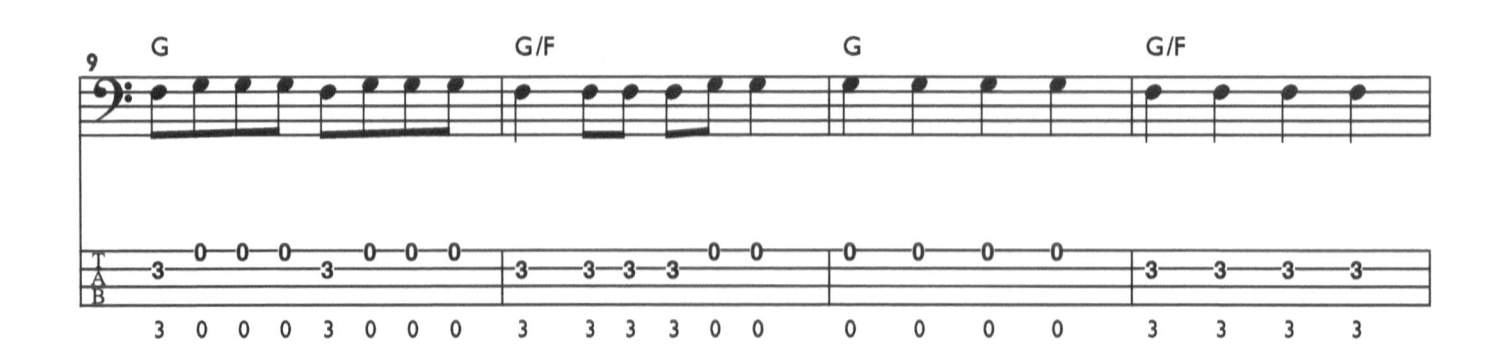

57

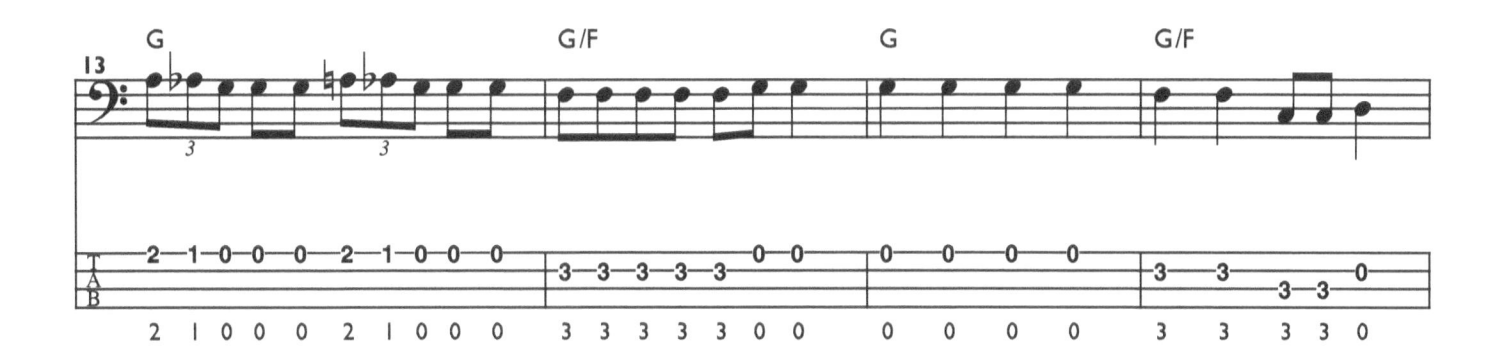

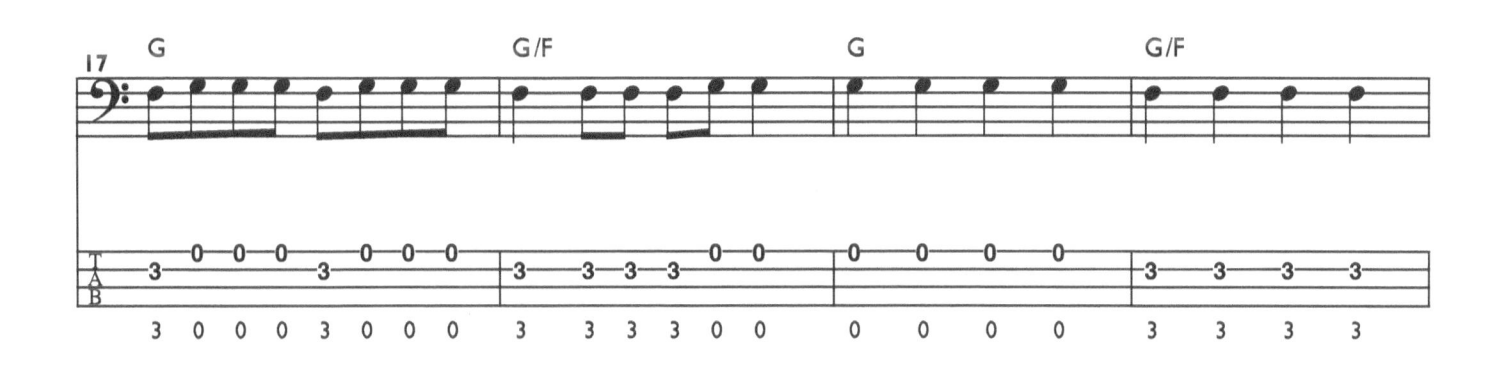

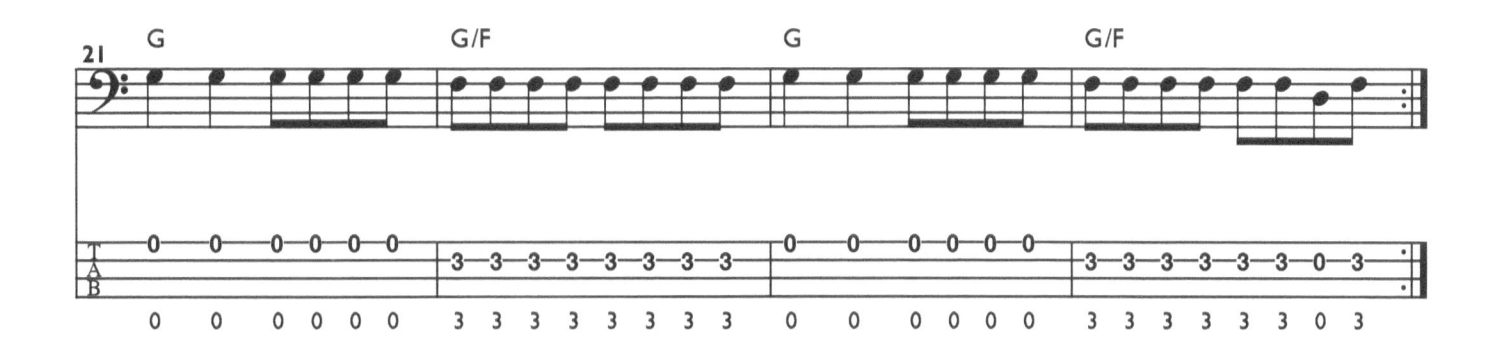

In the Style of Roger Waters (with Pink Floyd)

As a founding member, bassist, vocalist, and principal songwriter for Pink Floyd, Roger Waters has been on the cutting edge of progressive rock for many years. His style incorporates rock, jazz, and classical influences, sometimes including odd time signatures such as in the line below.

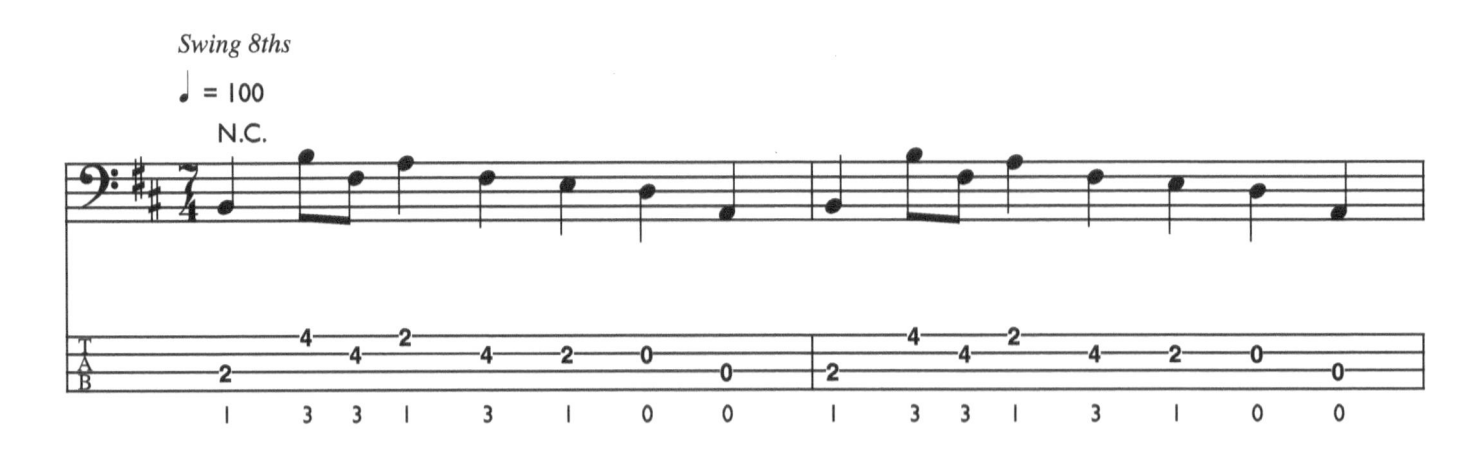

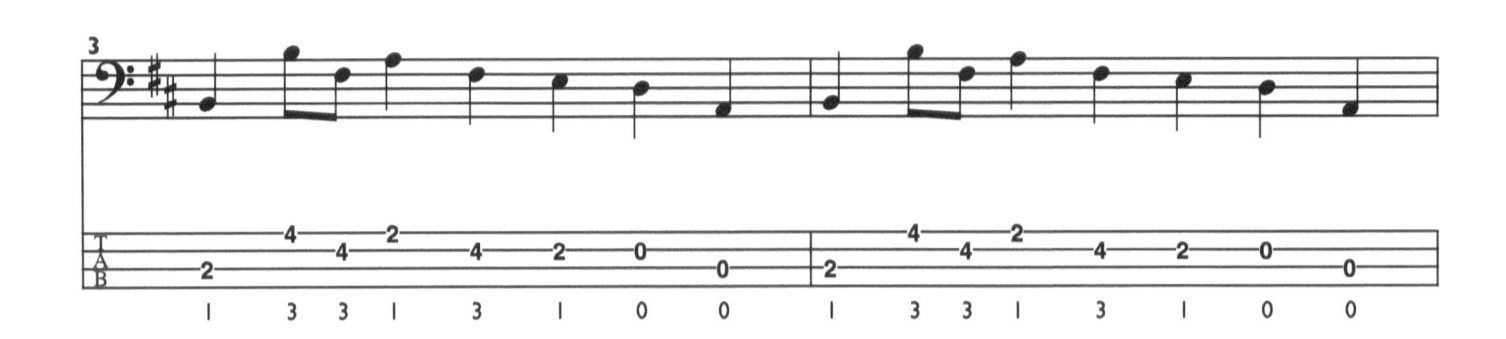

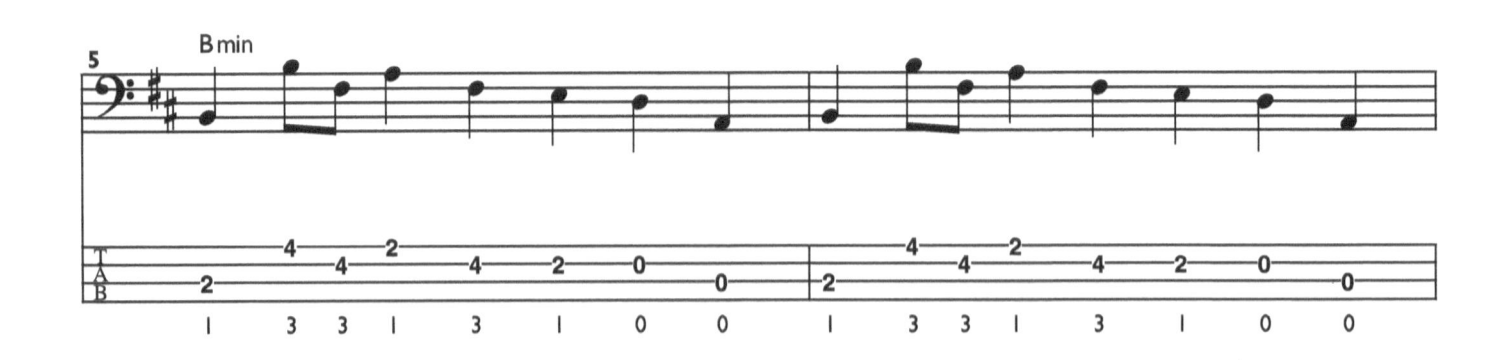

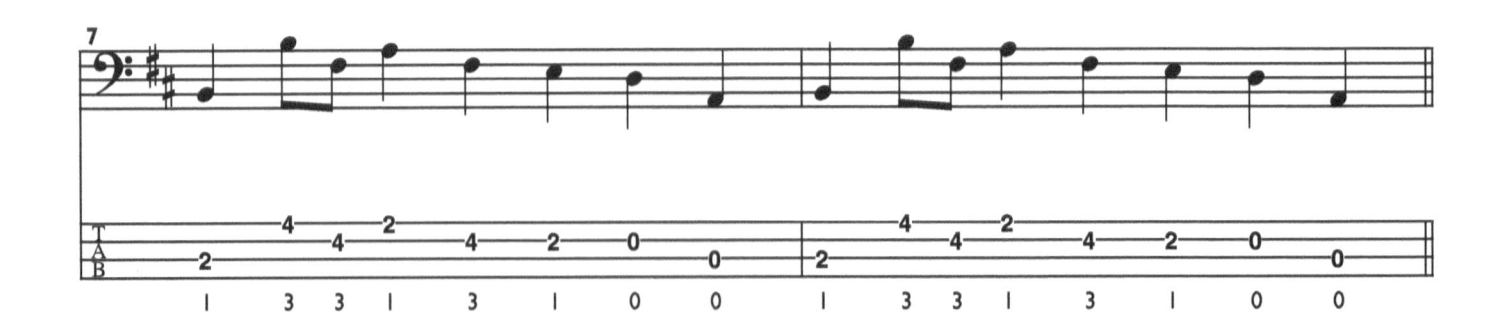

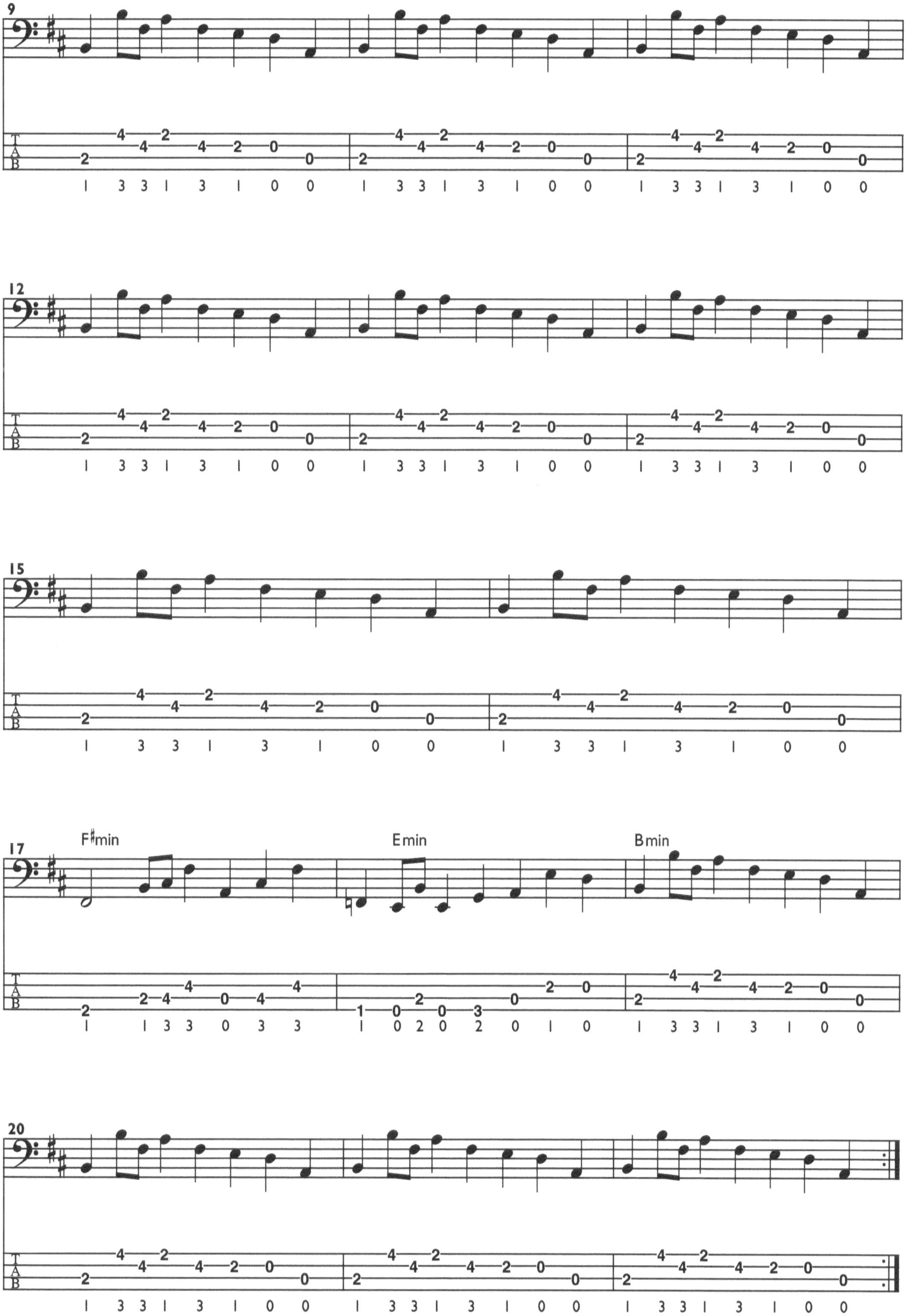
9
12
15
17
F♯min
Emin
Bmin
20
TAB

In the Style of Berry Oakley (with The Allman Brothers Band)

Berry Oakley, bassist for The Allman Brothers Band, was possibly the most important bassist in the southern rock genre. His melodic and flowing bass lines, together with the guitar playing of Duane Allman and Dickie Betts, helped create the band's distinctive sound.

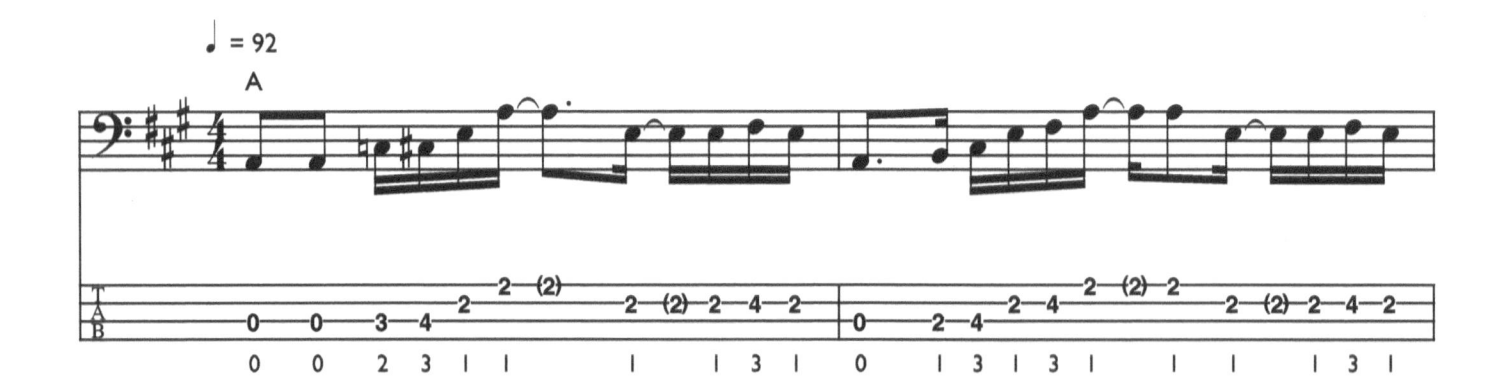

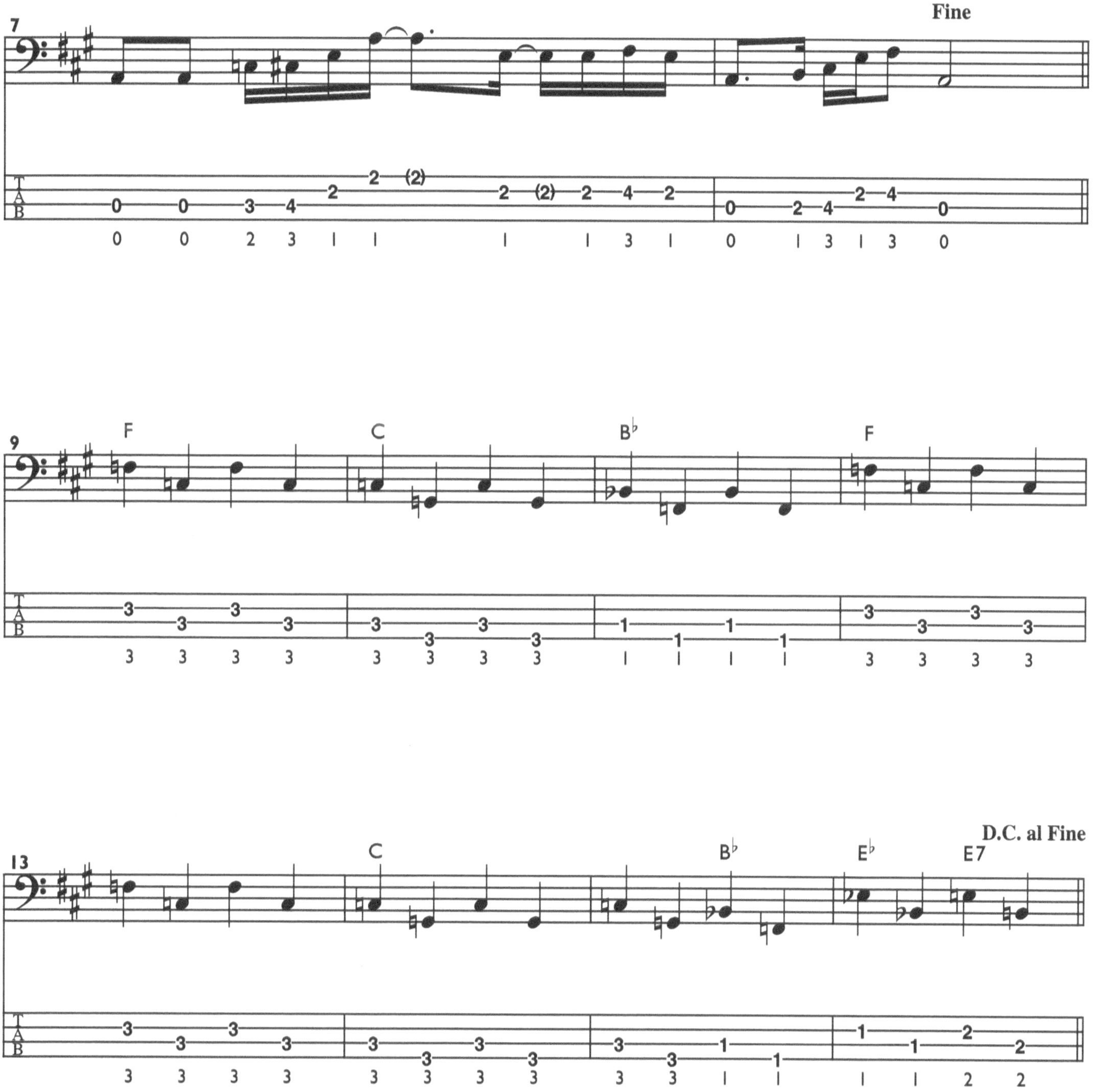
7
Fine
9
F
C
B♭
F
13
C
B♭
E♭
E7
D.C. al Fine

In the Style of Jason Newsted (with Metallica)

In many ways, Metallica is the quintessential heavy metal band and Jason Newsted, as the bassist for the band for more than 14 years, is one of the most important bassists in that genre. Newsted's strong sound and rhythmic intensity helped create the powerful sound and feel Metallica is famous for.

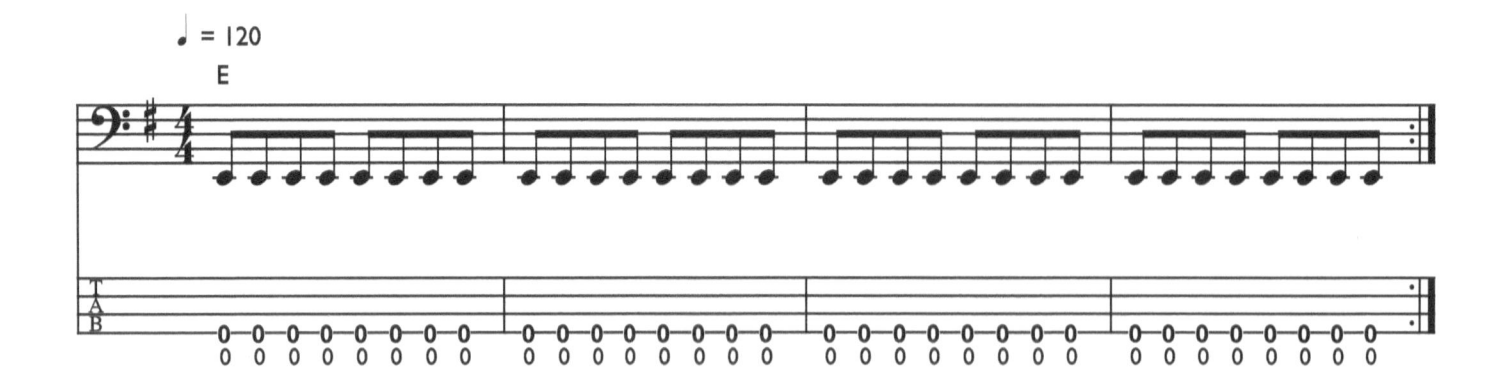

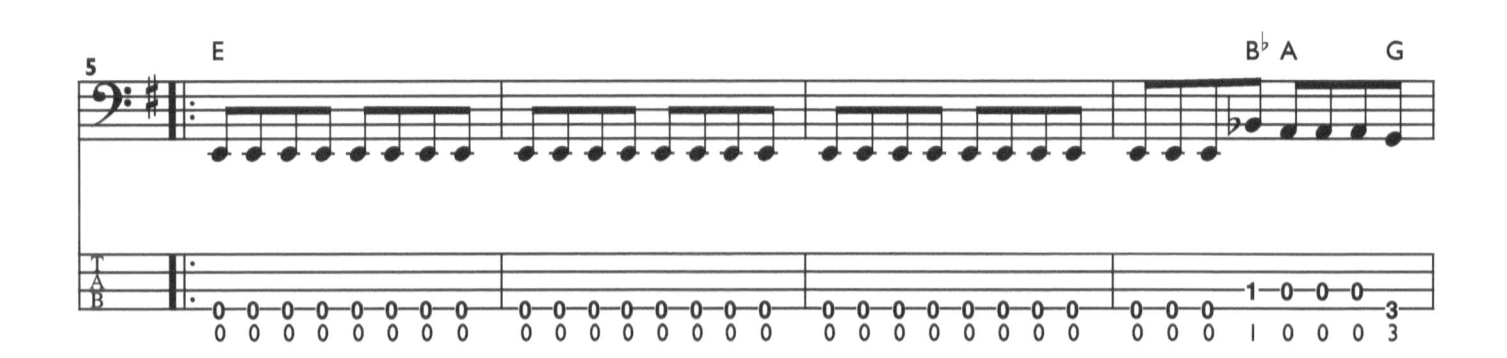

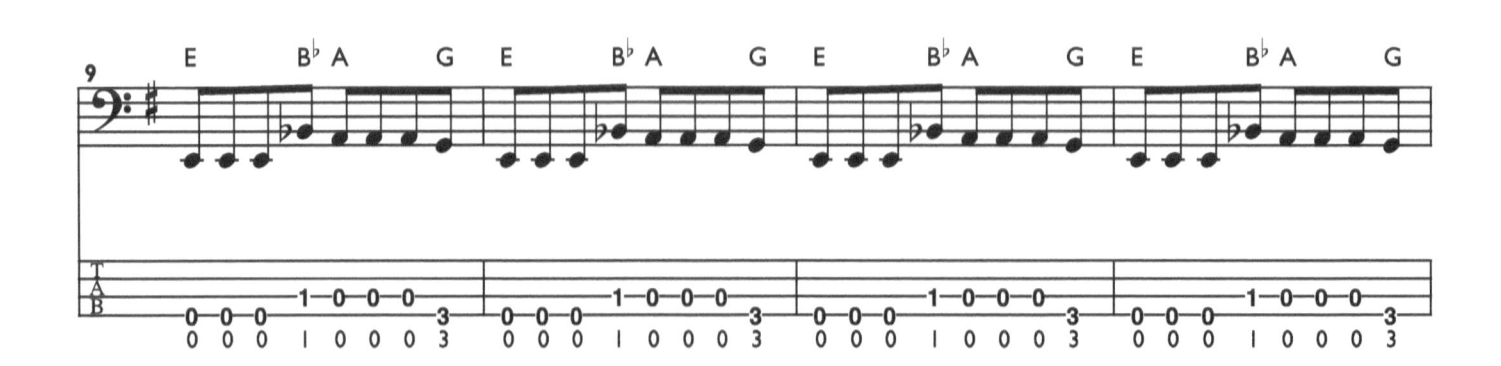

63

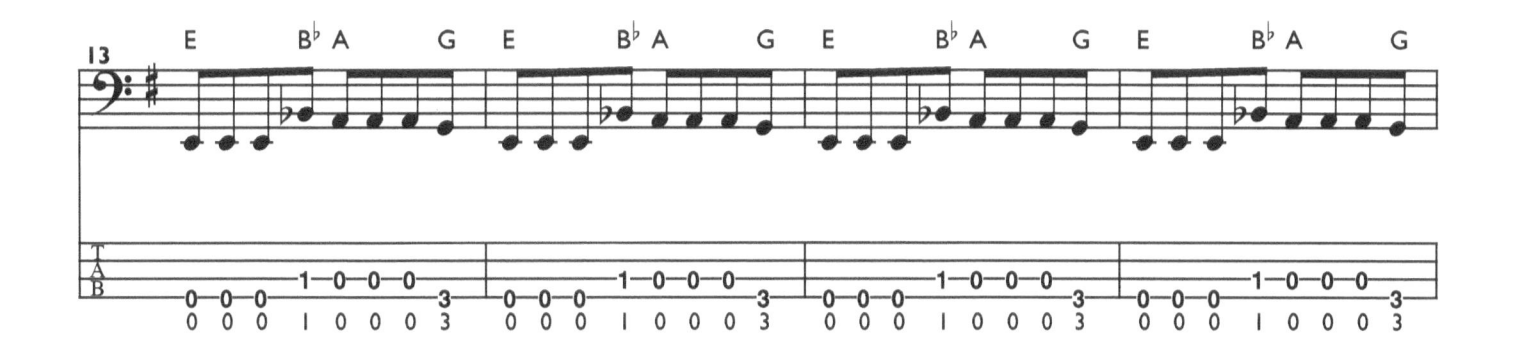

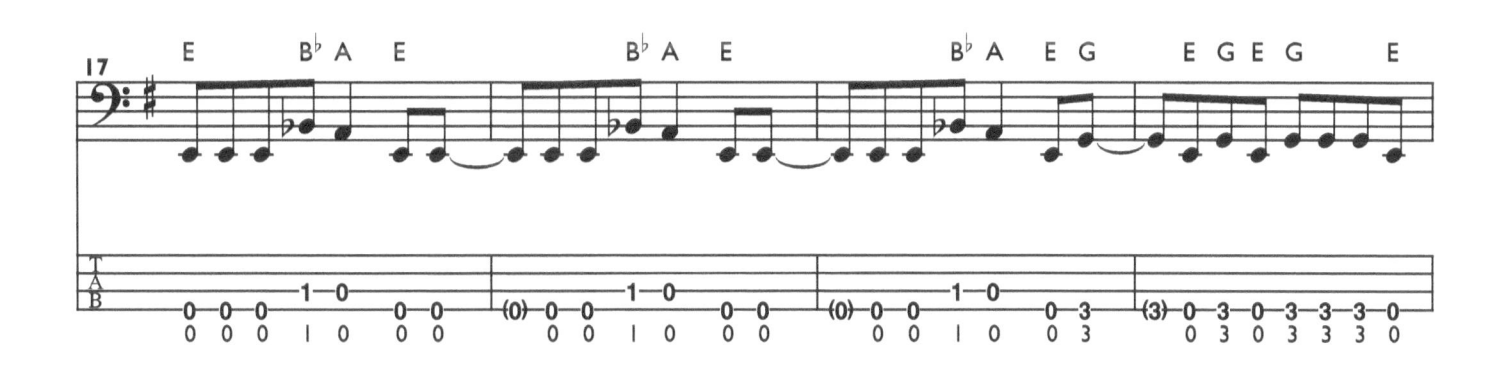

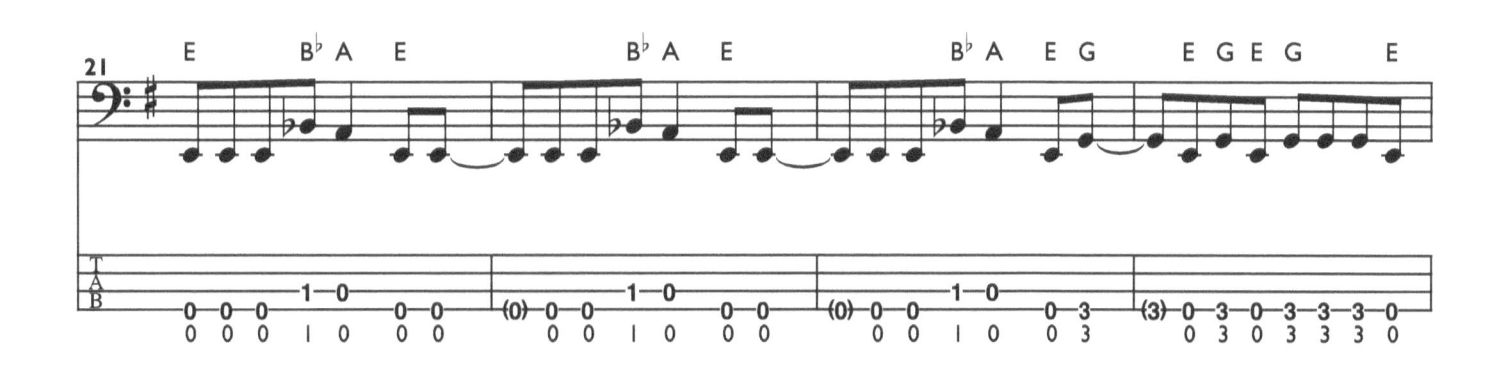

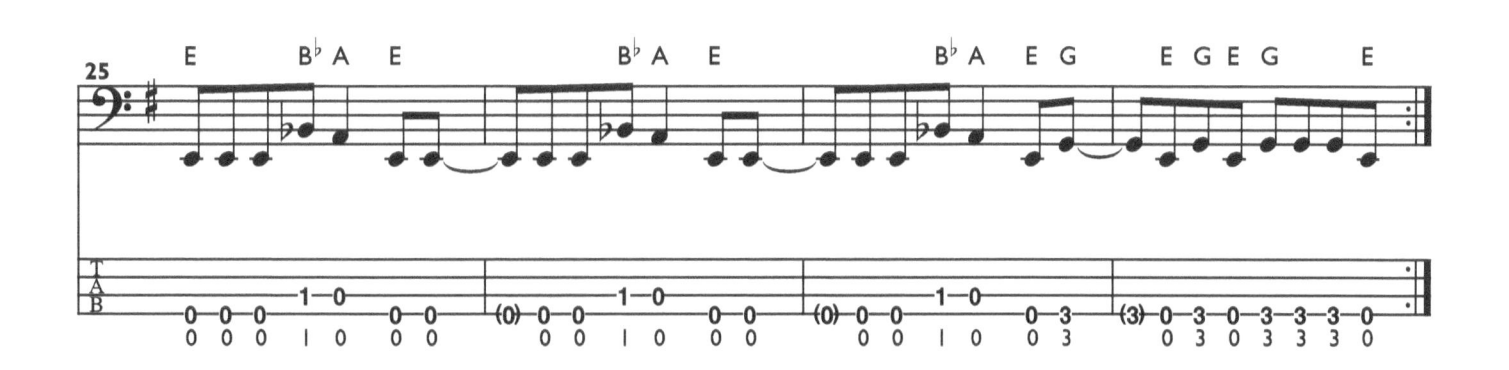

In the Style of Cliff Williams (with AC/DC)

AC/DC is considered one of the pioneers of heavy metal, but they are most often classified as "hard rock." Cliff Williams, the band's bassist since 1977, provides a solid musical foundation with his powerful, driving, no-frills bass lines.

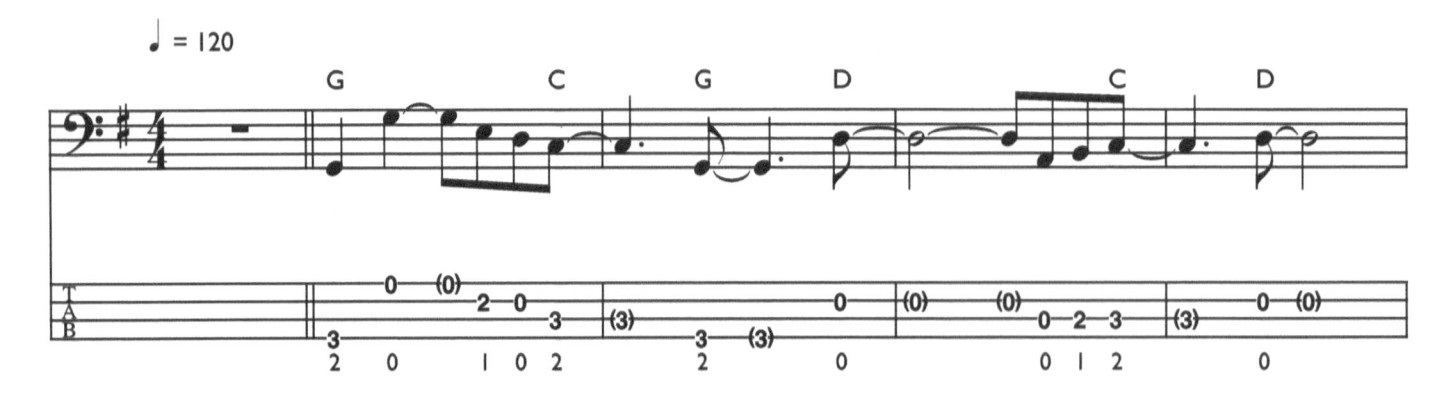

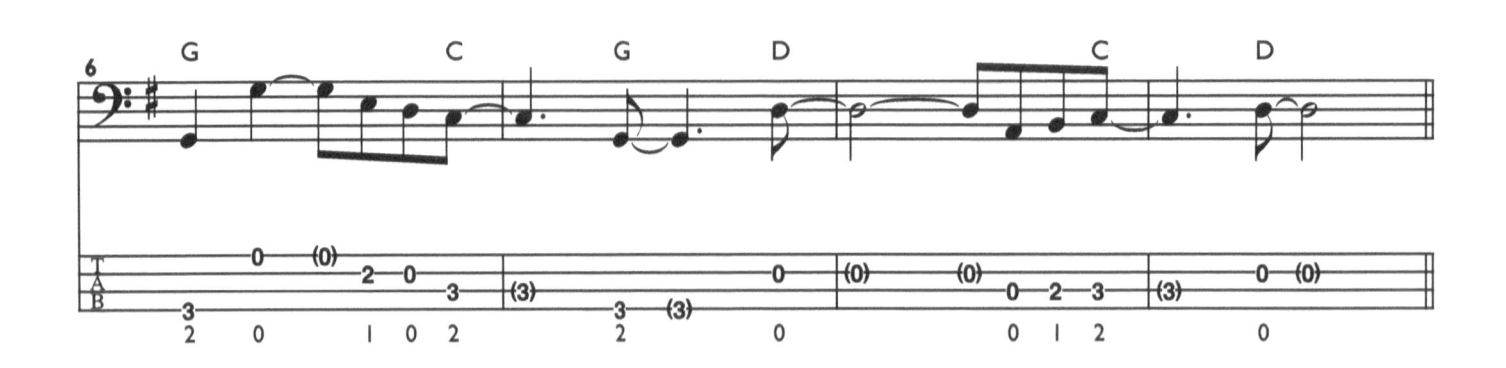

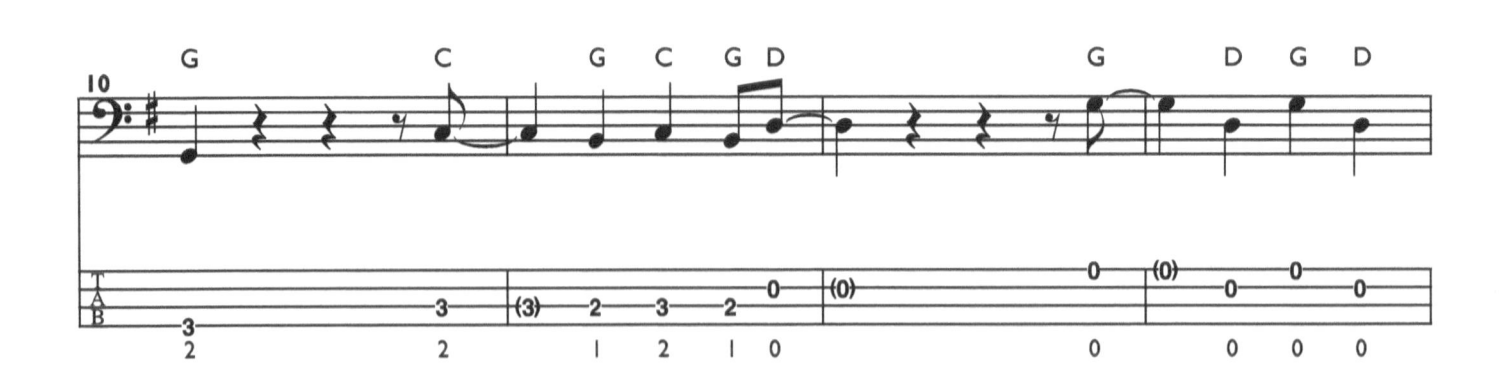

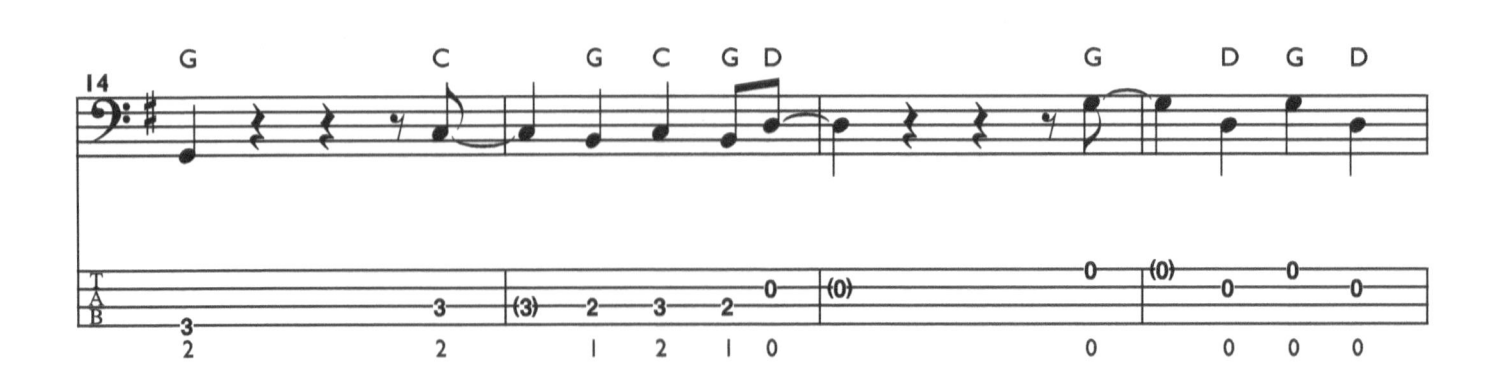

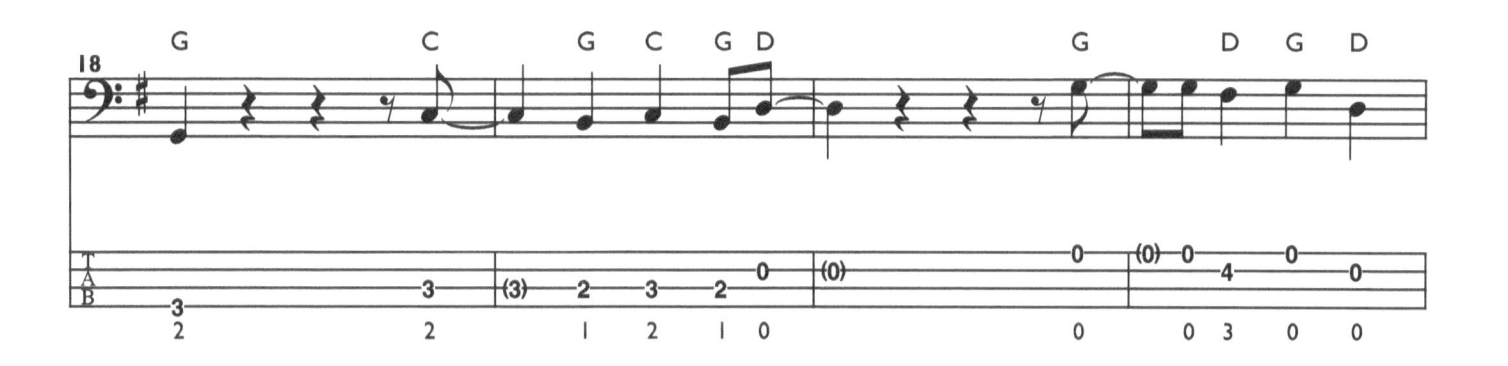

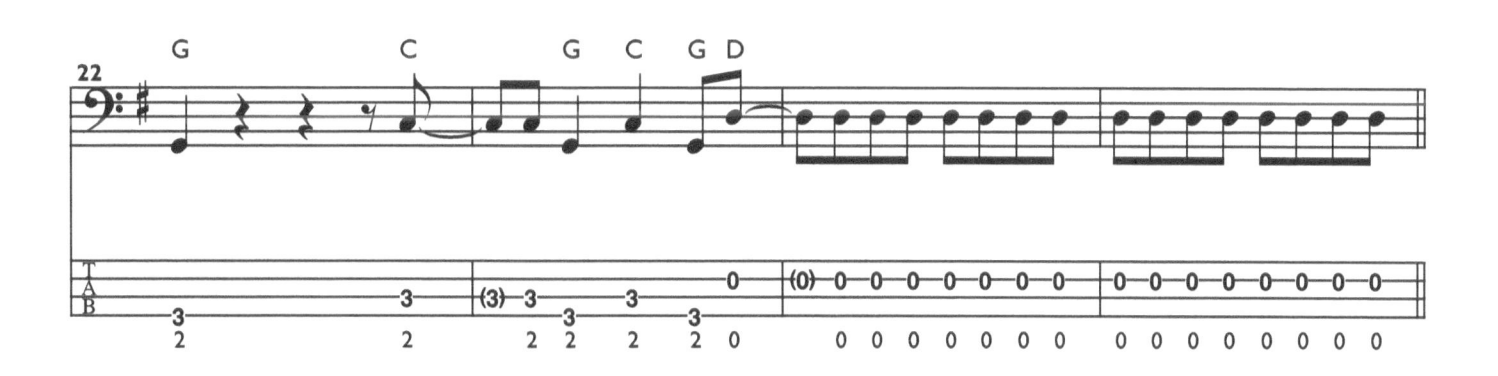

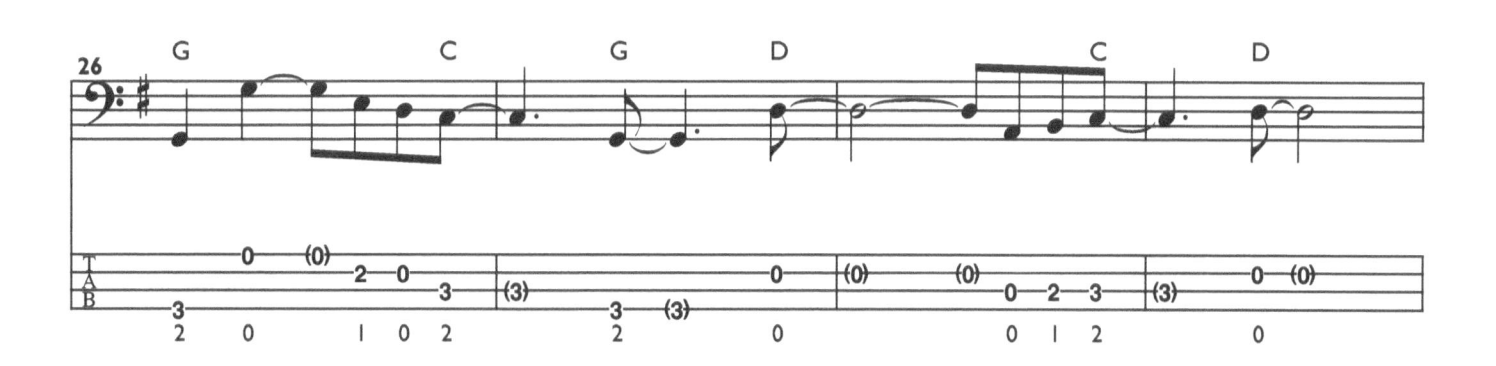

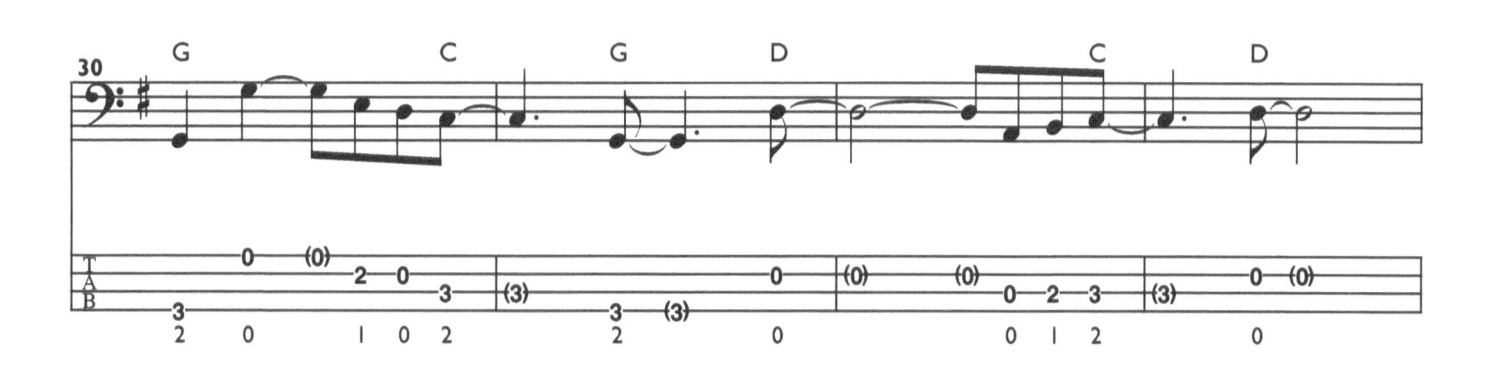

(Continued on next page)

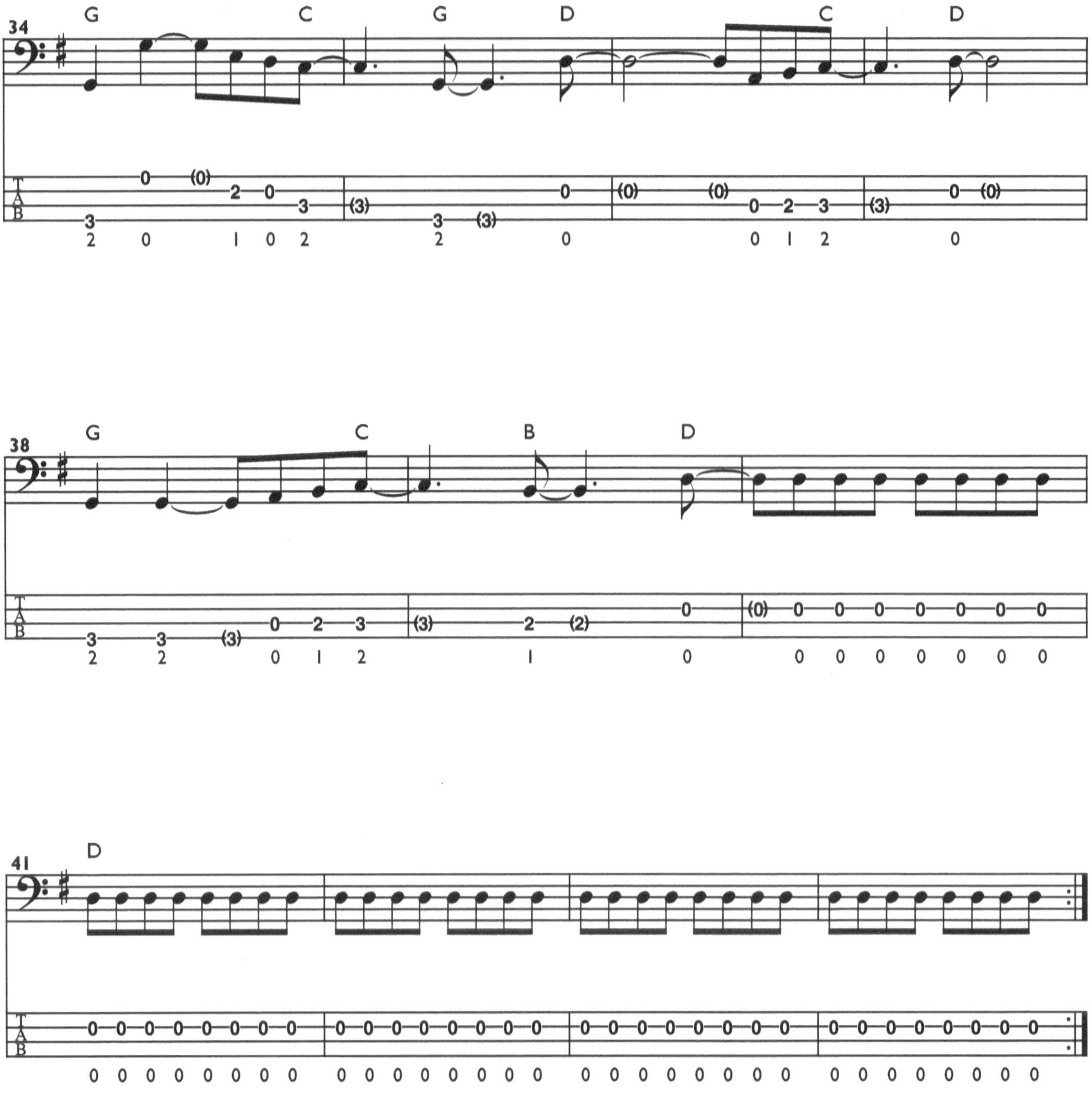
34
G C G D C D
TAB
38
G C B D
TAB
41
D
TAB

In the Style of Mike Dirnt (with Green Day)

Mike Dirnt is a founding member and integral part of the pop punk band Green Day. His strong and creative bass lines are an essential part of what makes up the band's sound.

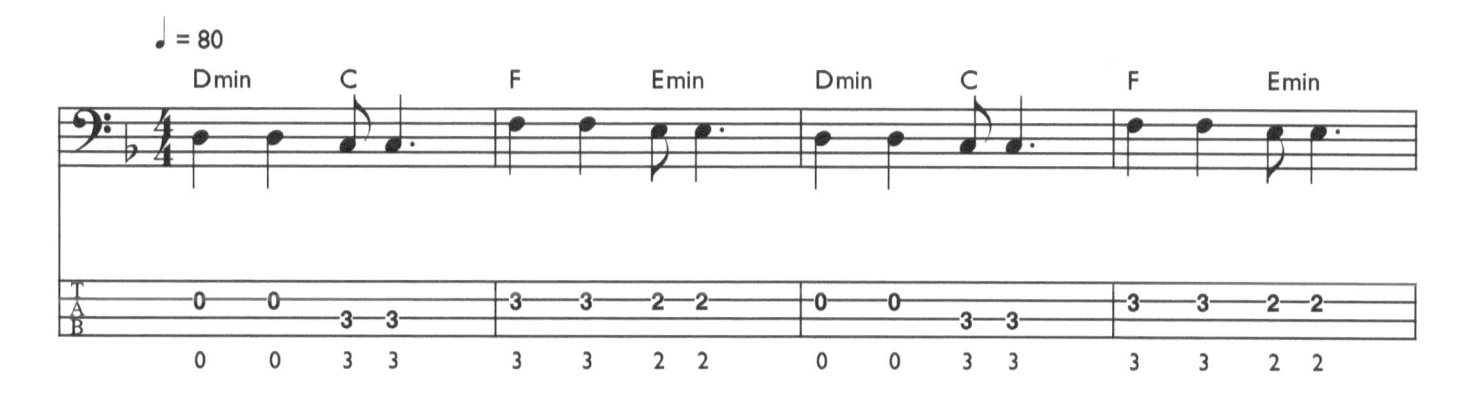

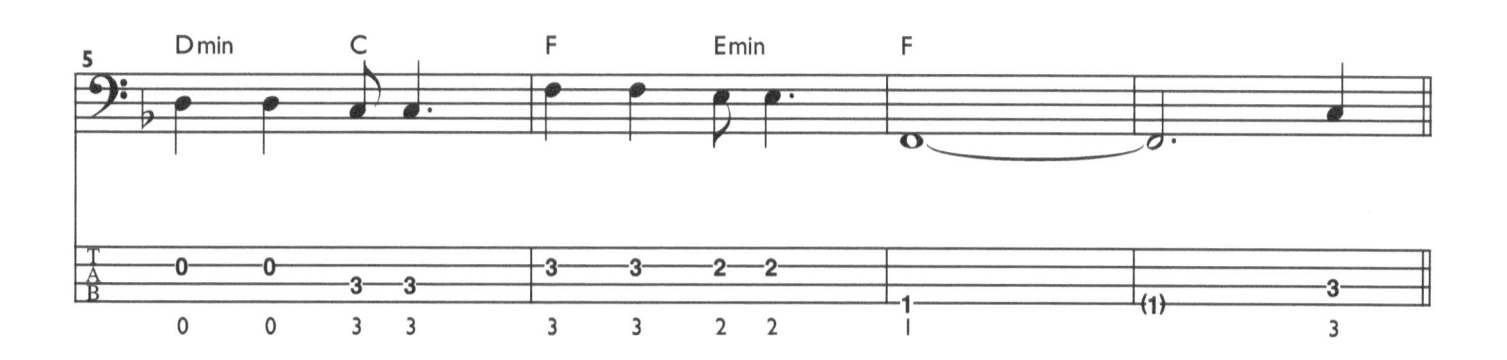

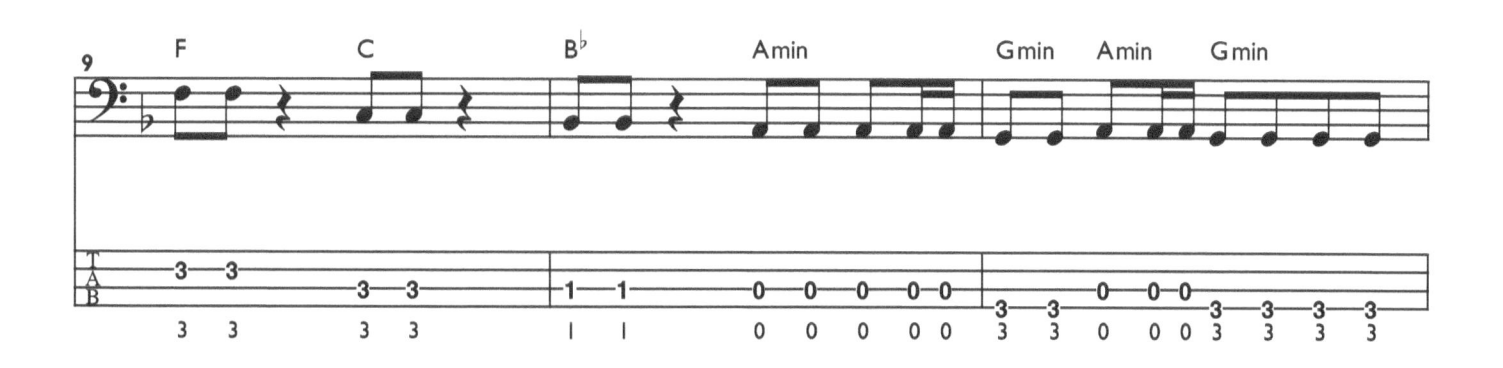

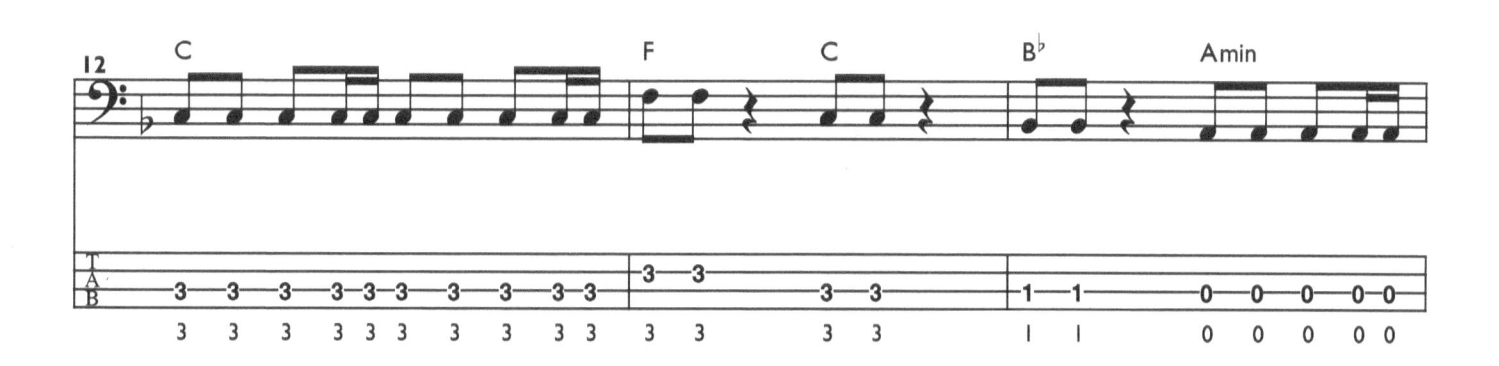

(Continued on next page)

15
Gmin Amin Gmin
C
B♭
B
C
19
Dmin
C
F
Emin
Dmin
C
F
Emin
23
Dmin
C
F
Emin
B♭
C
27
Dmin
C
F
Emin
Dmin
C
F
Emin
31
Dmin
C
F
Emin
F

35
C
Dmin C
B♭ Amin
Dmin C
39
F Amin
Dmin C
F Amin
B♭
43
C
Dmin C
F Emin
Dmin C
47
F Emin
Dmin C
F Emin
F

In the Style of Krist Novoselic (with Nirvana)

Following the huge success of Nirvana's single "Smells Like Teen Spirit," everyone took notice of grunge music and the Seattle sound. Krist Novoselic's bass lines were the foundation of the sound that carried Nirvana and Kurt Cobain to international fame.

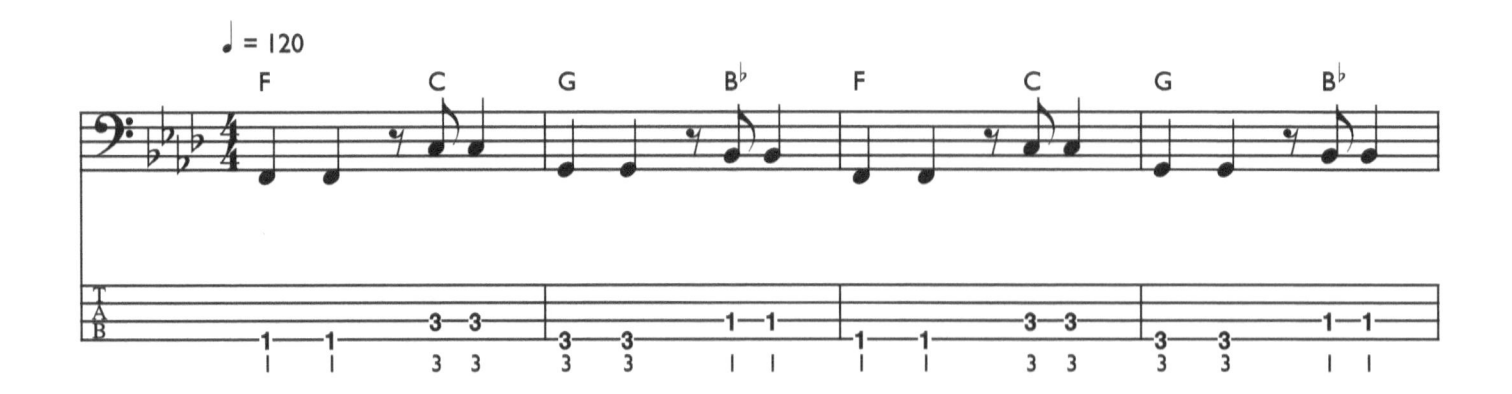

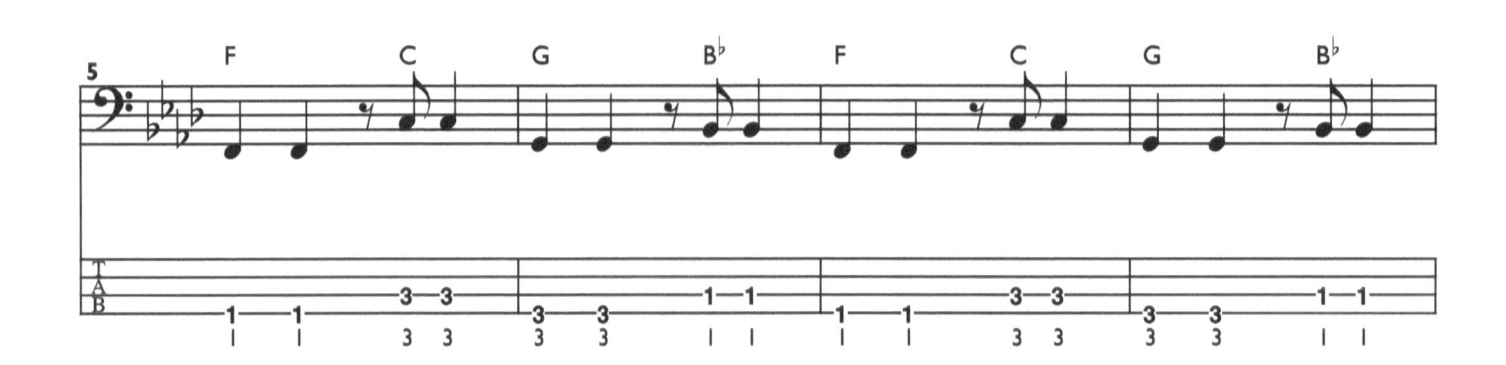

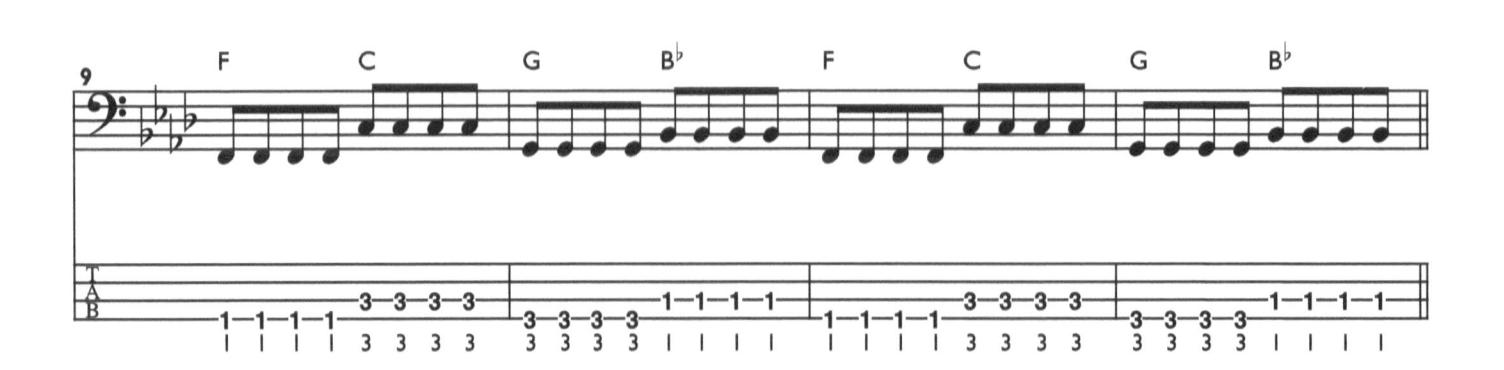

71

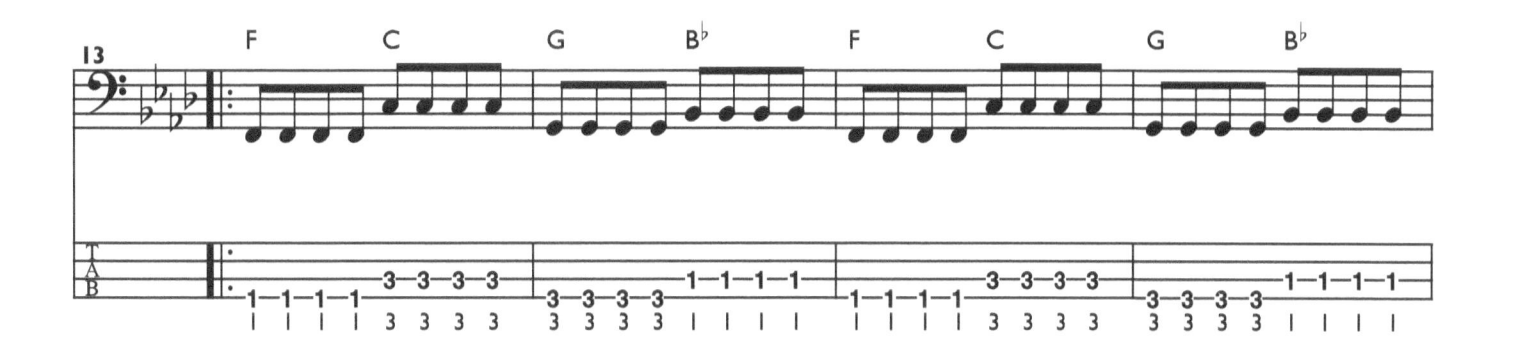

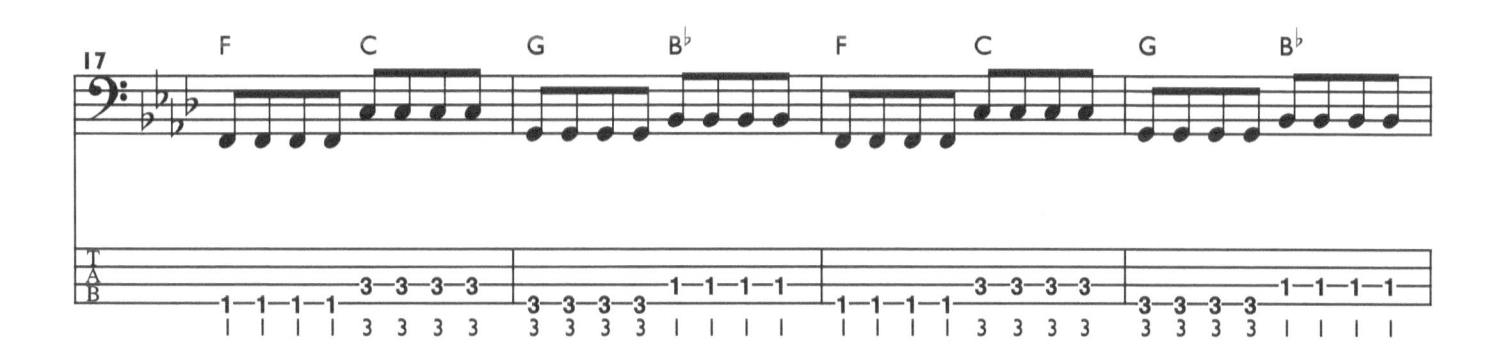

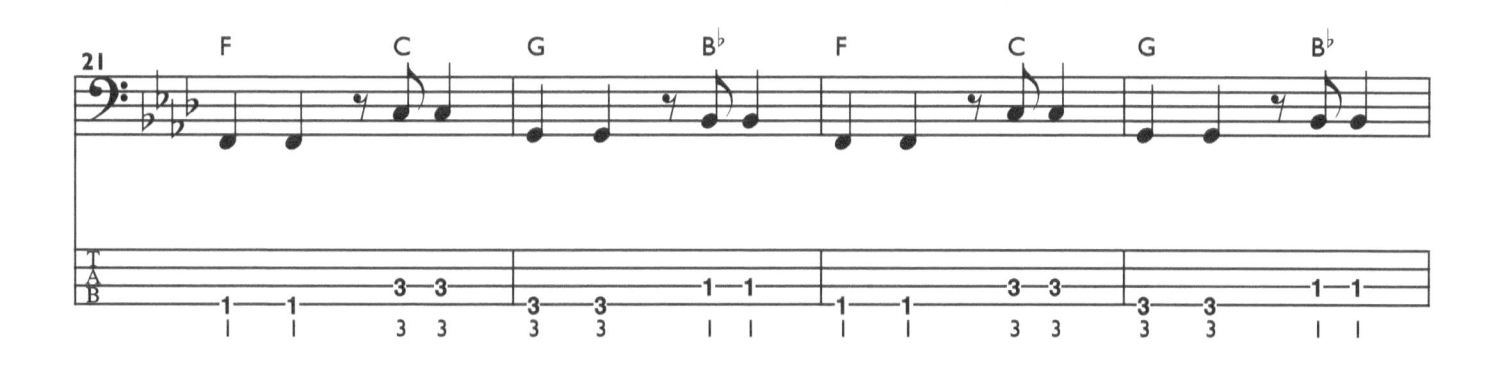

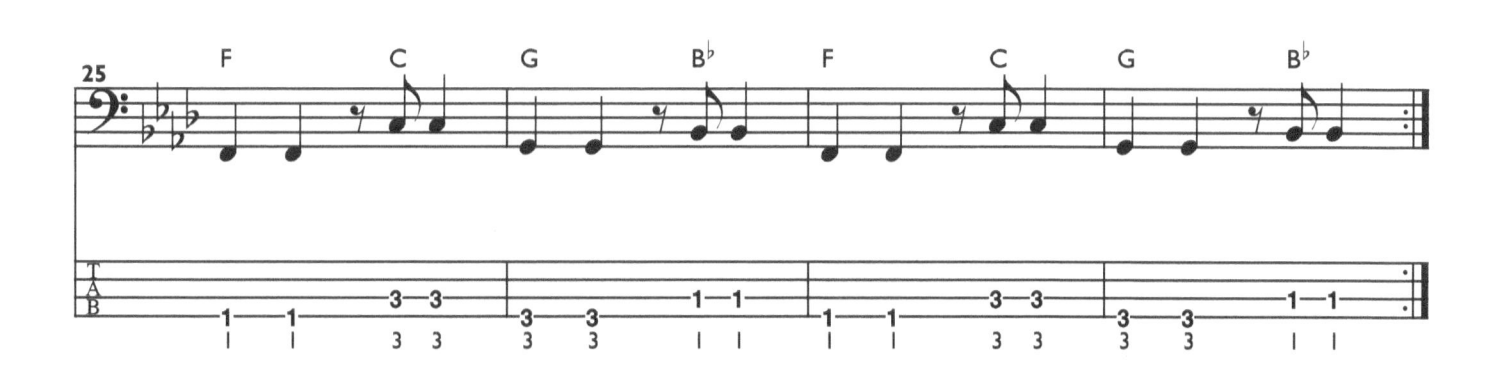

Chapter 4: Funk

A Brief History of Funk

The musical style we call "funk" was an off-shoot of soul and R&B and came to prominence in the 1960s. The first, and most important, band to consider its music "funk" was James Brown and His Famous Flames. Brown popularized and helped codify the funk style, first with the Famous Flames and later when his band changed its name to The J.B.'s. He was particularly insistent about one of funk's primary features: the rhythmic emphasis on the first beat of the measure. This groove, referred to as "hittin' on the one," was one of the key differences between the funk feel and jazz and R&B, which place emphasis on the backbeat (beats 2 and 4). In addition to this change in rhythmic emphasis, other differences include a more syncopated groove, static harmony, rhythmic hits, and lack of romantic lyrics and melodic content—all common in soul and R&B. Funk has been a popular and influential style for bass players, due to the fact that the bass takes such a prominent role in funk bands. The essential instrumental elements of a funk groove are the bass and drums, with the guitar and/or keyboard (and possibly horns) playing a less central and more complimentary role.

In addition to James Brown's groups, there have been many great funk bands. Another pioneer of the funk style was Sly Stone, with his band Sly & the Family Stone, which featured the groundbreaking bass stylings of Larry Graham. Their first recordings (and their performance at Woodstock) were crucial to introducing a wide audience to the funk style. Graham's signature "slap & pop" style (which he originated and refers to as "thumpin' and pluckin'") has since become a key part of funk bass playing and has been adopted by many great bassists. Another funk band which has had an enormous impact is the Oakland-based Tower of Power, whose bassist Francis "Rocco" Prestia perfected his own variation of funk bass playing. Prestia's style utilizes an impressive right-hand fingerstyle technique characterized by intricate sixteenth-note figures played in a tight ensemble fashion with drummer David Garibaldi and the Tower of Power horn section. Prestia's playing has had an influence on countless bassists, perhaps most notably the late bass virtuoso Jaco Pastorius.

The prominence of the bass in funk music has created funk bass stars like Larry Graham and Bootsy Collins. Collins played first with James Brown and then with another of funk's most important bandleaders, George Clinton, in his bands Parliament and Funkadelic. Funky bass players have since crossed over into other genres, like Marcus Miller with Miles Davis's band, Stanley Clarke with Chick Corea's Return to Forever, Victor Wooten with Bela Fleck and the Flecktones, and Flea with The Red Hot Chili Peppers. In addition, pop bands—like Level 42 led by bassist Mark King, The Brothers Johnson with bassist Louis Johnson, and Larry Graham's band Graham Central Station—all feature funk bassists.

Funk has had a large influence on many musical styles, and almost any type of music can be "funky" at times. Because of its syncopated beat and popularity for dancing, elements of funk have become a part of pop music around the world. The disco style, which became popular in the 1970s, was essentially a variation on funk (as is hip-hop), and many bands in various styles have incorporated the funk style into their repertoire, including jazz artists like Miles Davis and Herbie Hancock. In recent years, a new style has emerged, called drum and bass, which takes the funk groove to a new extreme; it doesn't just *feature* the bass and drums, those are the only two instruments in the band. Funk, like so much of popular music, is constantly changing and growing, and new funky bassists continue to appear on the scene.

> **Suggested Listening**
> - Bernard Odum and Fred Thomas (James Brown)
> - Francis "Rocco" Prestia (Tower of Power)
> - Paul Jackson (The Headhunters)
> - Larry Graham (Sly & the Family Stone, Graham Central Station)
> - The Bee Gees

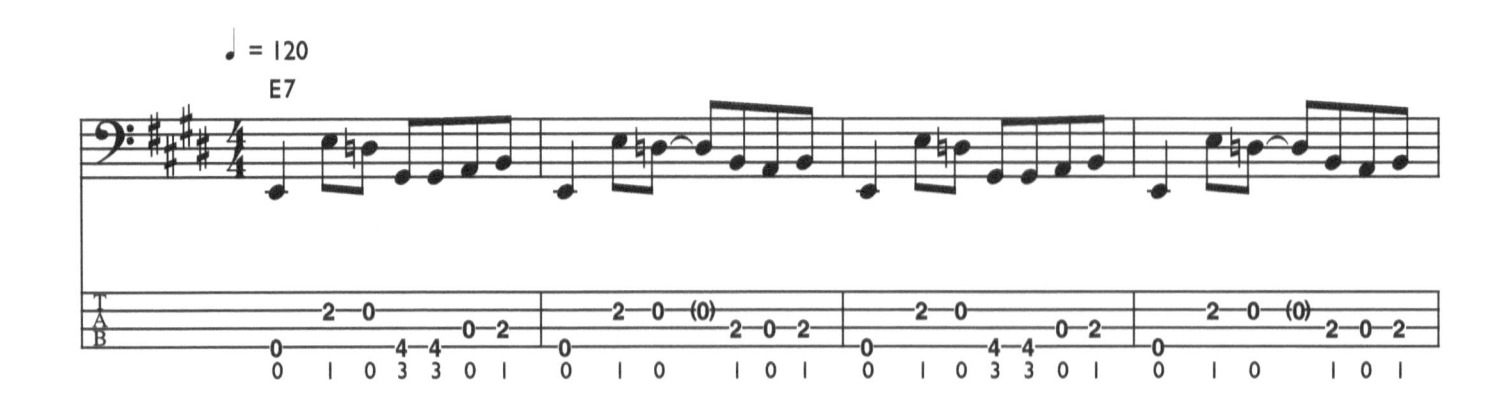

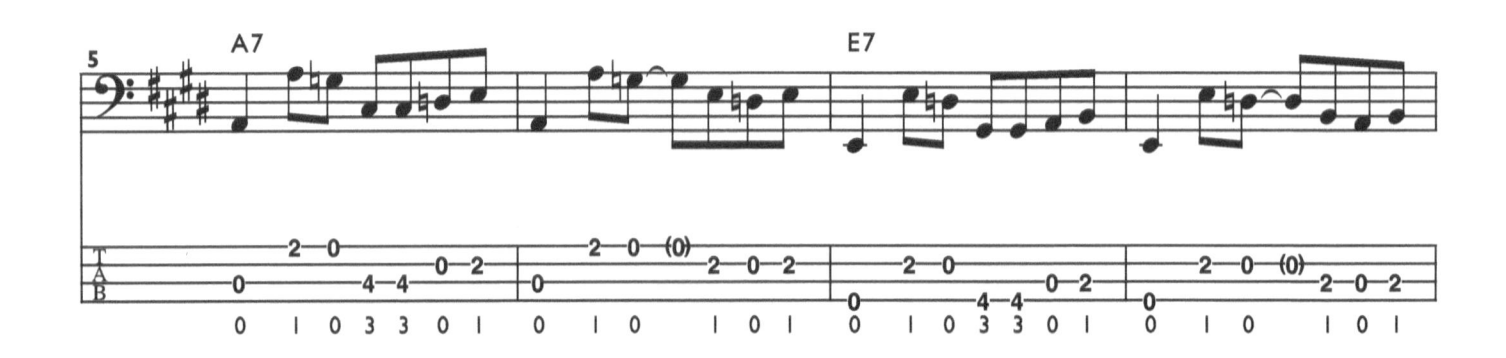

In the Style of Bernard Odum (with James Brown)

In the world of funk, simple is always best, and nobody has done simple and funky better than James Brown. Bassist Bernard Odum was the man who played the bass lines that made James Brown and His Famous Flames so funky. Like many of the early funk and R&B musicians, he was not well recognized for his work during his lifetime; but his solid, syncopated bass grooves were the foundation for the funky sound that made Brown famous.

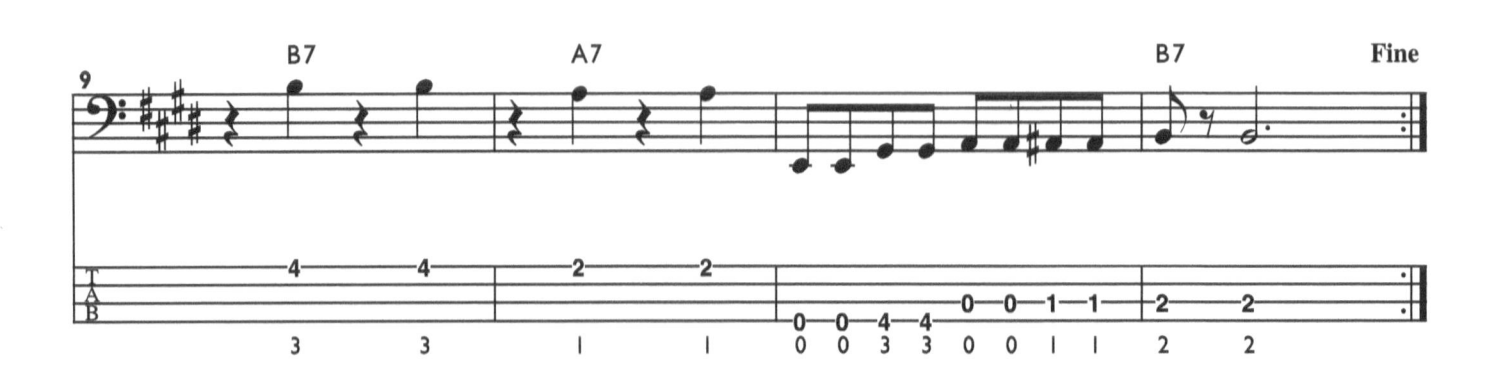

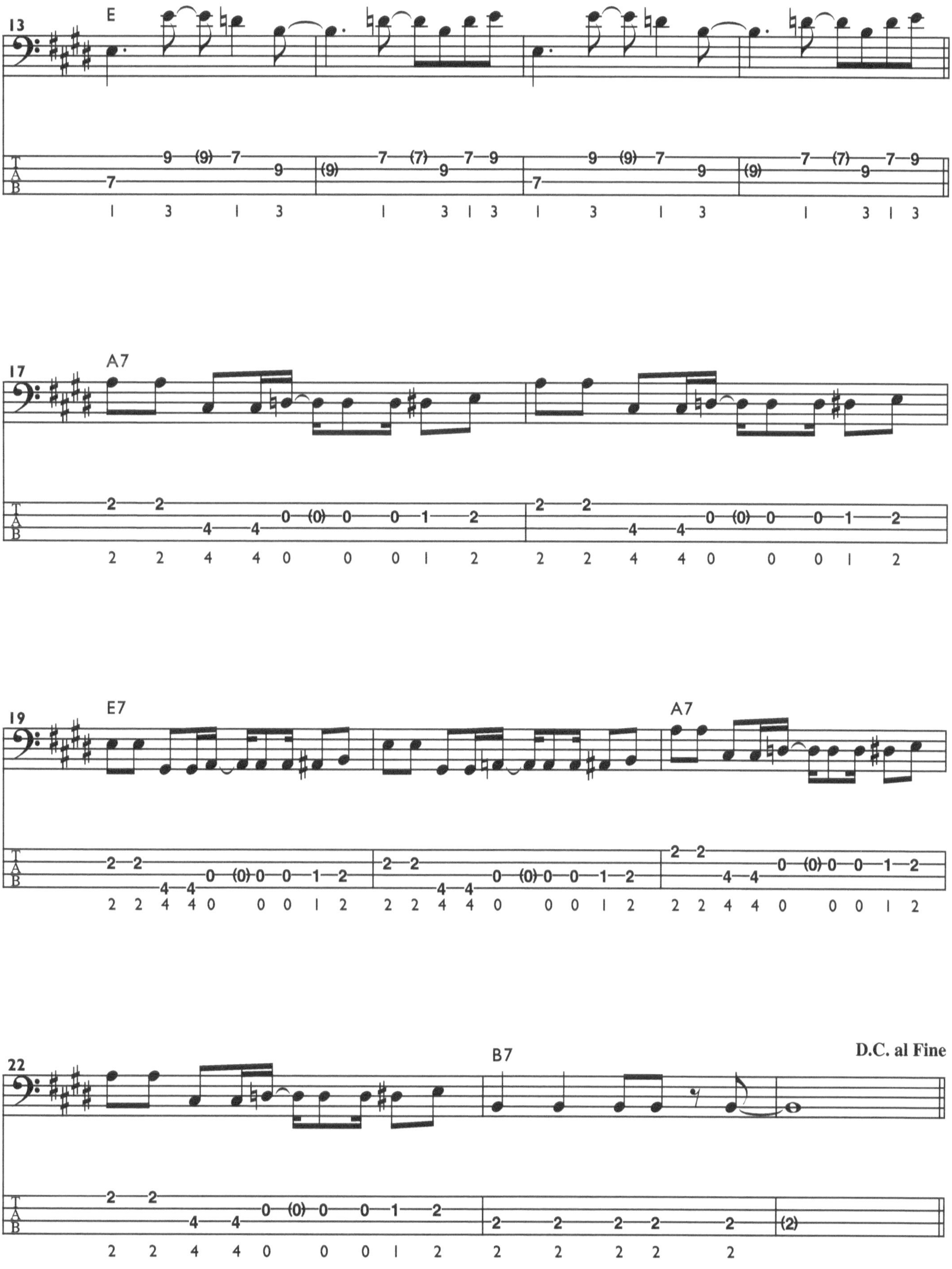
13
E
17
A7
19
E7
A7
22
B7
D.C. al Fine

In the Style of Fred Thomas (with James Brown)

Fred Thomas followed Bernard Odum in Brown's band when the Famous Flames became The J.B.'s. Thomas put his own personal spin on Brown's music. Here's a funky line in Thomas's style.

Fingerstyle Funk in the Style of Francis "Rocco" Prestia (with Tower of Power)

Francis "Rocco" Prestia is one of a kind. As the bassist for the super-funky band Tower of Power, he has been playing some of the funkiest bass lines ever for over 40 years. Prestia and drummer David Garibaldi have developed a way of playing funk that is all their own. Rocco's fingerstyle sixteenth-note grooves have influenced many great bassists.

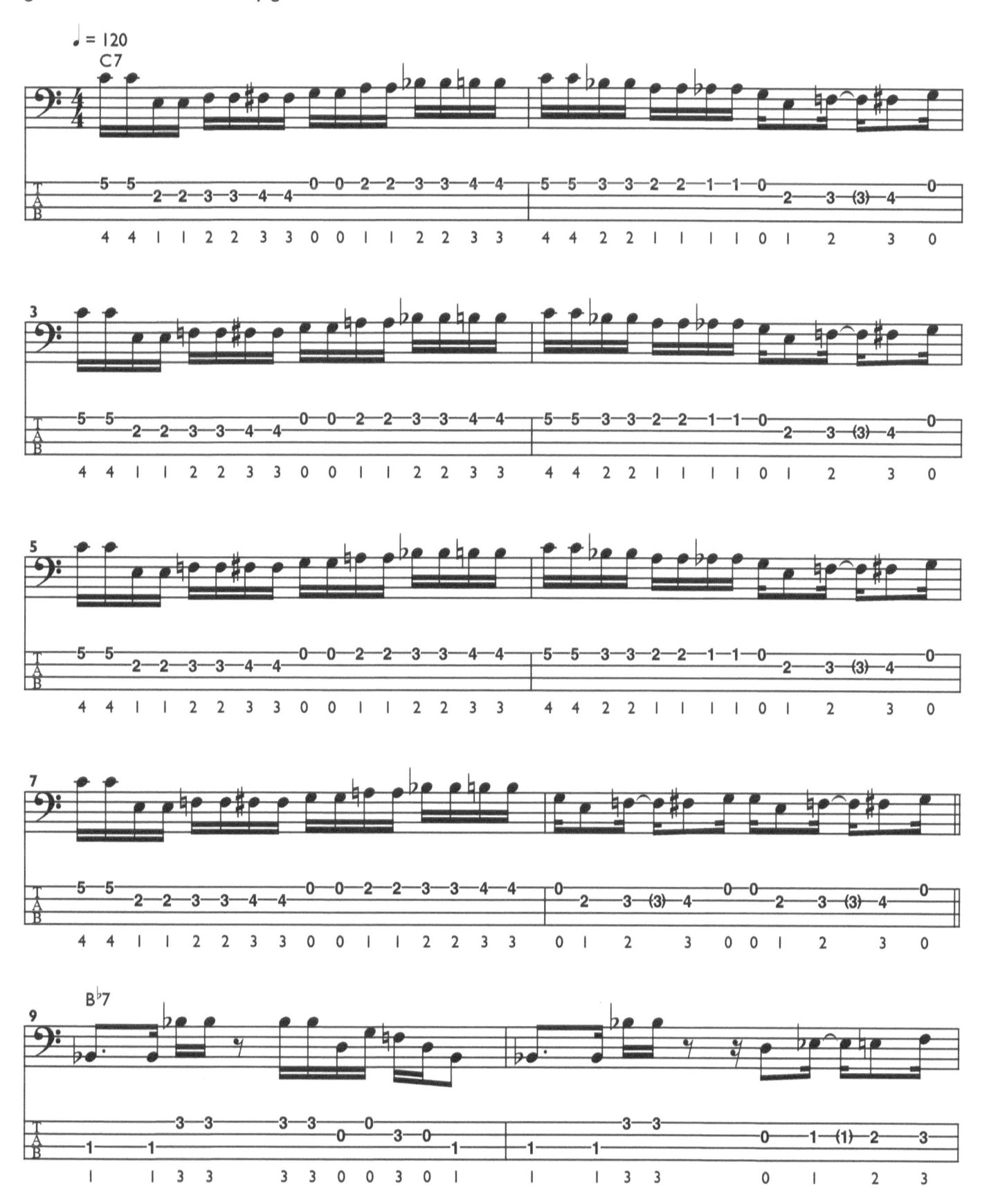

(Continued on next page)

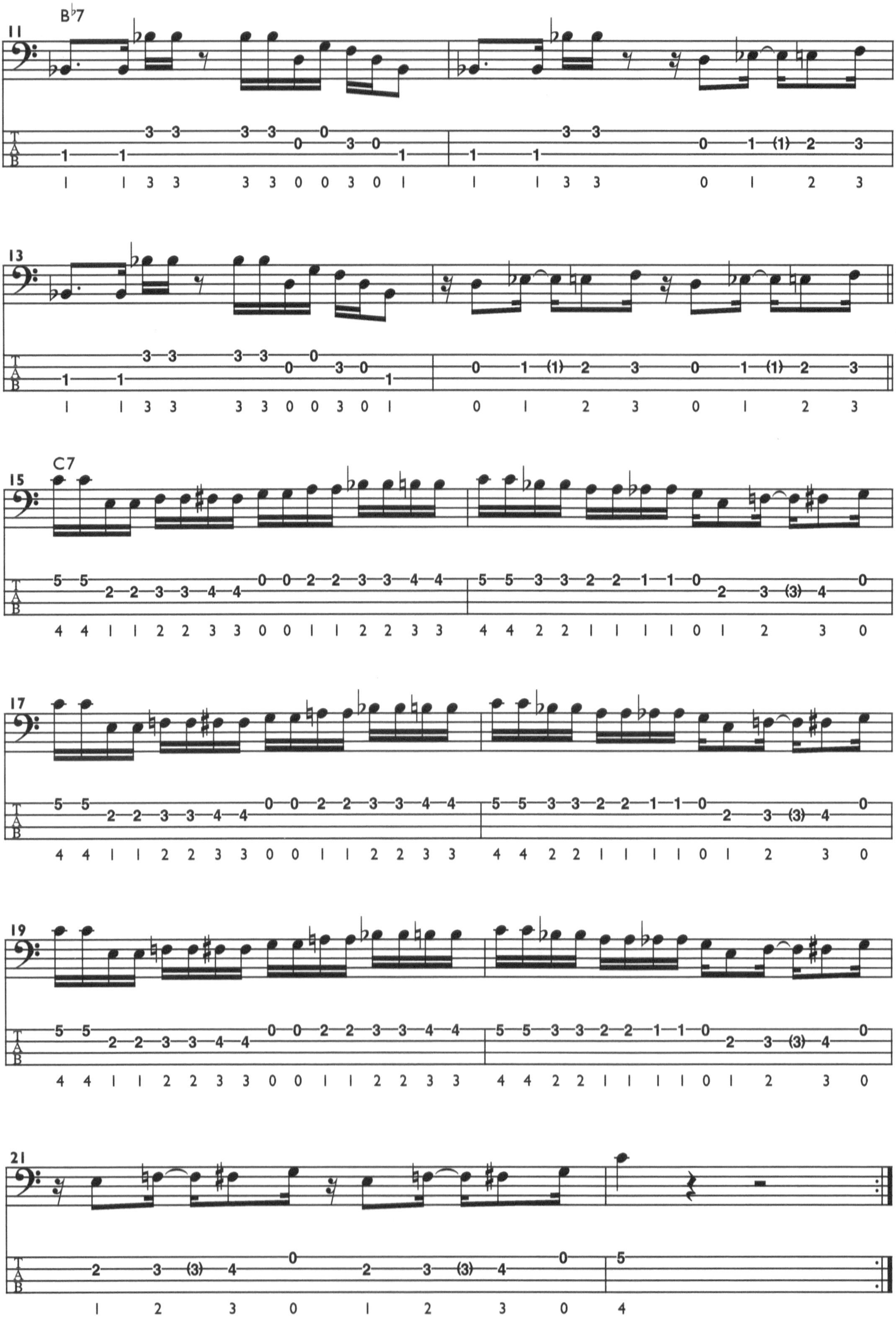
B♭7
C7

Another Line in the Style of Francis "Rocco" Prestia

Here's another funky example demonstrating Prestia's fingerstyle funk technique.

In the Style of Paul Jackson (with The Headhunters)

Paul Jackson is a brilliant bassist, as well as a highly trained and talented overall musician. He has performed with countless artists all over the world and has composed for nearly every possible ensemble and medium. His most famous work in the U.S. has been with the great jazz pianist Herbie Hancock in the seminal funk-jazz band The Headhunters.

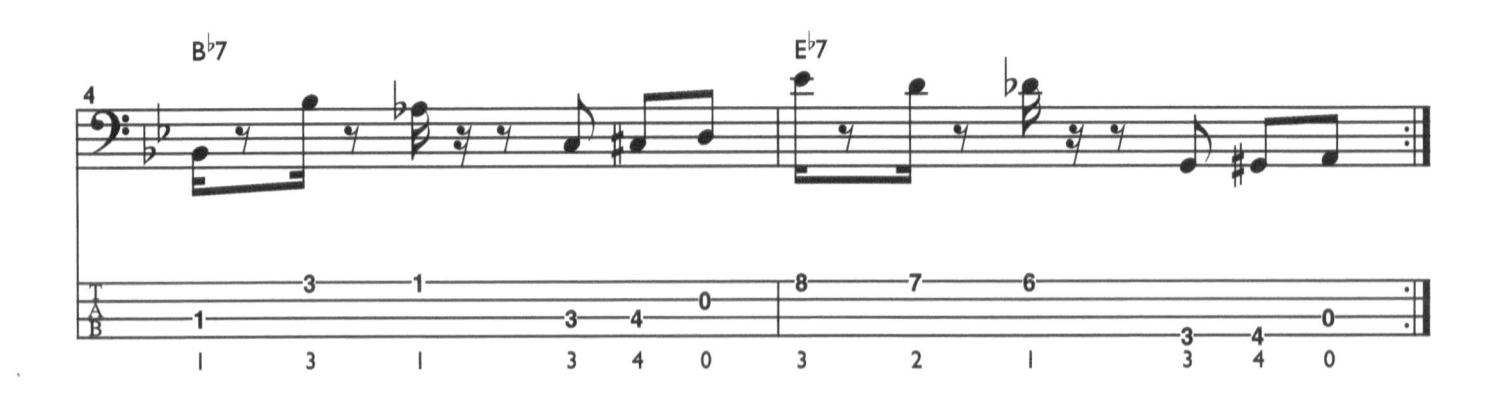

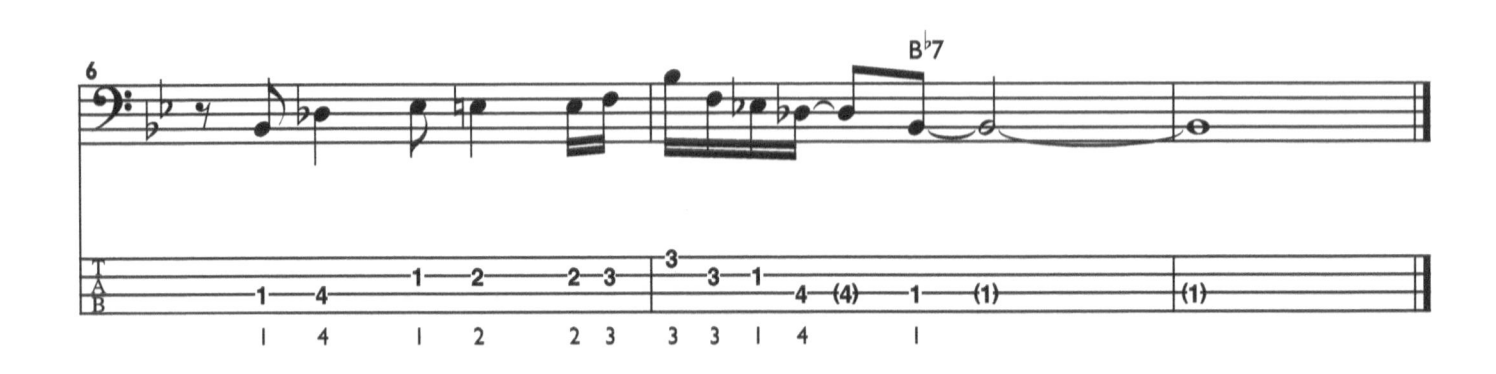

Introduction to Larry Graham and Slap & Pop

When the pioneering funk band Sly & the Family Stone became popular in the late 1960s, bassist Larry Graham turned bass playing on its head with his new right-hand technique. The style that Graham still refers to as "thumpin' and pluckin'" has become more commonly known as "slap & pop." Since Graham first introduced the world to the style, it has become a major component in funk bass playing and has been adopted by many great bassists including Marcus Miller, Flea, Stanley Clarke, and Victor Wooten. Graham's style was (and still is) unique, with its combination of fat "slapped" low notes, left- and right-hand muted strings, and snapped, or "popped," high notes. On the next page are a series of slap & pop grooves in Graham's style. Each groove builds on the one preceding it, adding rhythmic elements in each variation.

SLAP & POP NOTATION

The slap & pop style has a percussive quality produced by using two main techniques: slapping the string with the right-hand thumb and popping the string with the right-hand 1st finger. The style also makes use of muted notes, hammer-ons, and pull-offs. Below is a chart featuring brief explanations for some of these techniques and the abbreviations that appear in the music. The abbreviations appear above both the standard music notation staff and the TAB staff.

Slap & Pop Techniques	
S	**Thumb slap:** Strike the string with your right-hand thumb. The string should make a percussive sound as it strikes the fretboard.
P	**Pop:** Pluck, or "pop," the string with the 1st finger of your right hand. The string will snap back and strike the fretboard, creating a sharp, percussive sound.
H	**Hammer-on:** Play a note, then play a higher-pitched note on the same string by "hammering" onto the fret with another left-hand finger. Do not use your right hand for the second note; the sound comes from the left hand alone.
PO	**Pull-off:** A pull-off is the opposite of a hammer-on. Play a note, then play a lower-pitched note on the same string by quickly pulling your left-hand finger off the fret. The second note needs to be an open string or a note that is fretted beforehand. Do not use your right hand for the second note; the sound comes from the left hand alone.
X	**Muted note:** Gently touch the string with the fingers of the left hand, without pressing onto the fretboard, and pluck the string with your right hand. The result is a percussive sound with no discernible pitch.

In the Style of Larry Graham (with Sly & the Family Stone and Graham Central Station)

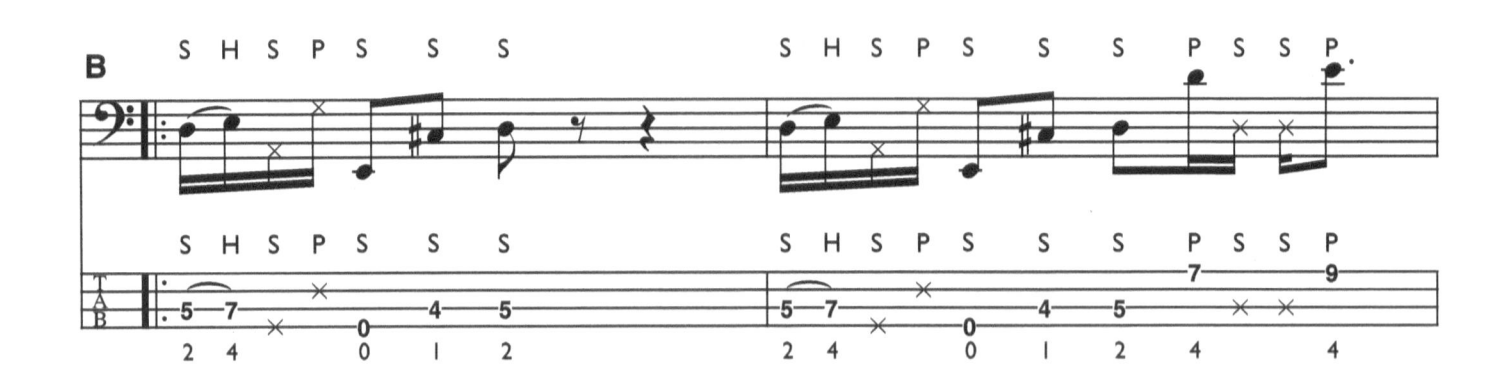

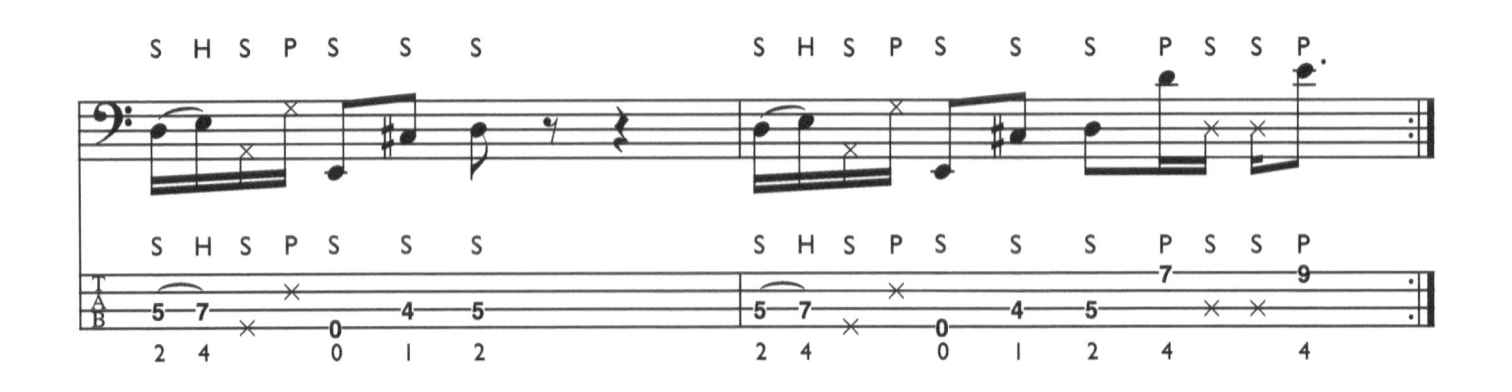

C

S P S S P S P S S P S P S S P S P S S P
TAB

D

S P S S P S P S P S P S P S P S P S S P S P S P S P S P S P
TAB

Disco

The funk style that developed in the 1960s gave birth to a new kind of dance music called "disco," which became enormously popular in the '70s. Because of the hit 1977 movie *Saturday Night Fever*, and its soundtrack by the Bee Gees, disco music was everywhere. Like funk, disco also featured the bass, with the grooves tending to be a little less syncopated and rhythmically varied than their funk predecessors.

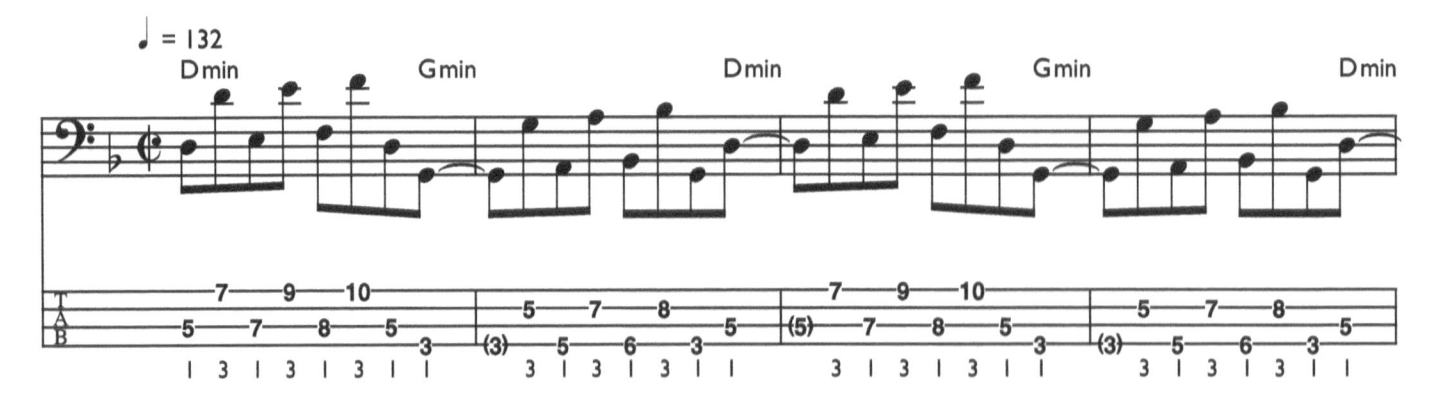

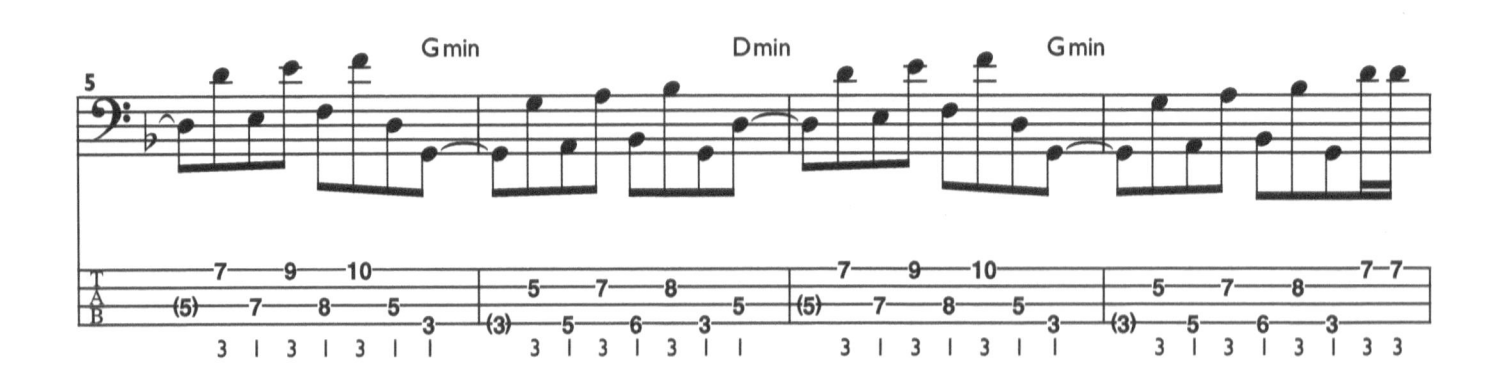

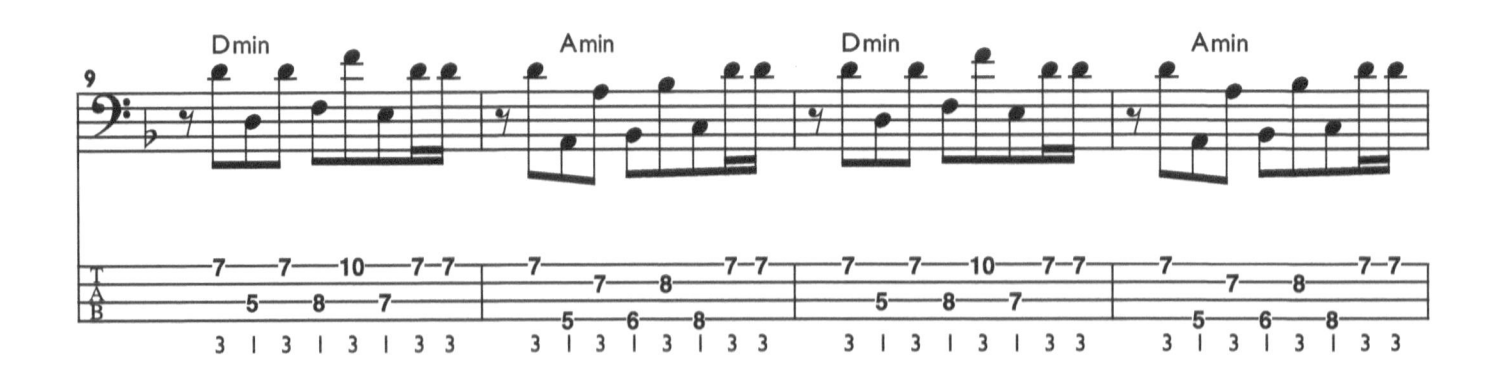

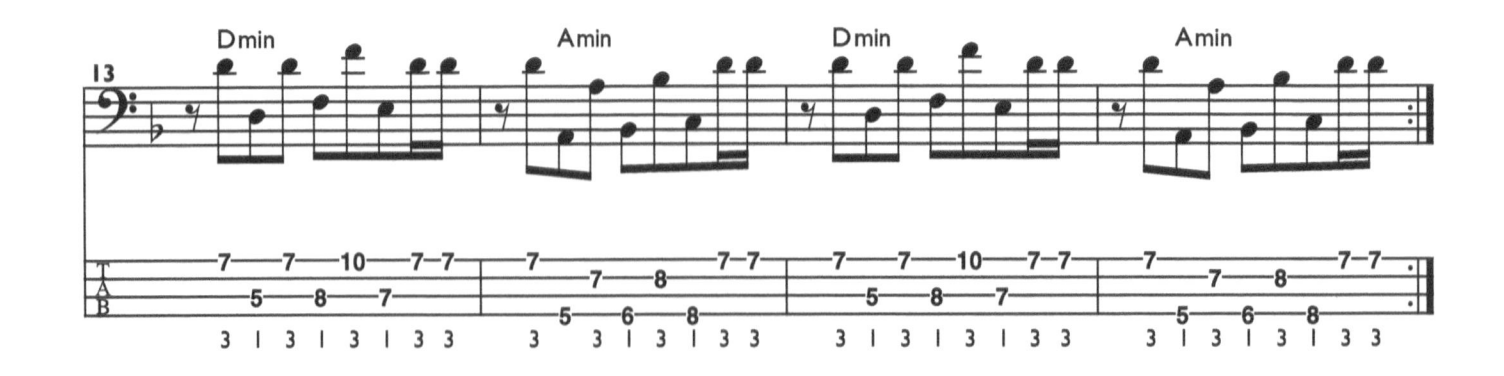

Chapter 5: Jazz

A Brief History of Jazz

The musical style we call jazz was born in the beginning of the 20th century. It is commonly believed that jazz was first played in New Orleans, and its greatest exponent is generally agreed to be the New Orleans trumpeter Louis Armstrong. The earliest New Orleans bands were marching bands, and they did not have bass players; the bass lines were played on a tuba or sousaphone instead. In a short time, though, the bands became stationary dance bands and began to use the double bass. With unamplified instruments, jazz bass playing started with a rudimentary timekeeping role, and early bass lines tended to be played with what is called a "two feel," referring to the style of playing on beats 1 and 3 of the $\frac{4}{4}$ measure. This style, which had been played by the sousaphone players, was continued by the bassists in traditional New Orleans-style bands in the teens and 1920s. Around that time, as many African-Americans, including many jazz players, began to migrate north to the industrial centers (like Chicago) in the mid-West and East, jazz's popularity increased tremendously. Jazz and jazz bass playing went through a variety of stylistic and technical changes, and in the 1930s through the 1940s, what is known as the swing style became popular. First in the "Chicago style" of dixieland playing, and then in the swing-style bands, the bass often played four beats to the bar, what became known as "walking bass." This style was further utilized and developed in subsequent jazz styles, including bebop, hard bop, modal, and the post-bop styles of the 1940s to 1960s. Bass players like Jimmy Blanton, who played with Duke Ellington's Orchestra, and later Paul Chambers with Miles Davis, Ray Brown with Oscar Peterson, and Scott LaFaro with Bill Evans propelled the walking bass style, as well as melodic bass soloing, to new heights. Most jazz bassists today commonly play a mixture of "two feel" and "walking" styles.

In addition, because of the many fine Latino musicians in jazz, the rhythms and styles of Latin music were incorporated into the jazz idiom. Brazilian styles like bossa nova and samba, as well as West Indian and Afro-Cuban rhythms, became important elements of jazz.

Aside from stylistic changes, an important change in jazz bass playing occurred in the 1950s, when the electric bass was introduced to jazz groups. The first notable bassists to play the electric bass in jazz were Monk Montgomery (in Lionel Hampton's big band and his brother Wes Montgomery's band) and Steve Swallow with guitarist Jim Hall's trio. Since that time, the electric bass has taken on an important role in jazz, particularly in the jazz-rock fusion style, which began in the 1960s with Miles Davis's album *Bitches Brew* and has continued with the playing of many brilliant electric bassists, including Marcus Miller, Stanley Clarke, Steve Swallow, and most importantly, the late, great electric bass virtuoso Jaco Pastorius.

As 21st century bassists, we are fortunate to have a wealth of bass playing to study and an enormous number of wonderful players to listen to, beginning with the 1920s and continuing through today. Like the old saying about pictures, a recording is worth a thousand words. The student is encouraged to listen to the recordings of the great jazz bassists in order to begin to understand their music and genius.

Suggested Listening
- Ray Brown (The Oscar Peterson Trio)
- Sam Jones (Cannonball Adderley)
- Ron Carter (Herbie Hancock, Miles Davis)
- Paul Chambers (Miles Davis, John Coltrane)
- Ahmed Abdul-Malik (Thelonious Monk, Coleman Hawkins, Toots Thielemans)
- Tommy Potter (Charlie Parker, Dizzy Gillespie)

Two Feel in the Style of Ray Brown
(with The Oscar Peterson Trio)

The "two feel" in jazz bass playing is both simple and complex. The brilliant bassist Ray Brown was a master of this style. It is simpler than playing walking bass in some ways because there are half as many notes, but doing it well is a difficult and subtle art. Pay close attention to note choice and time feel.

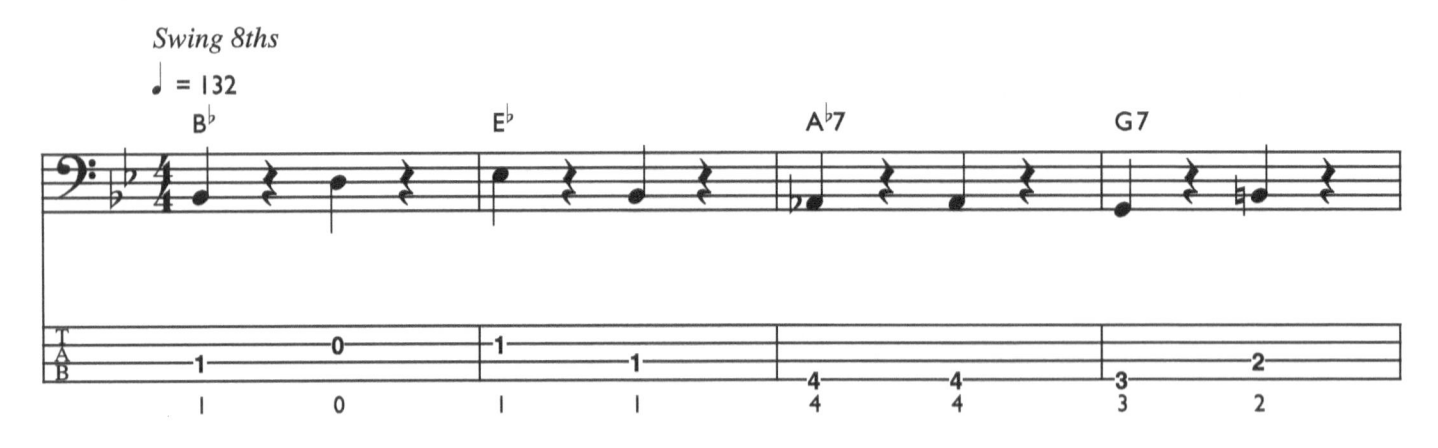

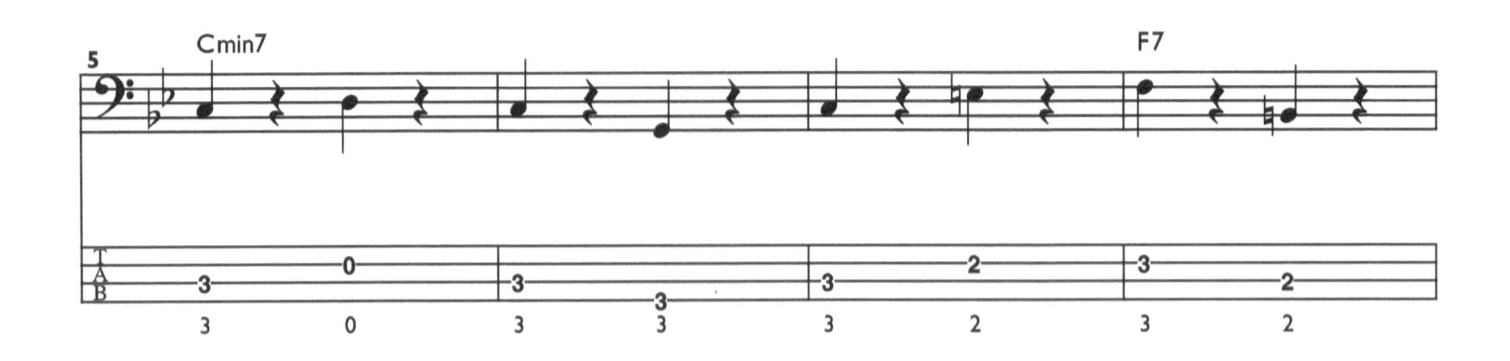

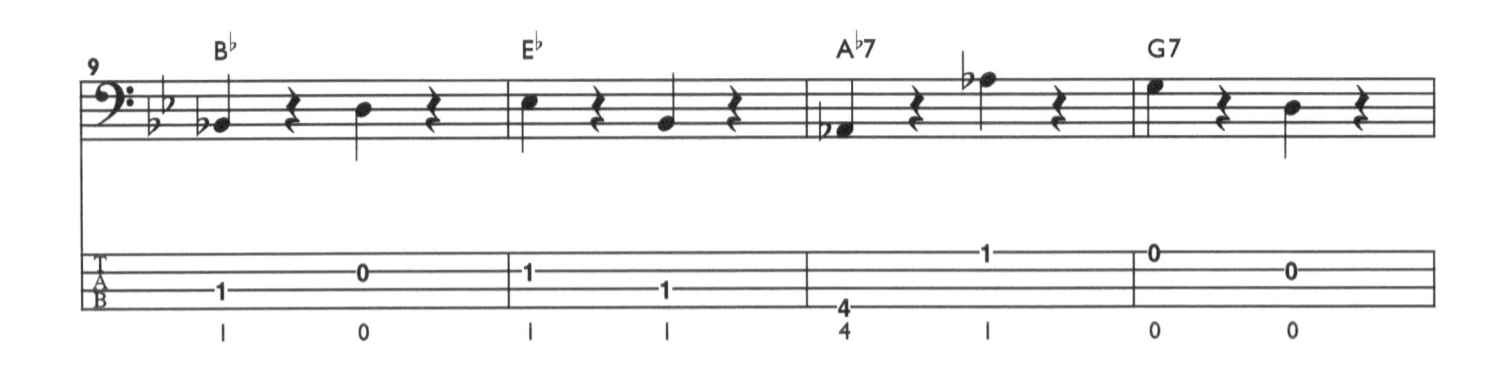

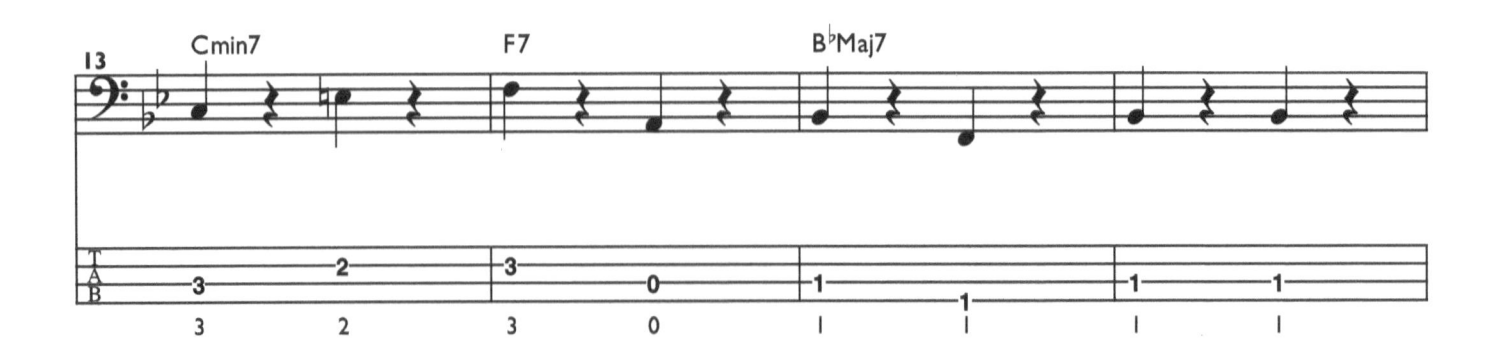

17
Amin7♭5 D7♭9 Gmin Amin7♭5 D7♭9 Gmin
21
Amin7♭5 D7♭9 Gmin Cmin7 F7
25
B♭ E♭ A♭7 G7
29
Cmin7 F7 B♭Maj7

Jazz Blues in the Style of Sam Jones (with Cannonball Adderley)

Sam Jones was a bassist's bassist. His sound and time were impeccable, and he was a master of the blues. In the years that he played with alto saxophonist Cannonball Adderley's band, Jones played many blues and blues-based compositions. Following is a jazz blues line in the style of Sam Jones.

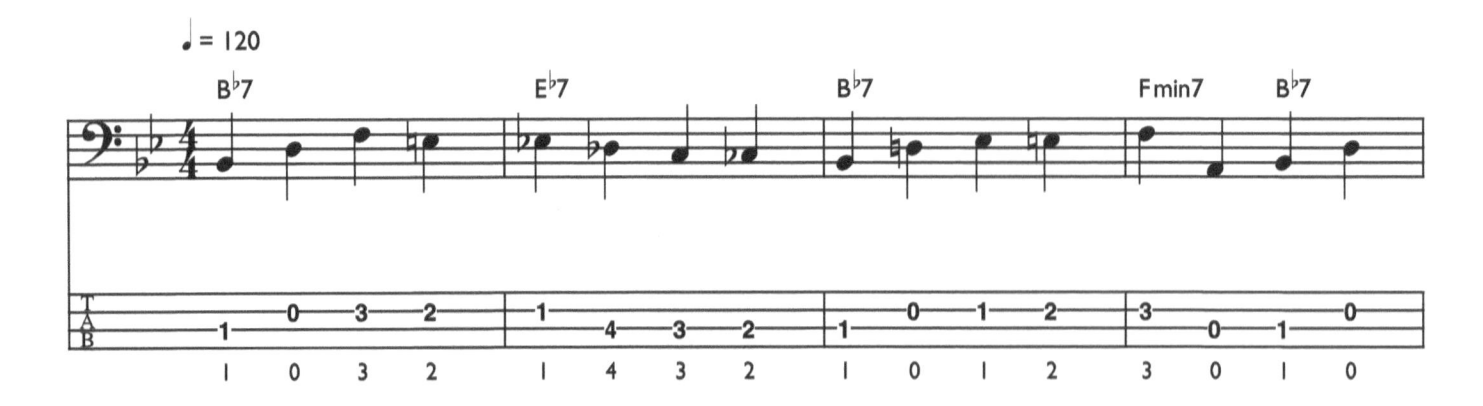

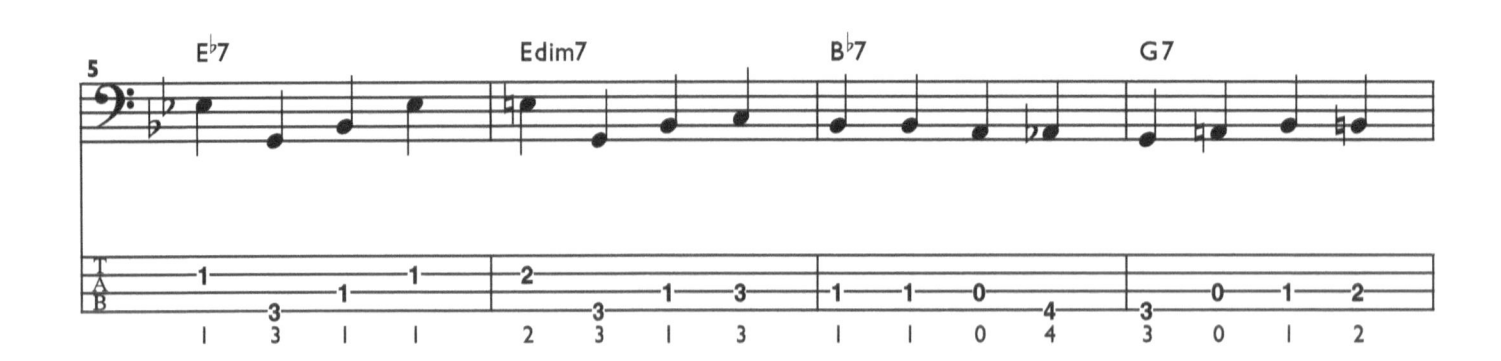

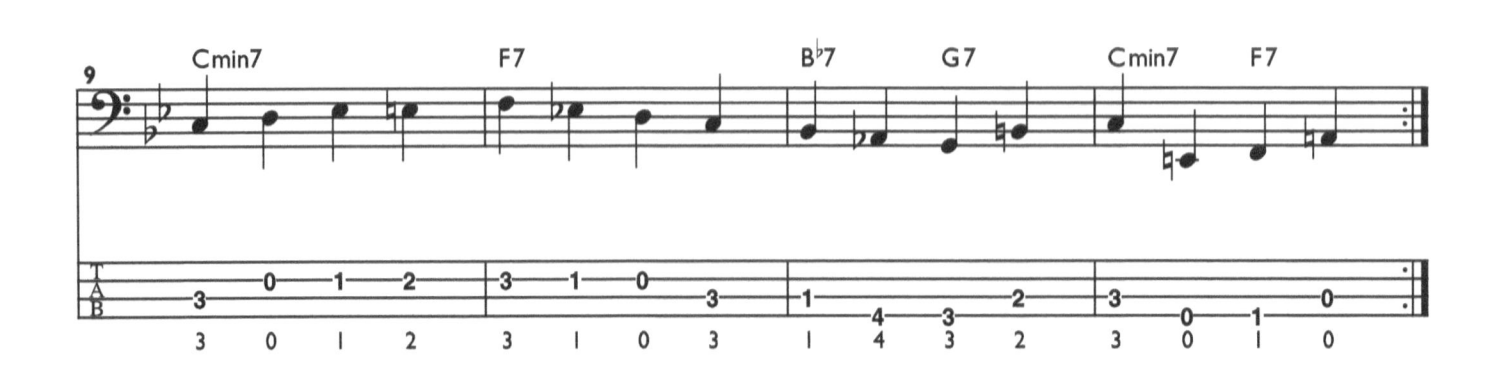

Blues in the Style of Ron Carter (with The Miles Davis Quintet)

Ron Carter is one of the most important bassists in jazz and has been since the 1960s when he played with The Miles Davis Quintet with Wayne Shorter, Herbie Hancock, and Tony Williams. That group broke new ground in jazz, and Carter's bass playing has done the same for jazz bass for over four decades.

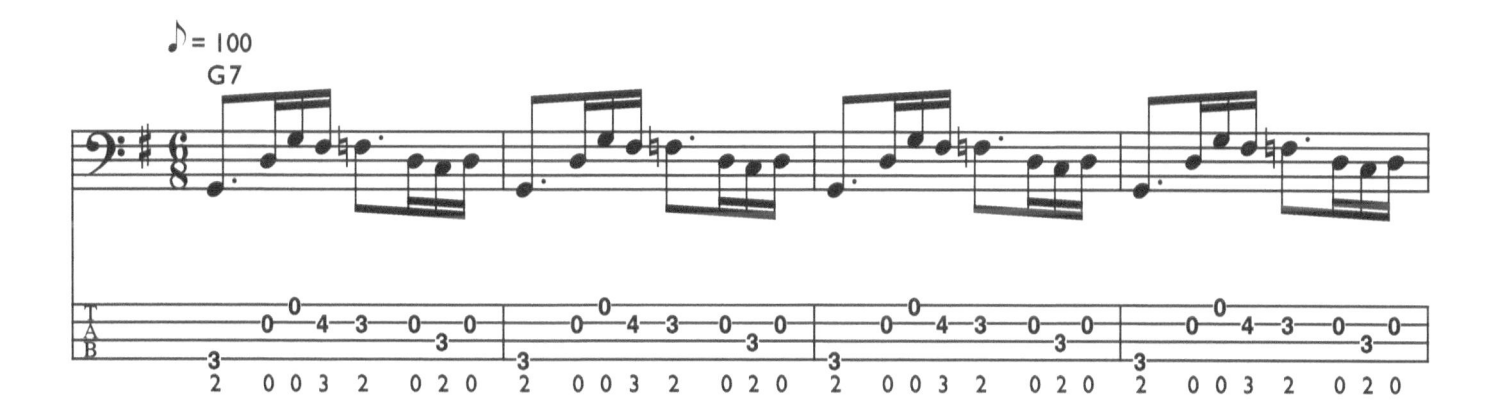

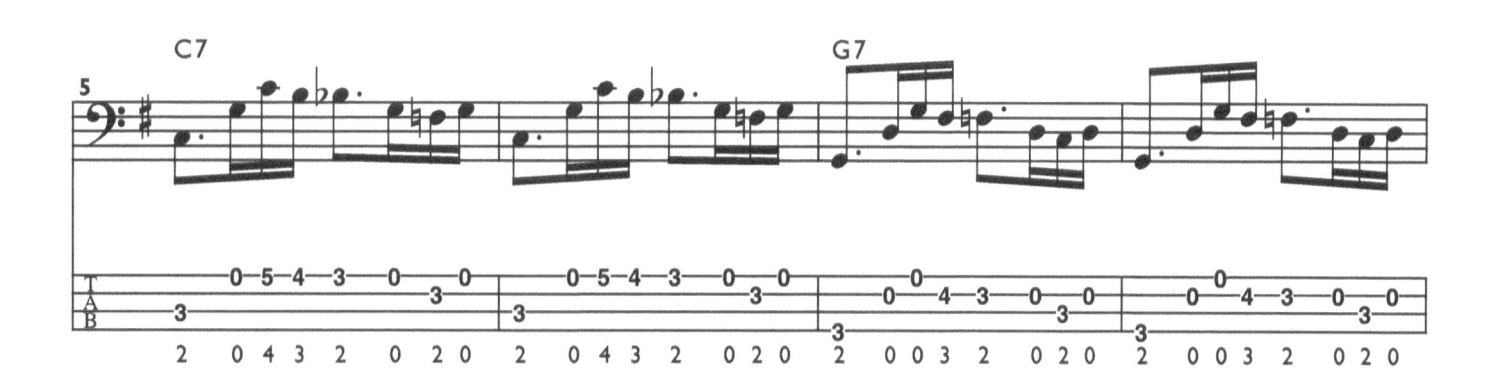

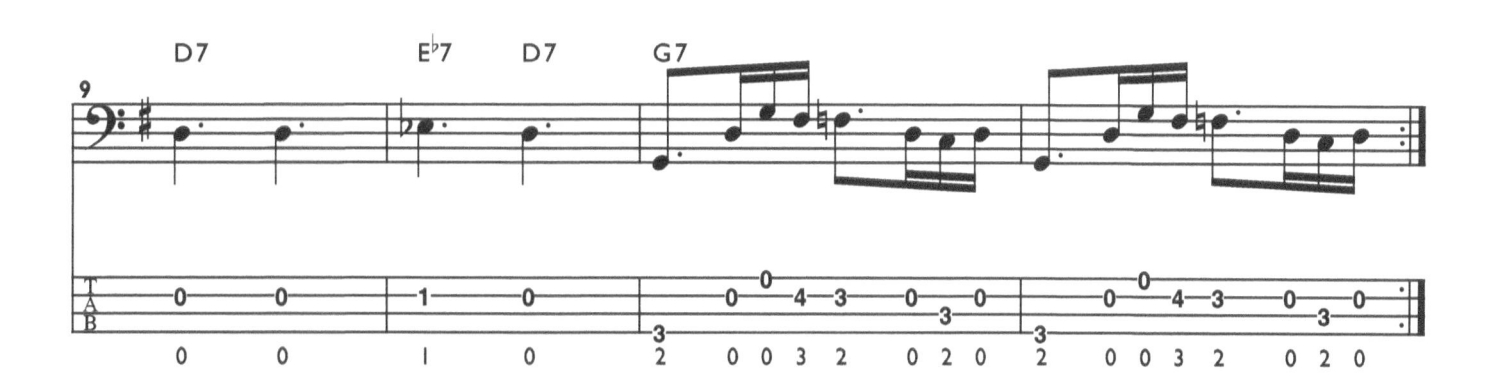

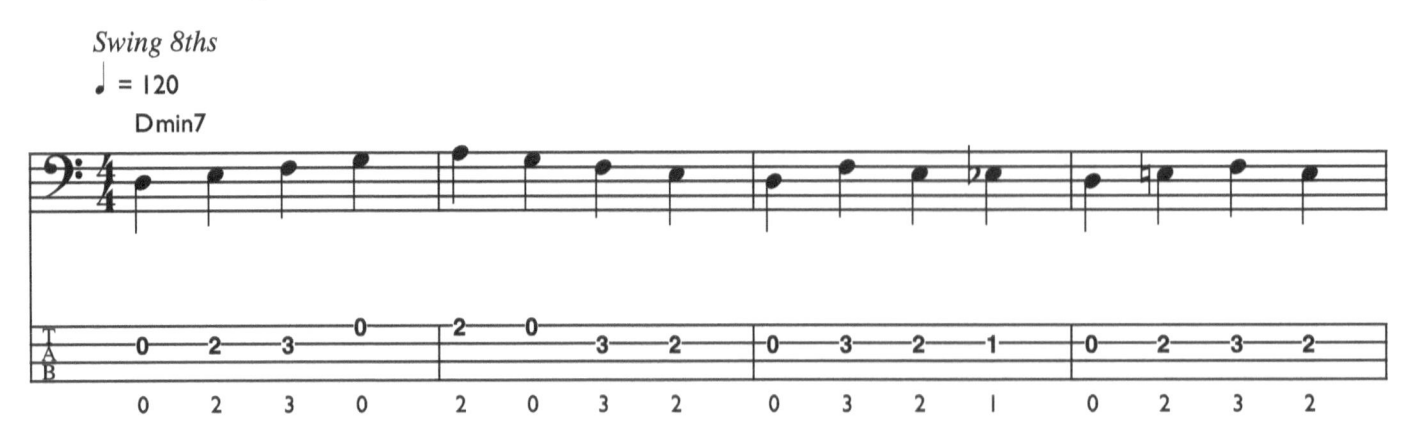

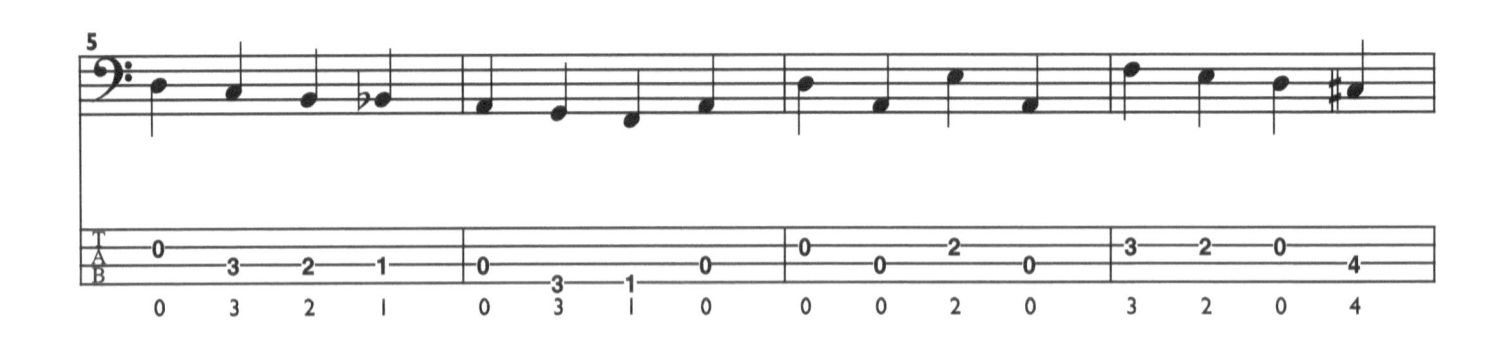

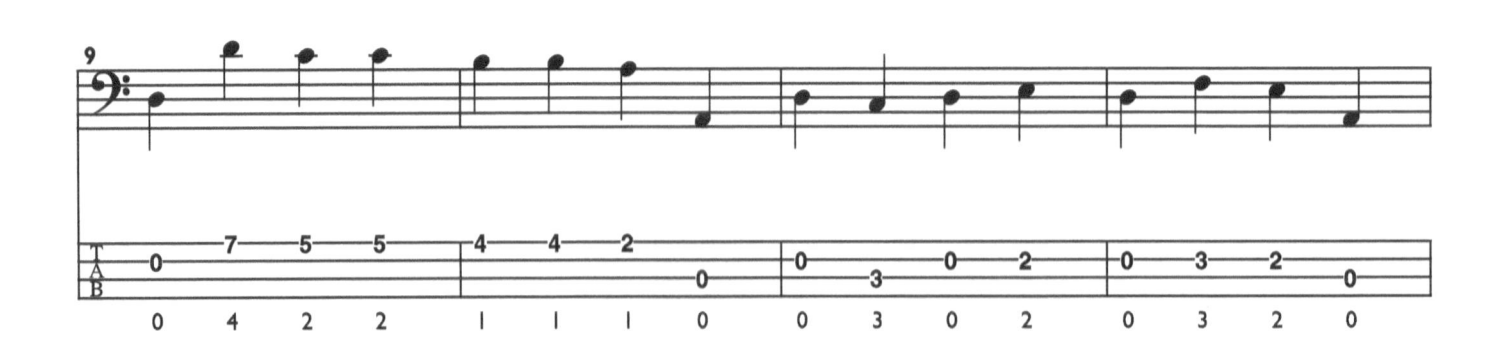

Modal Line in the Style of Paul Chambers (with Miles Davis)

In the 1960s, jazz musicians began to experiment with music that had static harmony, often using a single scale or mode. Players like Miles Davis, Bill Evans, and John Coltrane were influenced by French Impressionists Maurice Ravel and Claude Debussy, and began experimenting with this sound. Davis's most famous recording, *Kind of Blue* (1959), which features the virtuoso bass playing of Paul Chambers, is one of the first examples of this "modal" style. Following is a line using the Dorian mode, which consists of scale degrees 1–2–♭3–4–5–6–♭7.

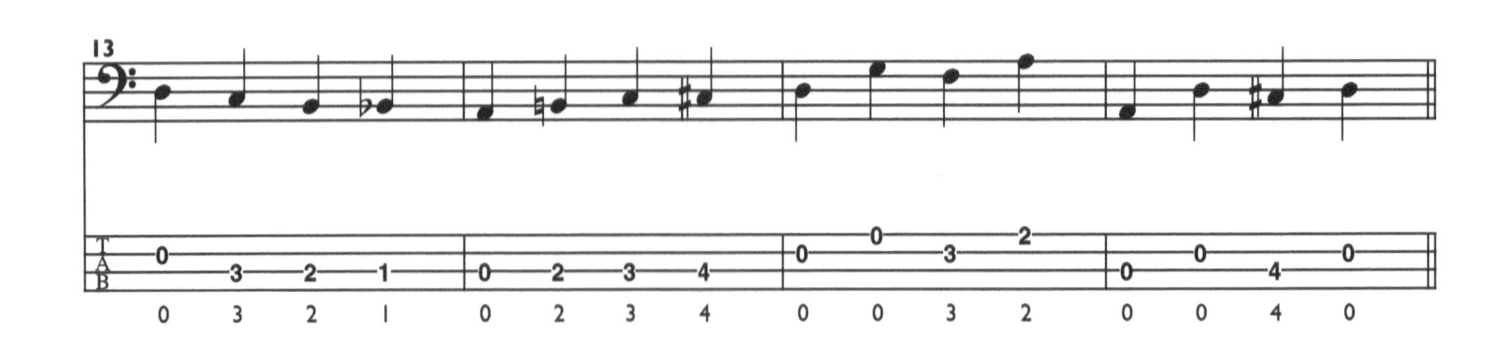

Swing 8ths

♩ = 120

Dmin7

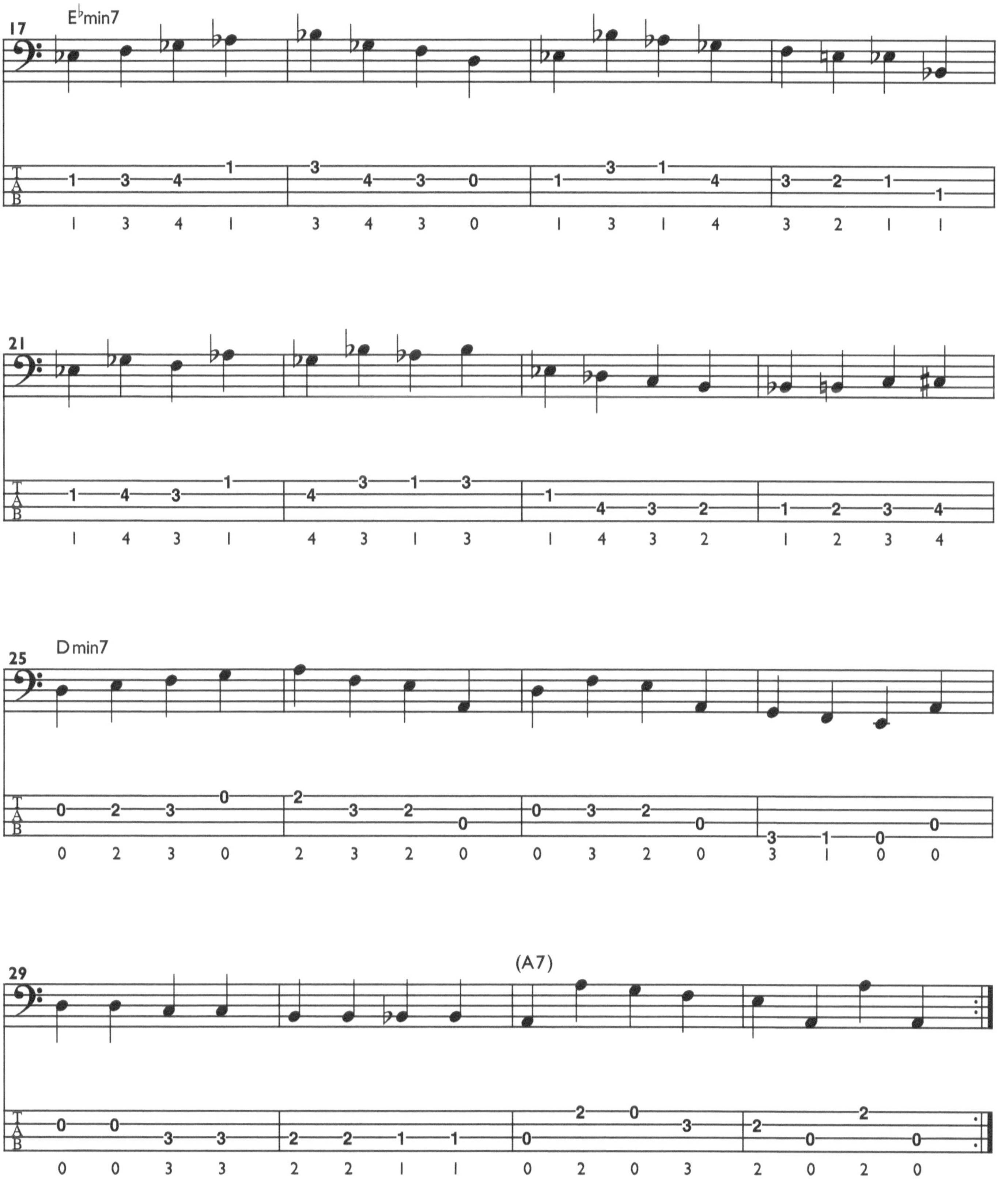
17
E♭min7
21
25
Dmin7
29
(A7)

Another Line in the Style of Ron Carter

Below is another line in Ron Carter's style. This one uses the quartal harmony that Herbie Hancock's band pioneered during the late 1960s. With quartal harmony, which builds chords in 4ths, instead of 3rds, Hancock found a different way of approaching the modal style that jazz players had been working on. Notice the 4ths in this line.

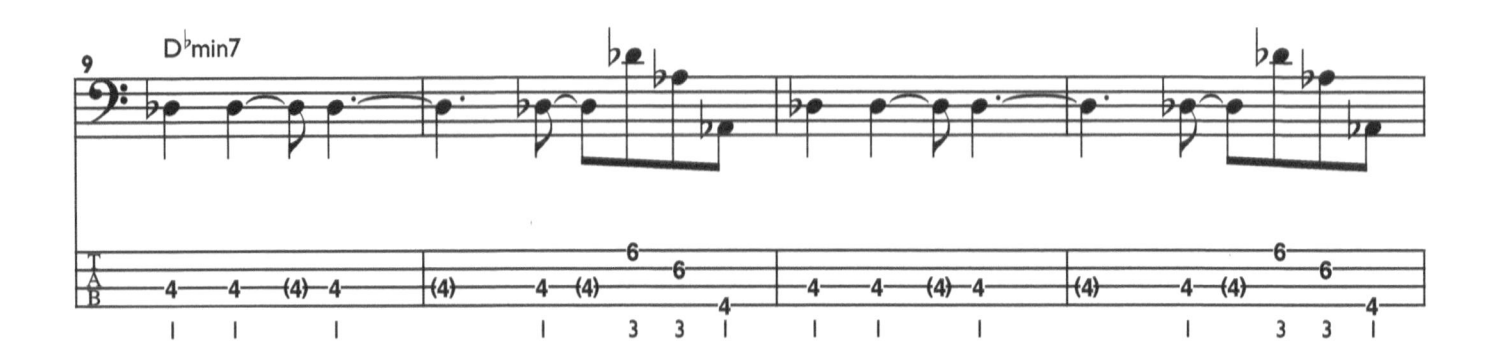

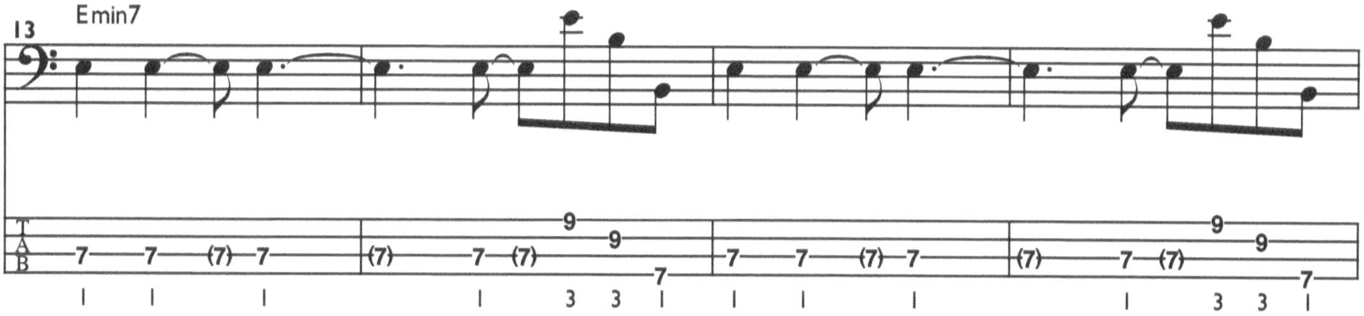
13
Emin7

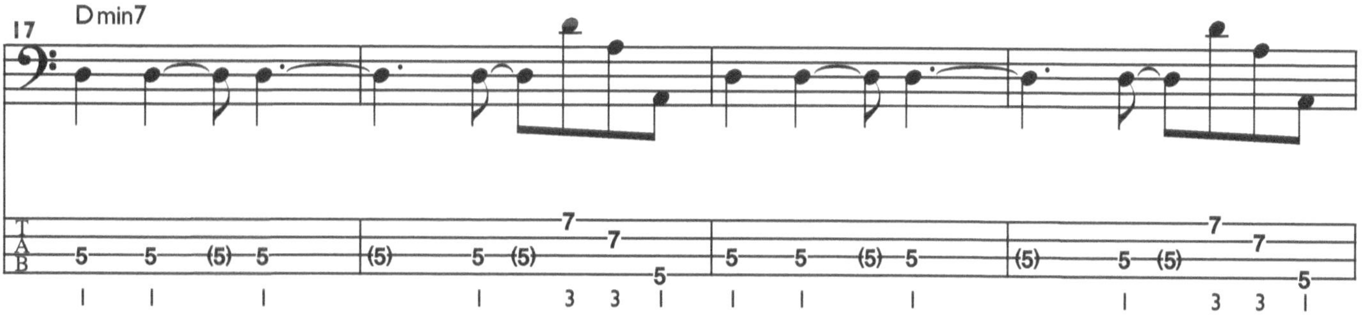
17
Dmin7

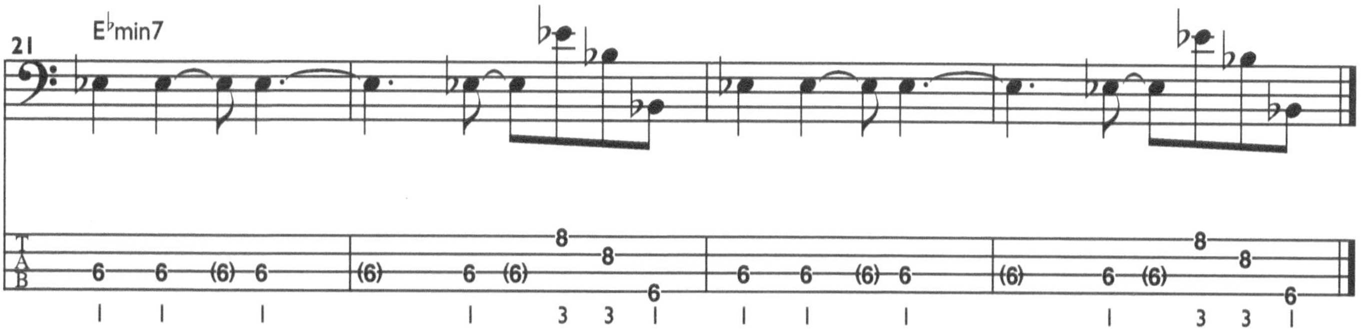
21
E♭min7

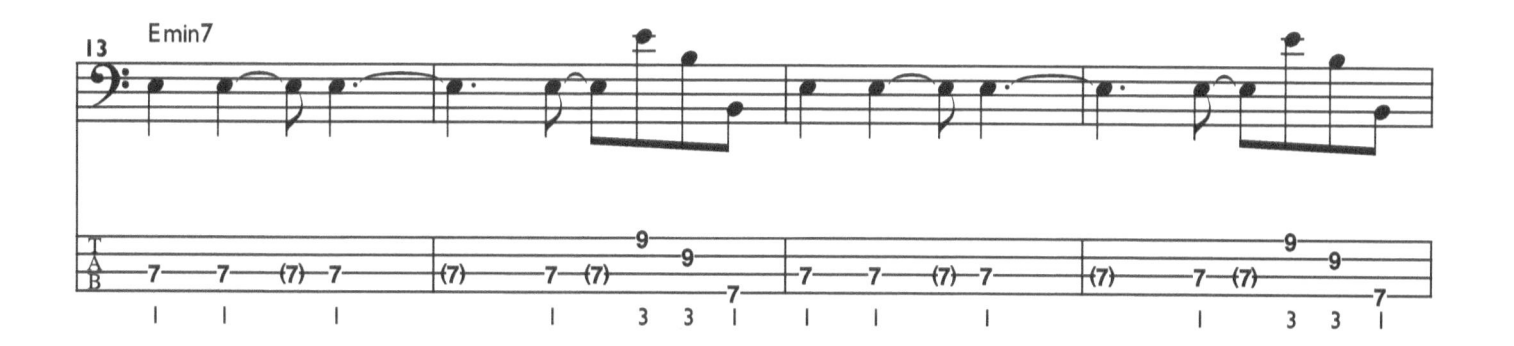

Minor Jazz Blues

The blues is generally played using dominant 7th chords. Sometimes, though, jazz musicians play a minor blues, which has a different sound resulting from the use of minor chords and minor scales. Notice how the harmony of the last four bars is different from the standard blues; instead of the standard V–IV–I turnaround, we have a ♭VI–V–i.

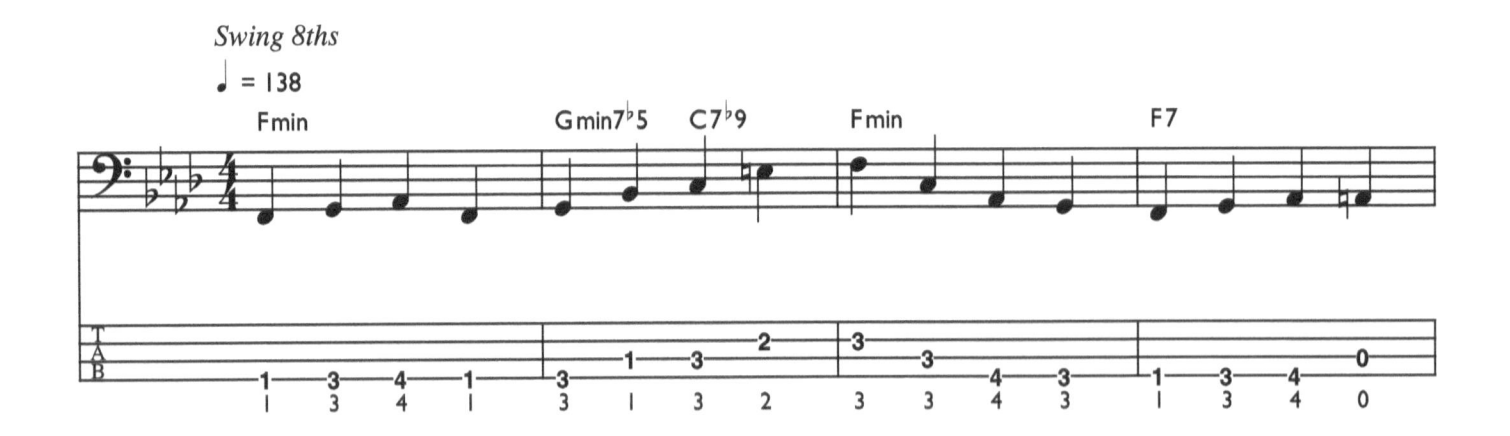

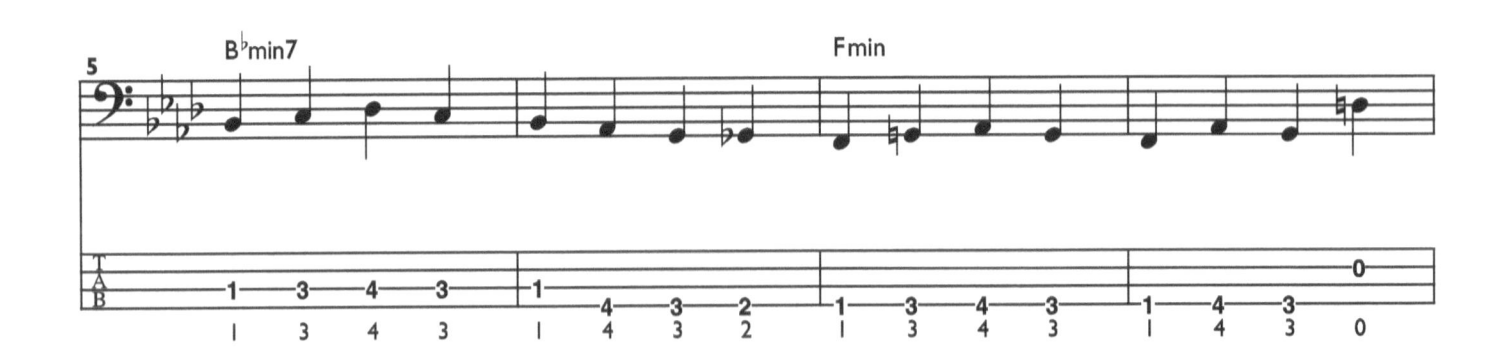

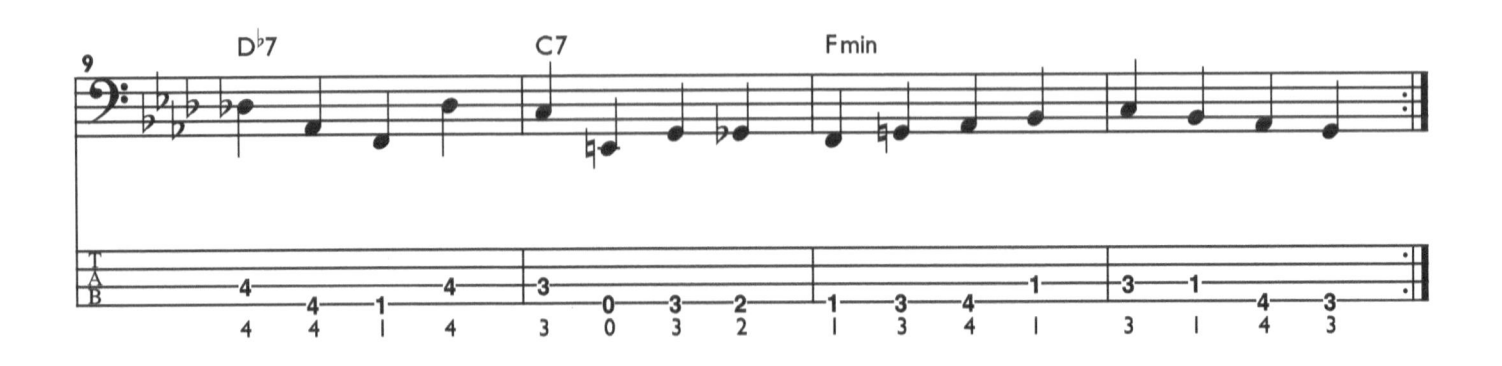

Bird Blues

Alto saxophonist Charlie Parker was one of the most important and innovative musicians in the history of jazz. Parker put his own spin on the blues. Because he was nicknamed "Yardbird," or "Bird" for short, jazz players often refer to this type of blues as "Bird blues." The difference in this type of blues is the harmony, particularly the first four bars.

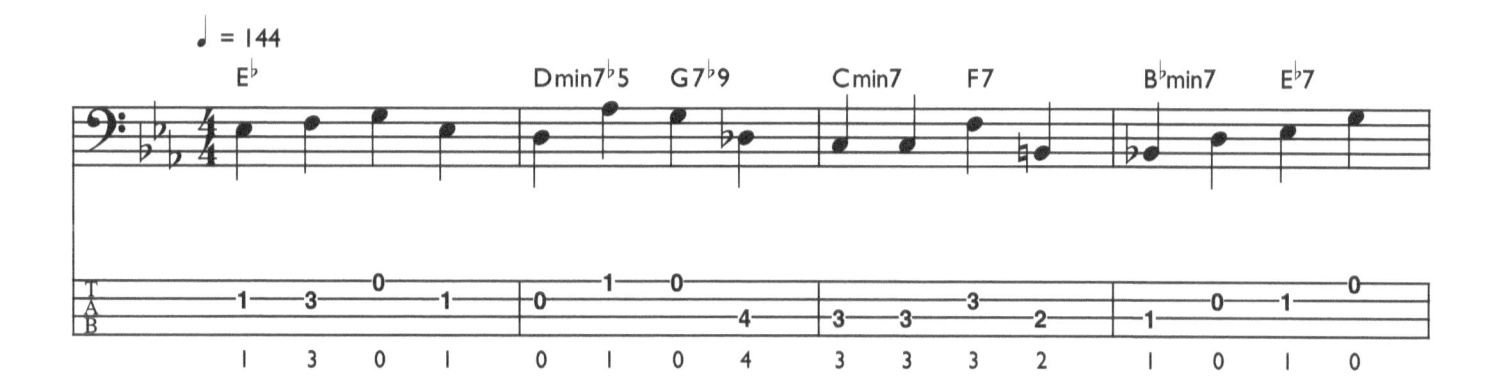

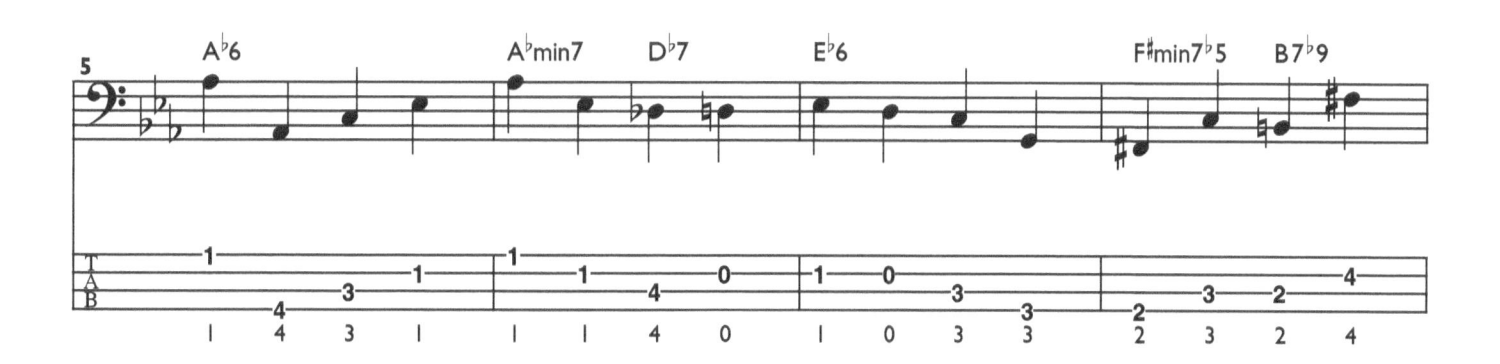

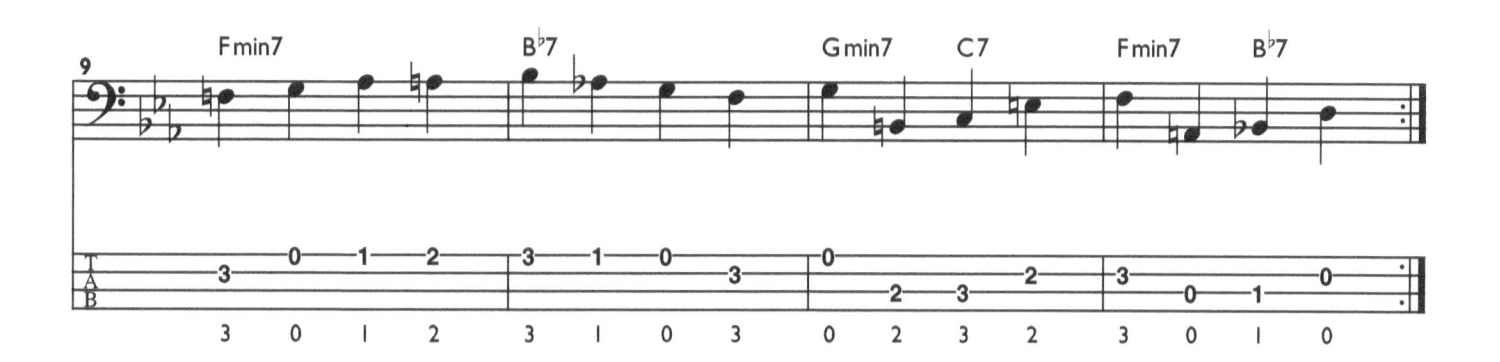

In the Style of Ahmed Abdul-Malik (with Thelonious Monk)

Bassist Ahmed Abdul-Malik played with the brilliant bebop pianist Thelonious Monk during one of the most important periods of Monk's career. Monk, like many jazz composers, used the harmony from the George Gershwin tune "I Got Rhythm" as a framework for some of his own tunes. Here is a line in Malik's style over what jazz players refer to as "rhythm changes."

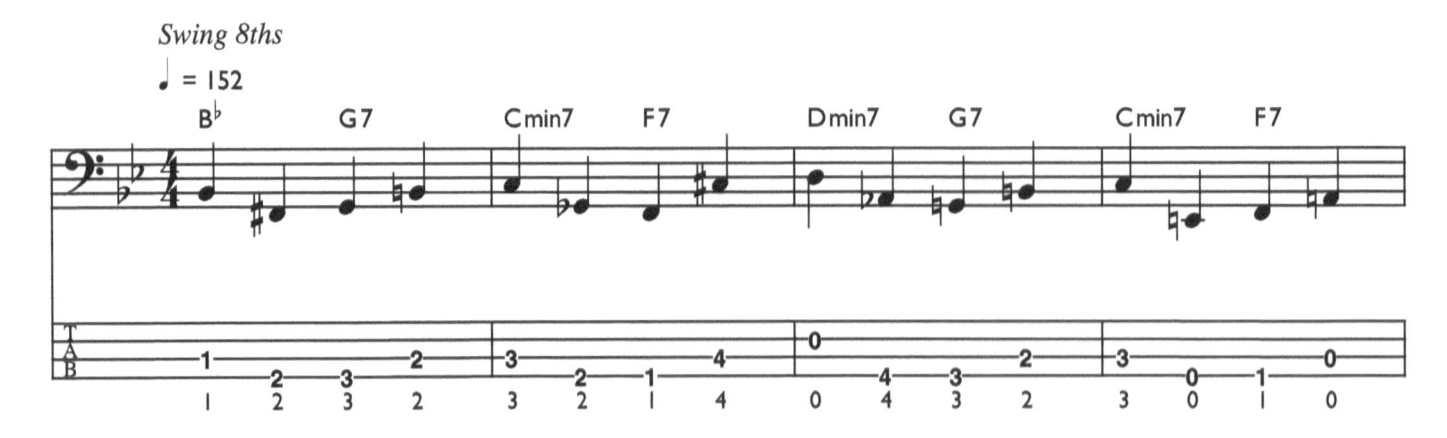

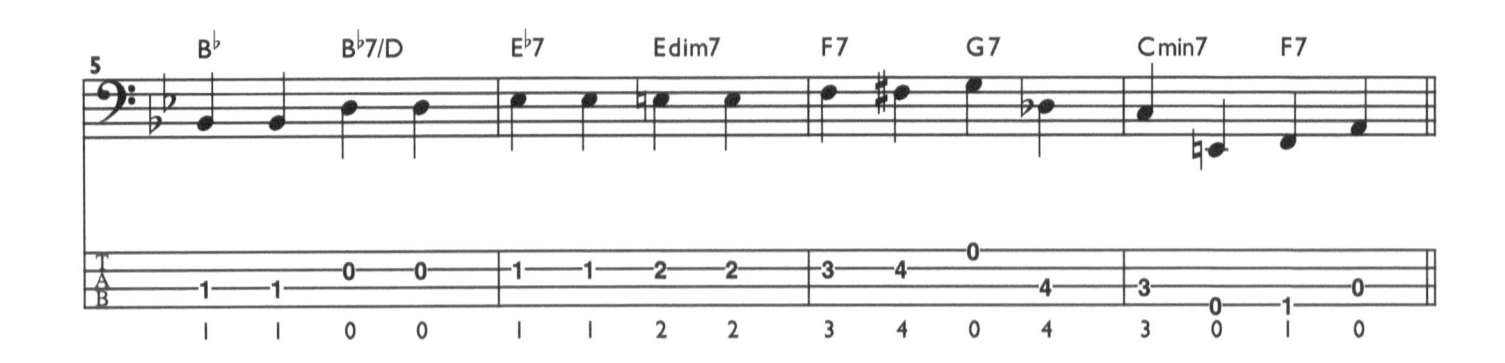

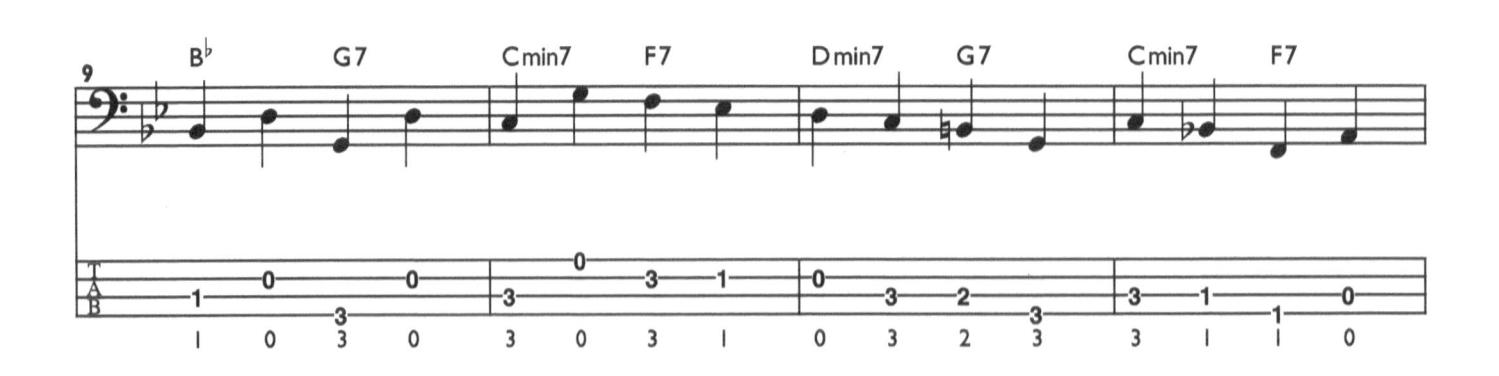

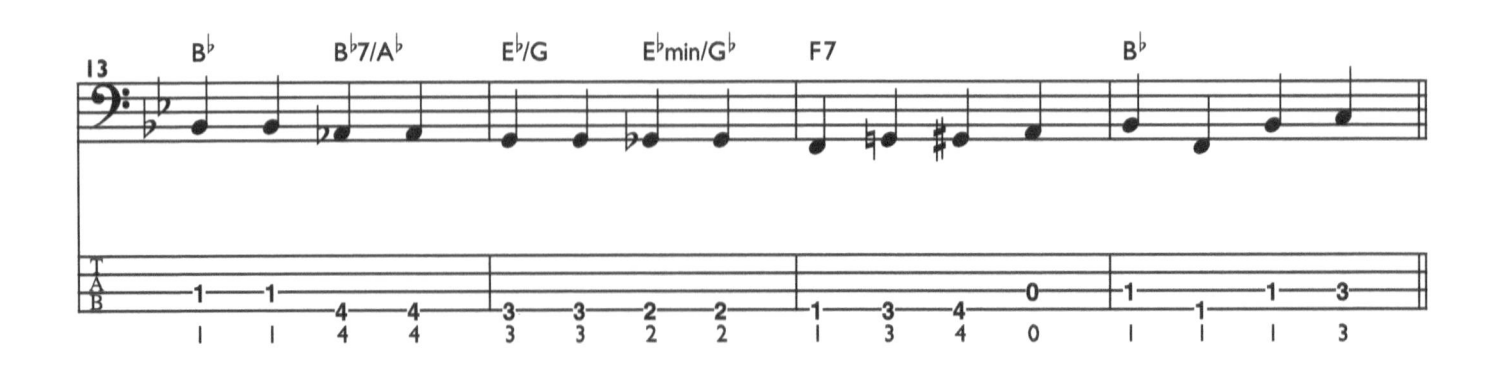

17
D7
G7
21
C7
F7
25
B♭
G7
Cmin7
F7
Dmin7
G7
Cmin7
F7
29
B♭
B♭7/A♭
E♭/G
E♭min/G♭
F7
B♭
(F7)

Ballad

Playing a jazz ballad is very different from playing a faster walking bass line. Let the notes ring, treating the quarter notes that are followed by rests more like half notes than quarter notes. Be sure to strive for strong time and forward motion without rushing.

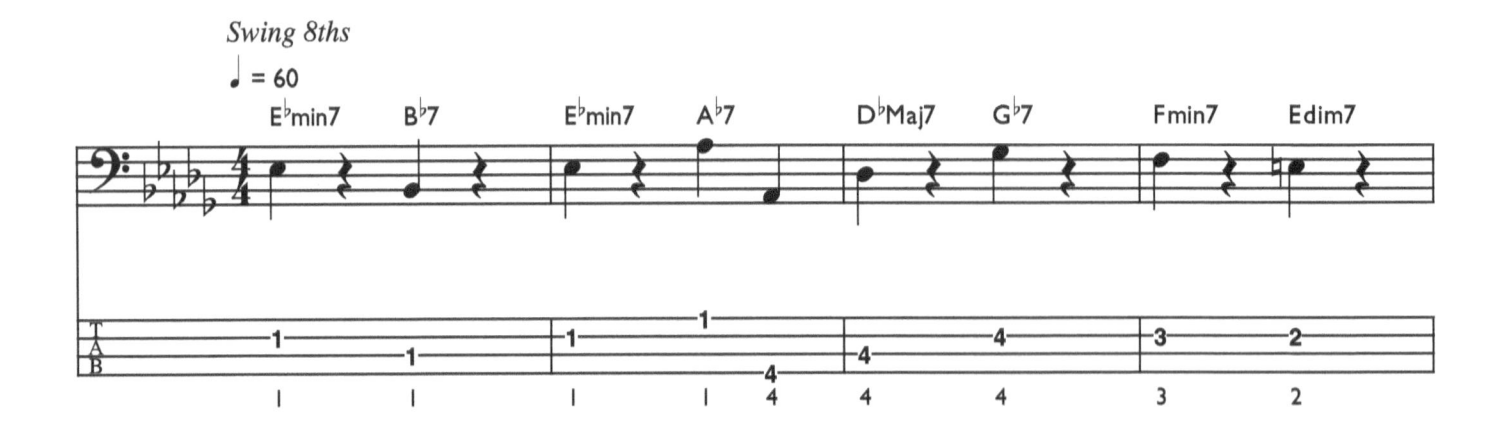

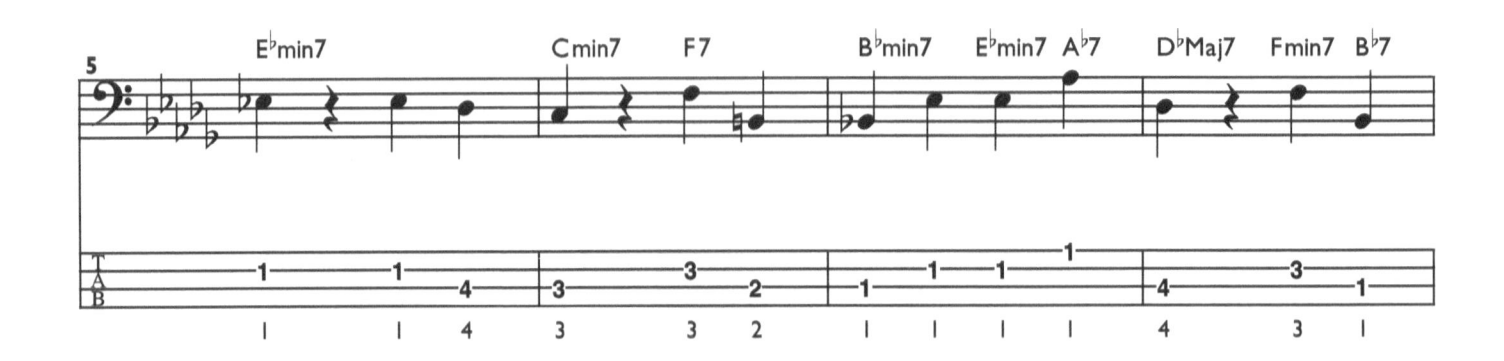

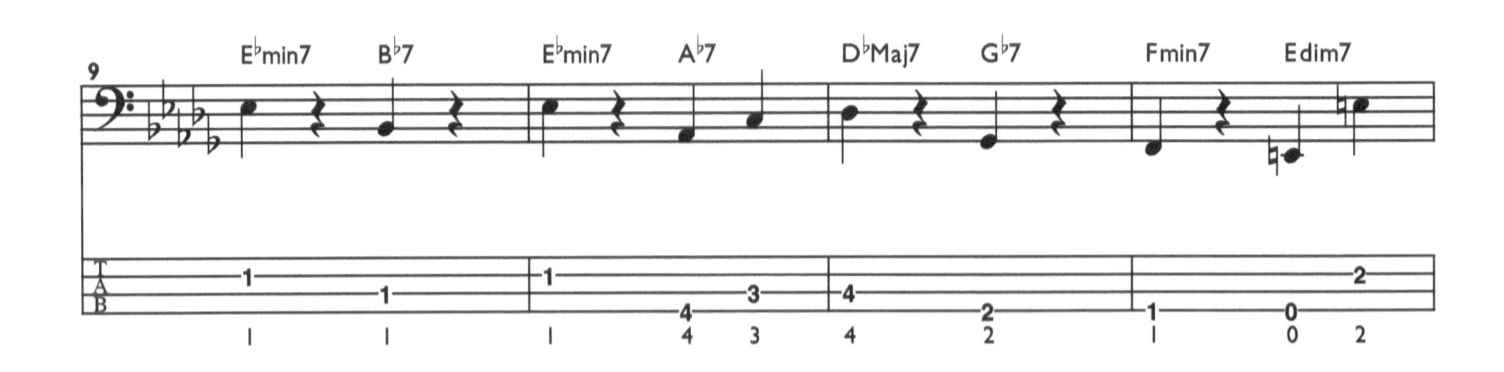

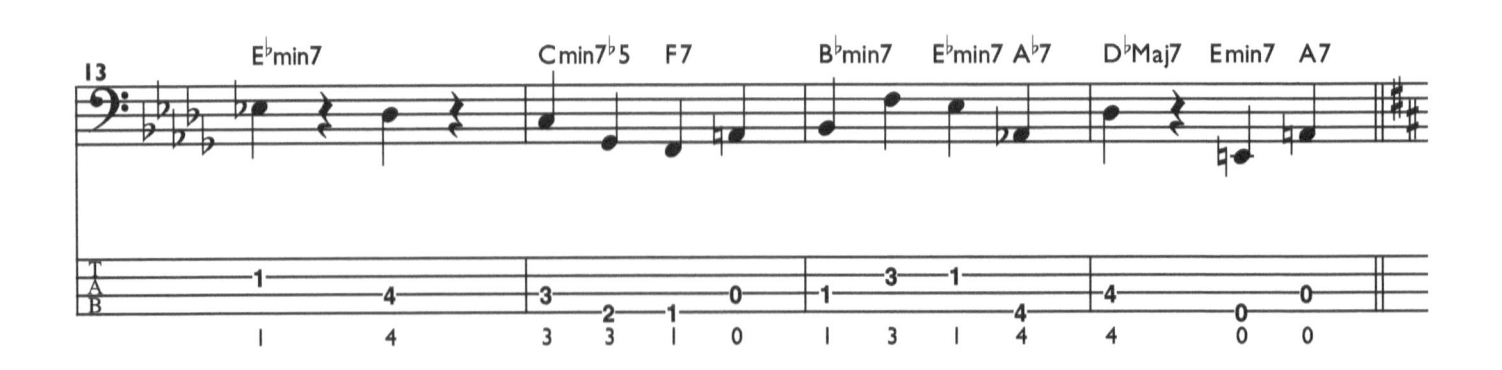

17
DMaj7 Emin7 F♯min7 Gmin7 C7 F♯min7 B7 Emin7 A7 DMaj7 A7
21
Dmin7 G7 Emin7 E♭dim7 Dmin7 G7 C7 B7 B♭7
25
E♭min7 B♭7 E♭min7 A♭7 D♭Maj7 G♭7 Fmin7 Edim7
29
E♭min7 Cmin7 F7 B♭min7 E♭7 E♭min7 A♭7 D♭Maj7

Jazz Waltz

The waltz was not common in the jazz style until Sonny Rollins began to play waltzes in the 1950s. Previous to that, Fats Waller had written his wonderful "Jitterbug Waltz," but that was a rare exception. With Rollins' reintroduction of the waltz, jazz players began to play in 3/4 time much more often, and the "jazz waltz" became a standard part of the jazz repertoire. In 1962, virtuoso harmonica player and guitarist Toots Thielemans had a hit with his jazz waltz "Bluesette."

25
B♭
Amin7♭5
D7♭9
Gmin7
C7
31
Fmin7
B♭7
E♭Maj7
E♭min7
A♭7
37
D♭Maj7
D♭min7
G♭7
BMaj7
43
Cmin7
F7
Dmin7
D♭7
Cmin7
F7

In the Style of Tommy Potter
(with Charlie Parker and Dizzy Gillespie)

Tommy Potter was a great bassist who played with Charlie Parker and Dizzy Gillespie from 1947 to 1950. During that time, Parker and Gillespie were on the cutting edge of the new music they helped invent—bebop. With its fast tempos and complex harmonies, bebop has become the technical benchmark for jazz players. Following is a line in the style of Tommy Potter playing over a Charlie Parker chord progression. Even though it is in a different key, notice the similarity between this harmony and "Bird Blues" (page 95).

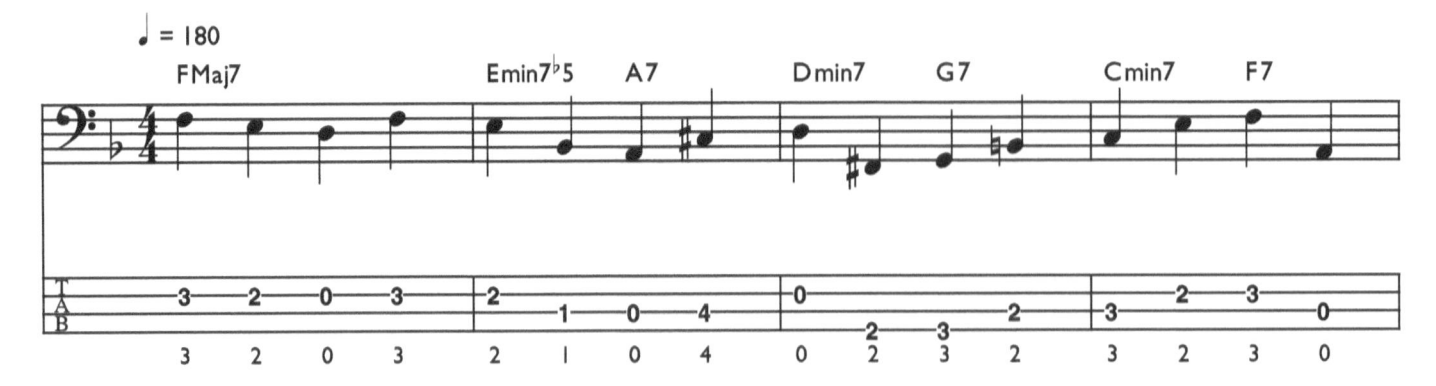

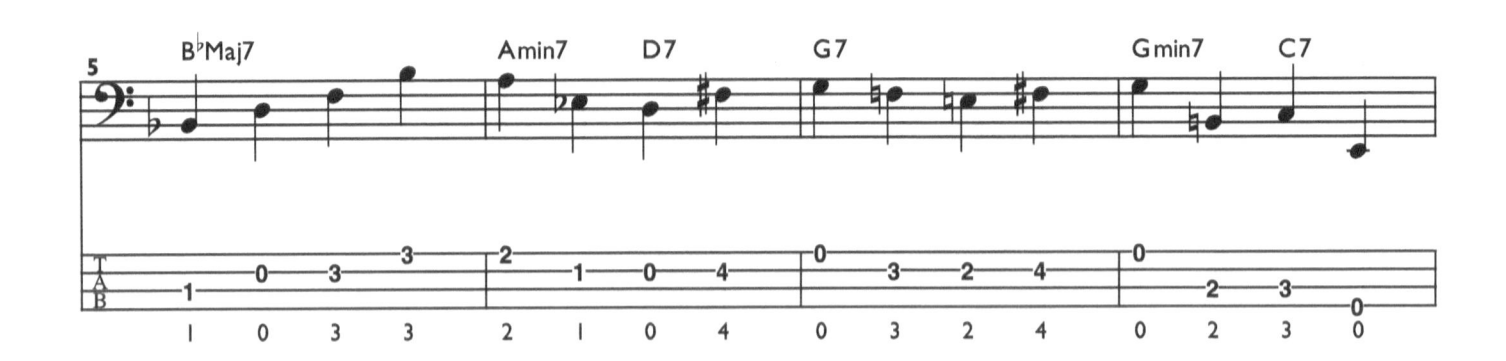

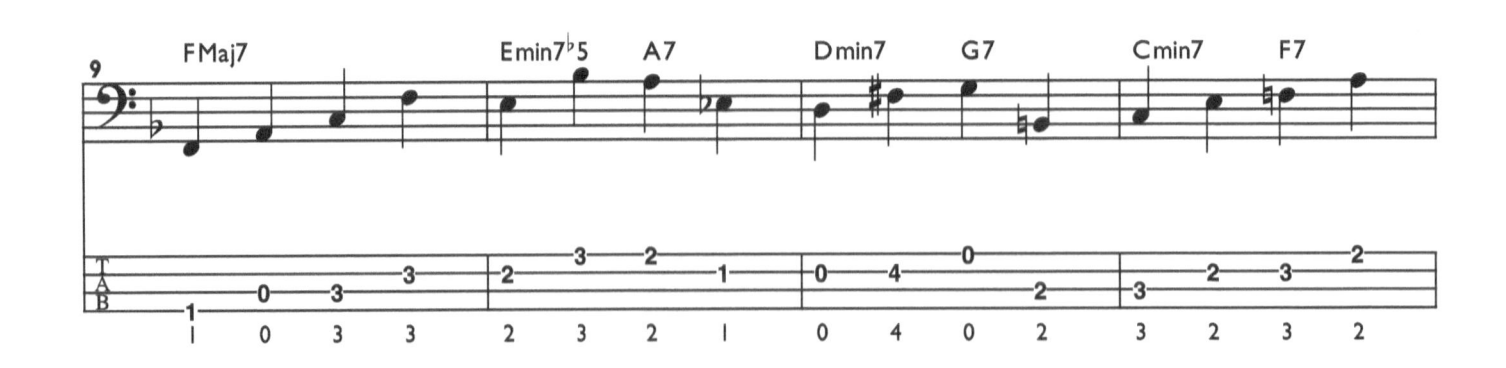

17
Cmin
Cmin7
F7
B♭7
B♭6
21
E♭min7
A♭7
D♭min7
Gmin7♭5
C+7
25
FMaj7
Emin7♭5
A7
Dmin7
G7
Cmin7
F7
29
B♭Maj7
Amin7♭5
D7
Gmin7
C7
FMaj7

In the Style of Paul Chambers (with John Coltrane)

Paul Chambers was one of the greatest double bassists to ever play the instrument. He is best known for his work with The Miles Davis Quintet from 1955 to 1963, but he also played with many of the most famous jazz musicians of his time, including Thelonious Monk, Wes Montgomery, and John Coltrane. Following is a line in the style of Paul Chambers on a chord progression by Coltrane. Learn this line slowly at first, then gradually increase the tempo.

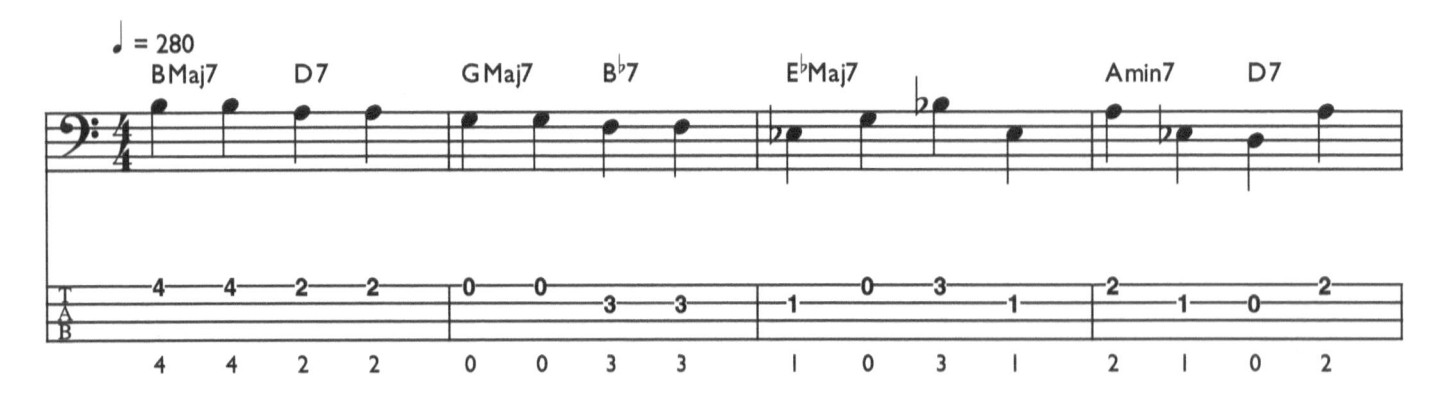

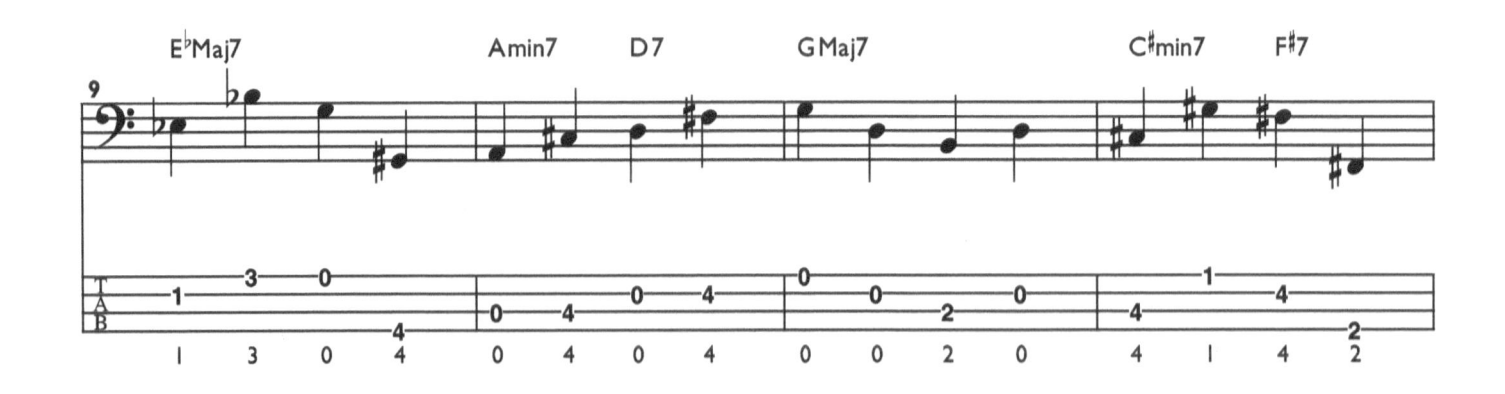

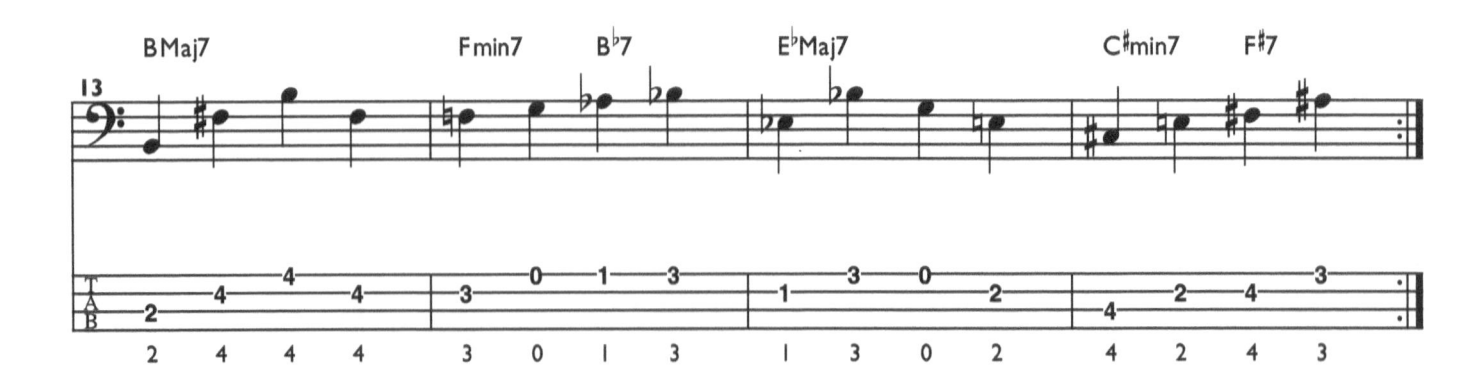

Chapter 6: World Music

A Brief History of World Music

The term "world music" was coined in the 1960s as an ethnomusicological term, but it wasn't until the late '80s that it began to be used as a marketing tool by the music industry. Exactly what world music is is hard to pin down, but it's safe to say it encompasses many of the musical styles that come from outside of our Western culture. While that leaves a lot of open territory, some of the world's musical styles have been, and are, more present than others on the Western scene. The first and most notable examples of this "world" phenomenon are now staples of Western pop music, although they were not categorized as world music at the time they were introduced. Polish polka, Latin American styles like Argentine tango and Brazilian bossa nova and samba, Caribbean styles like calypso, and reggae and ska styles from Jamaica, are all well-established examples of foreign styles that have become part of Western popular music. In more recent years, we've seen the introduction of classical and folk musics from around the world as well as pop music from places like Africa, India, and South and Central America. In some cases, this music is more or less "pure" in its derivation from one particular culture, like the Cuban music and musicians presented in the film and recording *The Buena Vista Social Club*. But more and more, thanks to the globalization of the world, popular music is blending and melding styles. The results of this phenomenon were seen as early as the 1950s with the mambo style, which became a huge hit all over the country. Mambo was a musical style created in New York City by Cuban immigrants, the most notable of whom was the great Cuban bassist Israel "Cachao" López, who is considered by many to be the originator of mambo. Mambo incorporated African rhythms with Cuban melodies and the improvisational and harmonic elements of jazz, and was in many ways a forerunner to the salsa style, which has continued on a similar path. Early ska musicians and reggae pioneers like Bob Marley and Peter Tosh drew on U.S. and British rock and soul artists as inspirations for their unique style, and African pop musicians like King Sunny Adé, Fela Kuti, Ladysmith Black Mambazo and Johnny Clegg—as well as many musicians from the Middle East and Asia—are all doing much the same thing in blending the sounds of their local culture with Western pop music to varying degrees. Particularly notable are the African bassists who have enriched popular bass playing in recent years. Probably the first of these to be widely heard is the South African bassist Bakithi Kumalo, whose wonderful fretless playing on Paul Simon's hit album *Graceland* introduced American ears to a new style. More recently, bassists like Richard Bona and Etienne Mbappé, both from Cameroon, have introduced a new virtuosity, blending their African styles with Western jazz and pop bass playing.

Needless to say, the world music genre is a big tent, and it is not within the scope of this book to represent it all. The following examples are a sample meant to encourage more investigation into the many styles and musicians playing great world music. Now, with the advent of the internet and even more accessible recording and playback technology, music is becoming more global all the time.

In the list to the right, asterisks (*) indicate the bass players.

Suggested Listening
- Bossa nova: Stan Getz, Antonio Carlos Jobim
- Samba: Sérgio Mendes
- Calypso: Bob Cranshaw* (Sonny Rollins)
- Reggae: Aston Barrett* (Bob Marley and The Wailers)
- Ska: Joe Gittleman* (The Mighty Mighty Bosstones)
- South African: Bakithi Kumalo* (with Paul Simon on *Graceland* and on Kumalo's own recordings)

Bossa Nova

The bossa nova style was born in the 1950s in Brazil. Combining elements of the samba style (page 108) with romantic melodies and eloquent lyrics, bossa nova became the music of sophistication. Saxophonist Stan Getz brought the sound of bossa nova to the U.S. with his recording *Jazz Samba* in 1962, introducing U.S. listeners to one of the fathers of bossa nova, the great Brazilian composer Antonio Carlos Jobim. Following is an example of a bossa nova bass line.

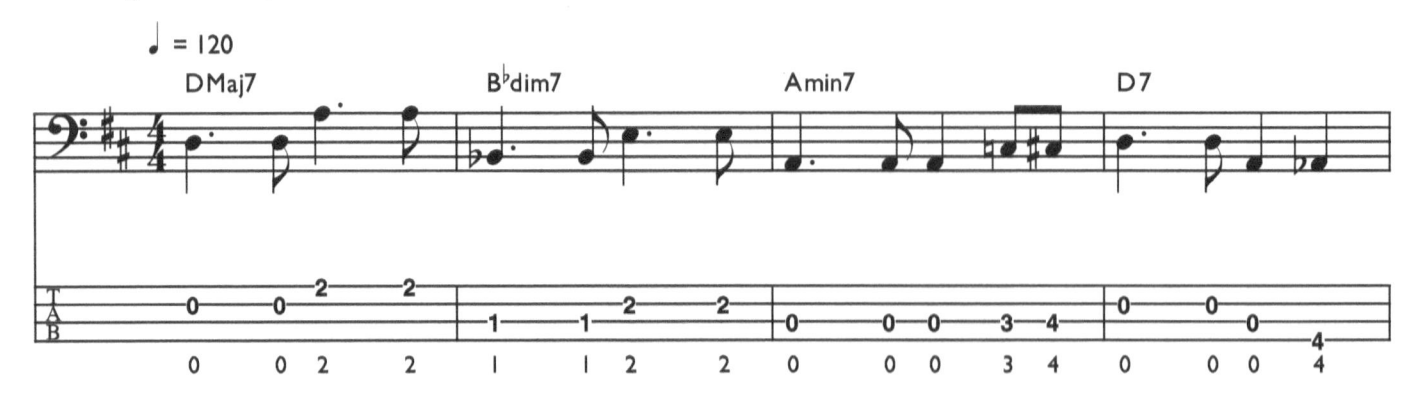

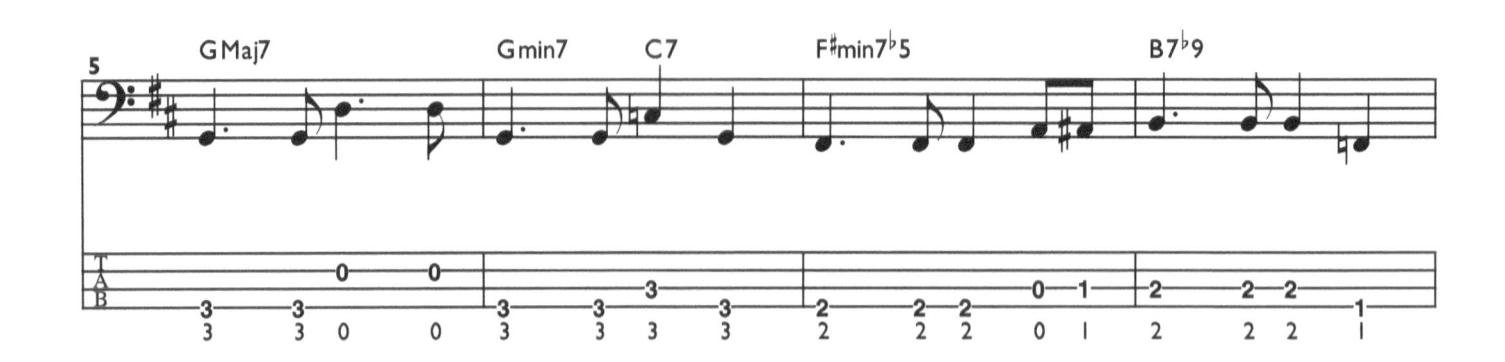

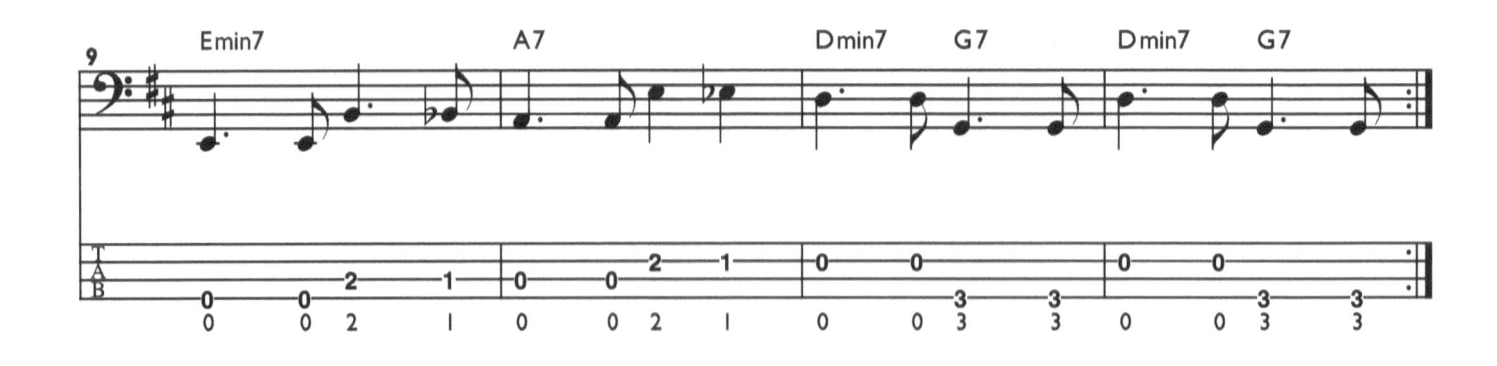

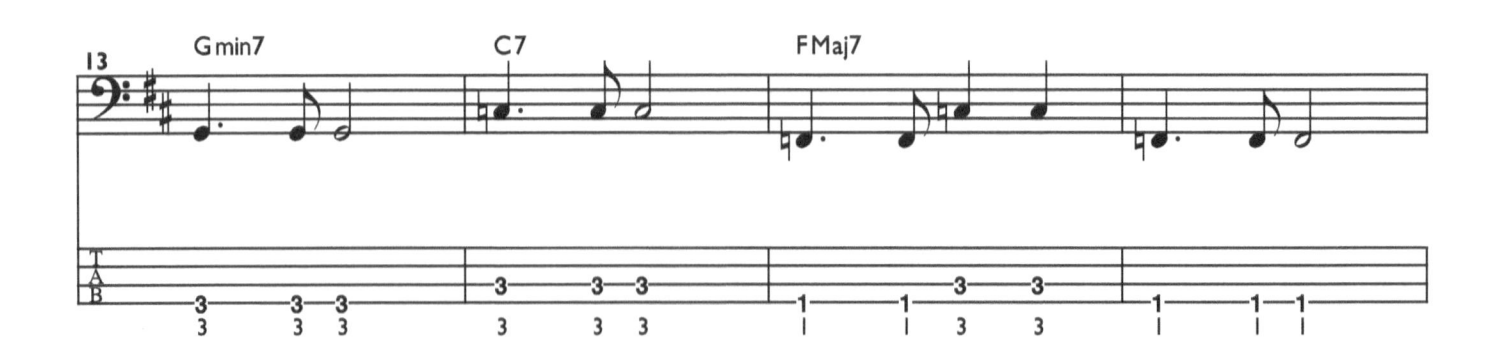

Fmin7 B♭7 E♭ Emin7 A7
DMaj7 B♭dim7 Amin7 D7
GMaj7 Gmin7 C7 F♯min7 B7
Emin7♭5 A7 Dmin7 G7 Dmin7 G7

Samba

Samba is a style that has been the dominant popular music in Brazil for more than 100 years, and has been part of the popular music of the United States since the 1950s. Songs like "Summer Samba" and "One Note Samba" became pop hits and created an awareness of—and love for—the Brazilian musical culture that exists to this day.

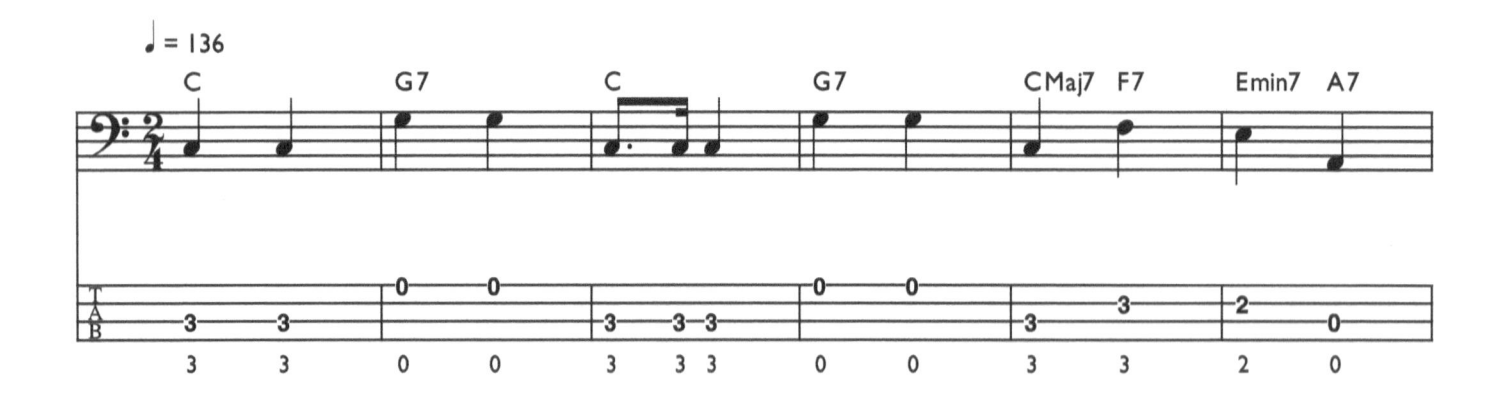

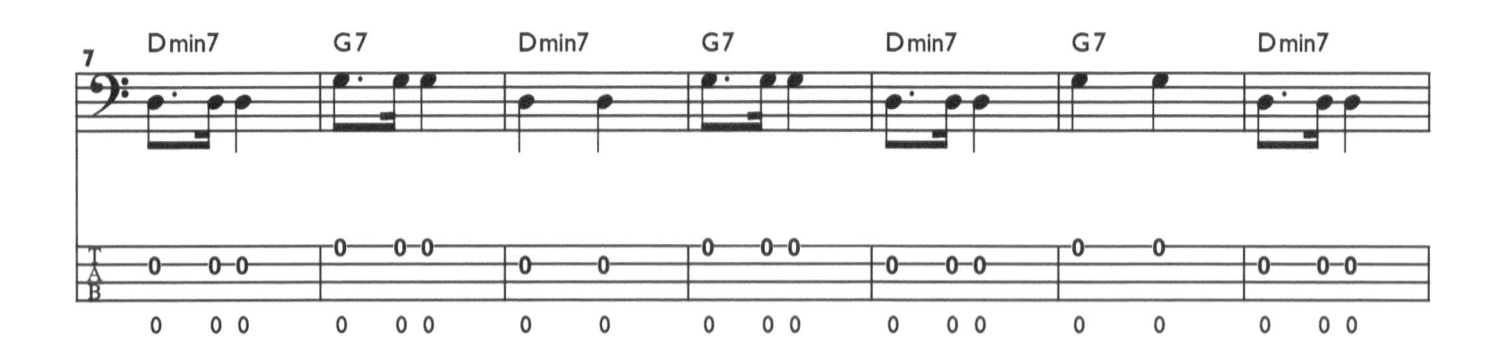

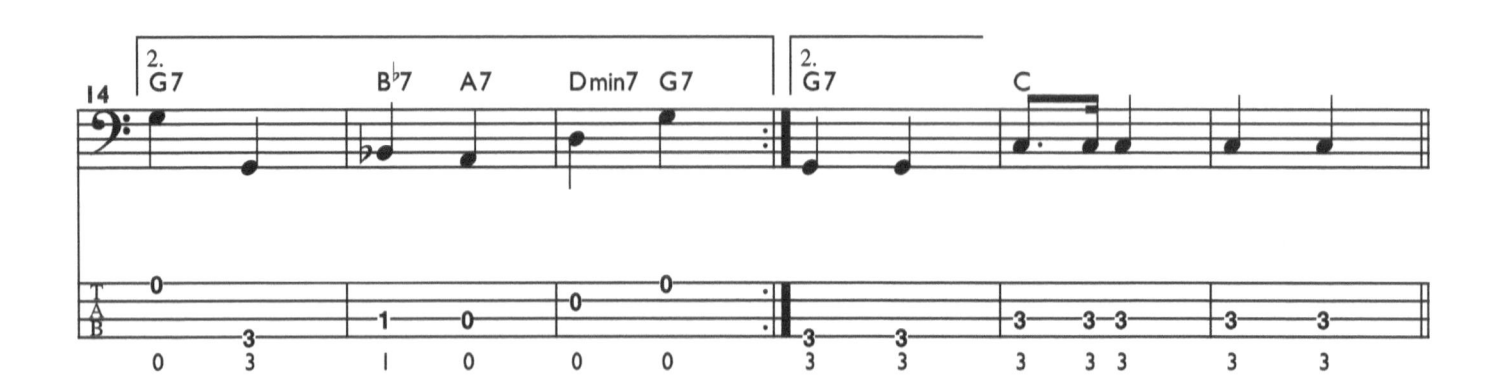

20
Gmin7 C7 FMaj7 Fmin7 B♭7 Emin7 A7 Dmin7 G7
28
CMaj7 G7 CMaj7 G7 CMaj7 F7 Emin7 A7 Dmin7 G7
36
Dmin7 G7 Dmin7 G7 Dmin7 G7 CMaj9

Calypso in the Style of Bob Cranshaw (with Sonny Rollins)

Calypso is a musical style that originated in the islands of Trinidad and Tobago and was popularized in the U.S. by artists like singer Harry Belafonte and jazz saxophonist Sonny Rollins. Rollins, whose parents were from the West Indies, was in a unique position to incorporate this style into his music. When he recorded his calypso tune "St. Thomas," Bob Cranshaw (Rollins' bassist for more than 50 years) was in the band. Following is a calypso line in Cranshaw's style.

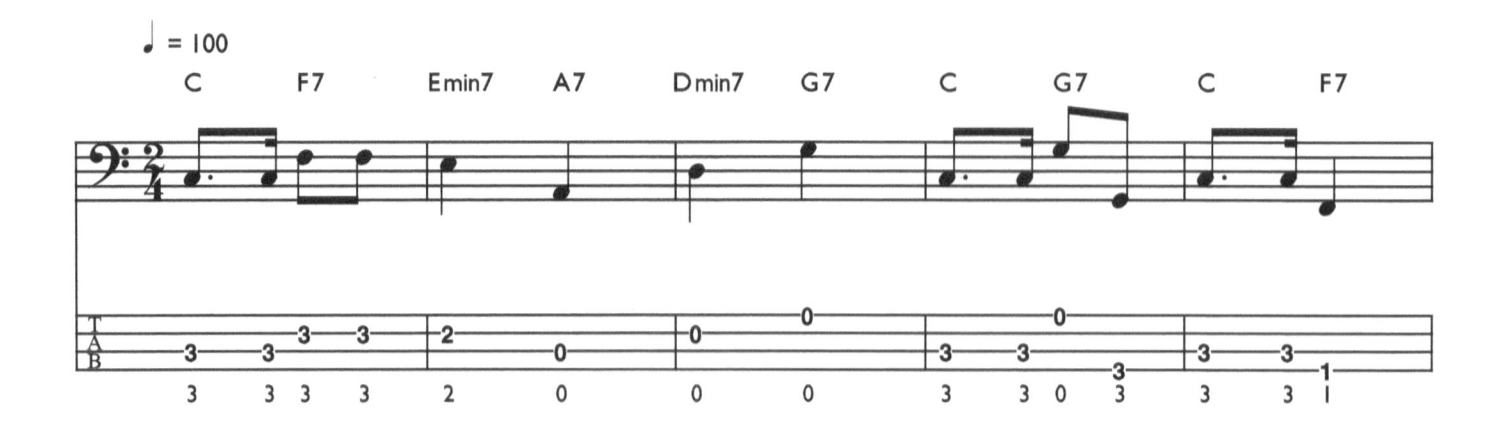

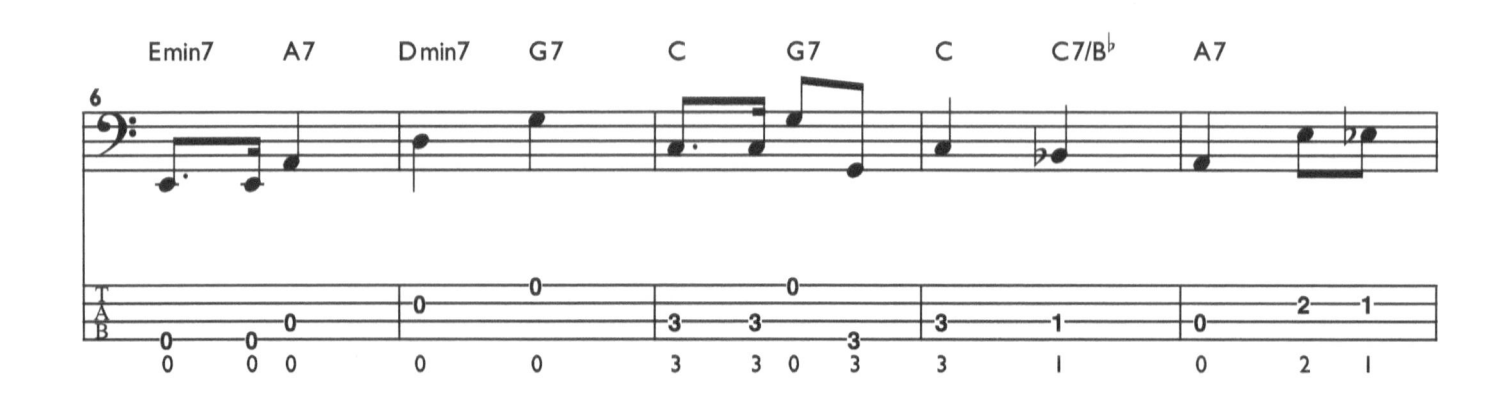

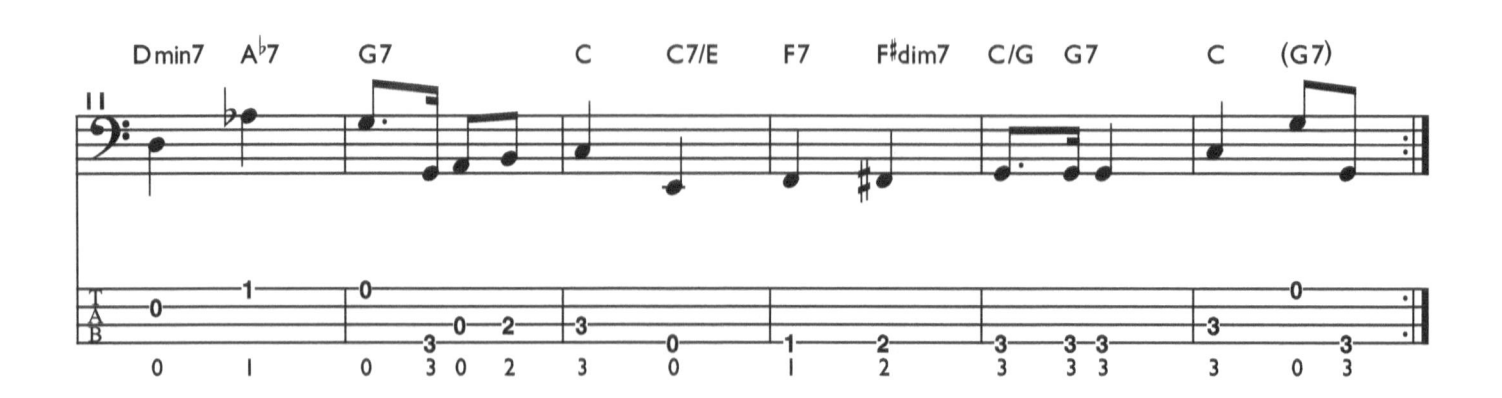

Reggae in the Style of Aston Barrett
(with Bob Marley and the Wailers)

Bob Marley and the Wailers put reggae music on the world map in the late 1960s and early '70s, and Wailers bassist Aston "Family Man" Barrett played a big part in creating their sound and all of their success. Reggae has since become part of the international pop music scene, and its influence can be heard in many kinds of music. Barrett is still playing and, these days, serves as the bandleader of The Wailers as they continue to tour the world.

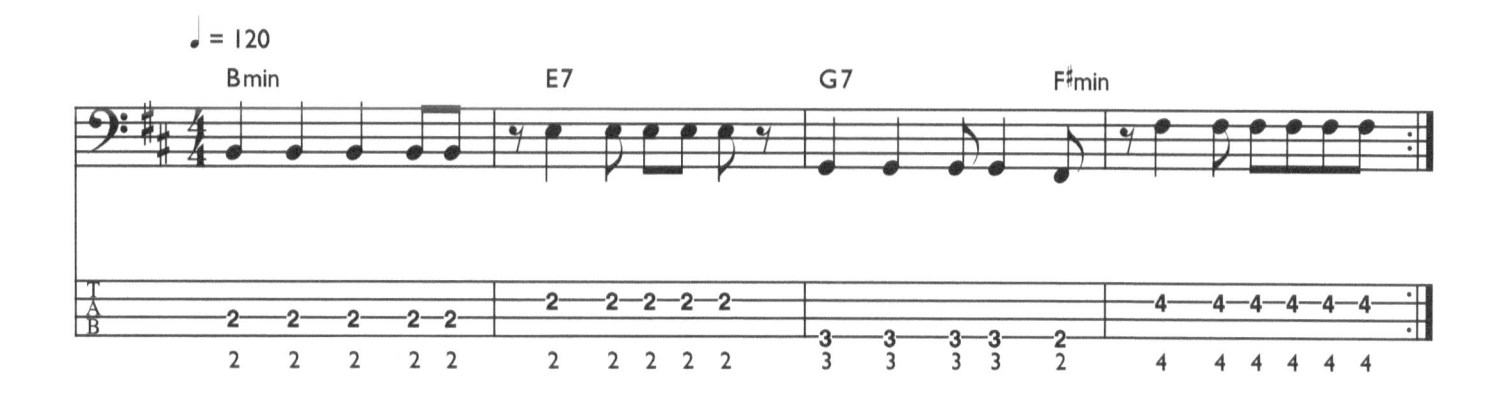

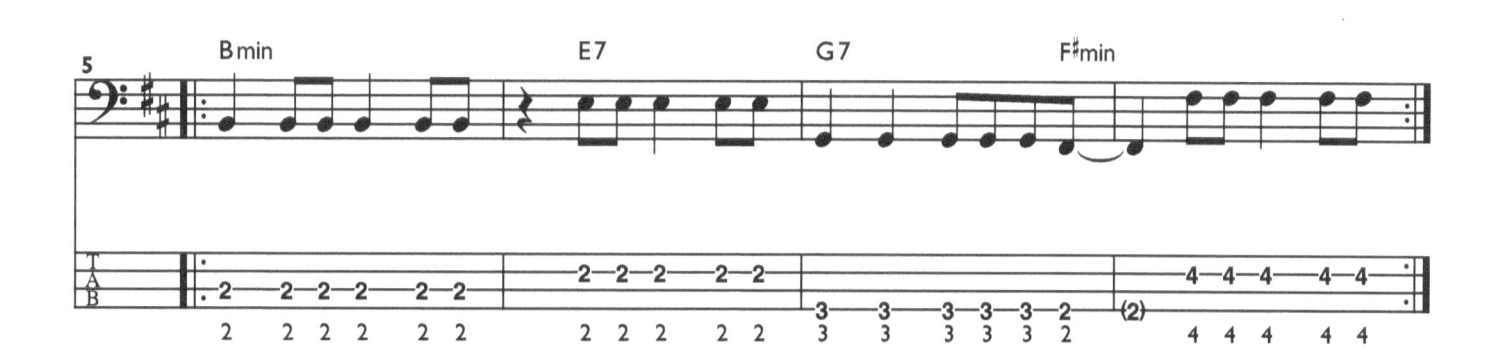

Ska in the Style of Joe Gittleman (with The Mighty Mighty Bosstones)

The ska style is in many ways the ultimate world music. Originating in Jamaica, it migrated to England in the '70s (known as ska's "second wave") and then the U.S. in the '90s (ska's "third wave"). Throughout its migration, the style developed and evolved, merging with other styles like rock, punk, and hardcore. The Boston-based band The Mighty Mighty Bosstones is the quintessential ska band from the 1980s and '90s, the period during which the style became popular in the U.S. Bosstones bassist Joe Gittleman is one of the most accomplished players in the style.

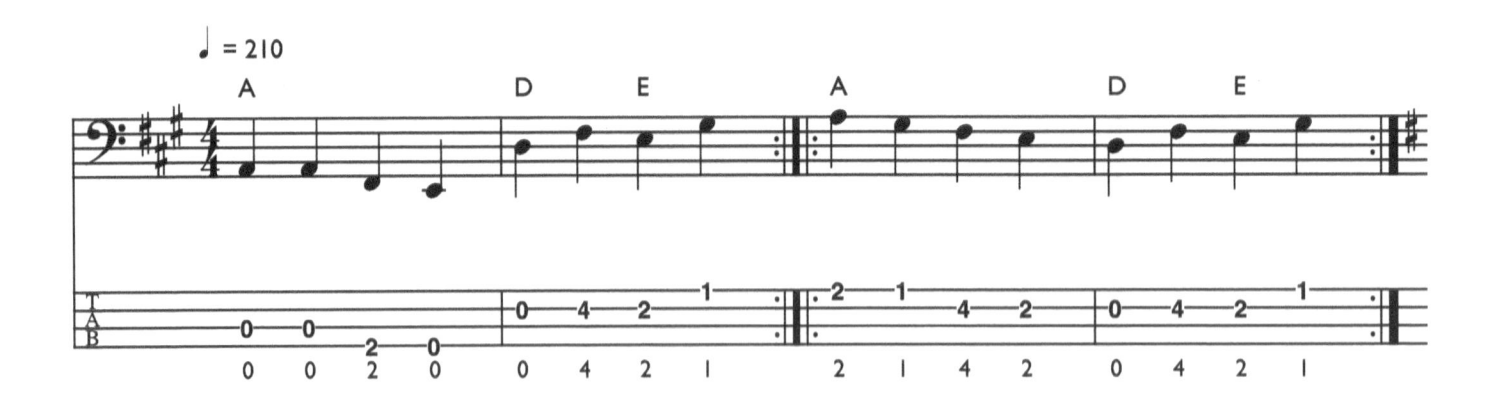

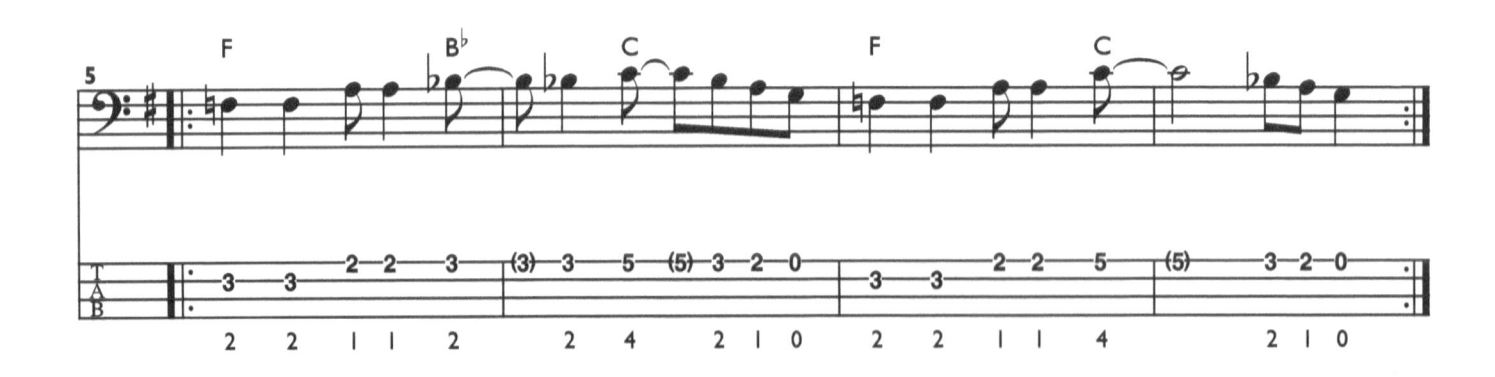

South African/American Pop in the Style of Bakithi Kumalo (with Paul Simon)

Paul Simon's 1986 album *Graceland* was one of the first hit recordings in the U.S. to feature African music played by African musicians. Bakithi Kumalo's wonderfully expressive fretless bass playing was one of the musical highlights of the recording. Kumalo grew up in South Africa's Soweto, an urban area in the city of Johannesburg, and continues to make fantastic recordings of his South African/American world music.

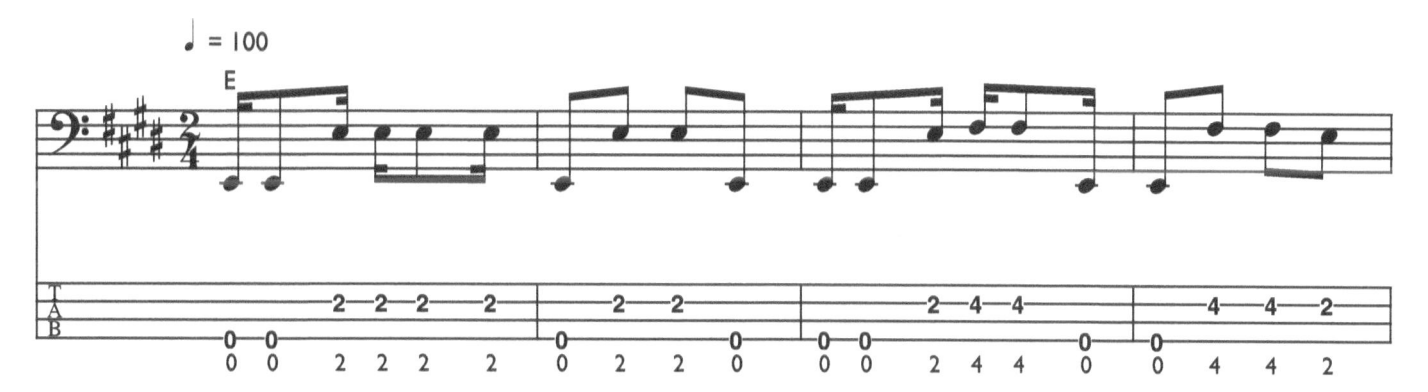

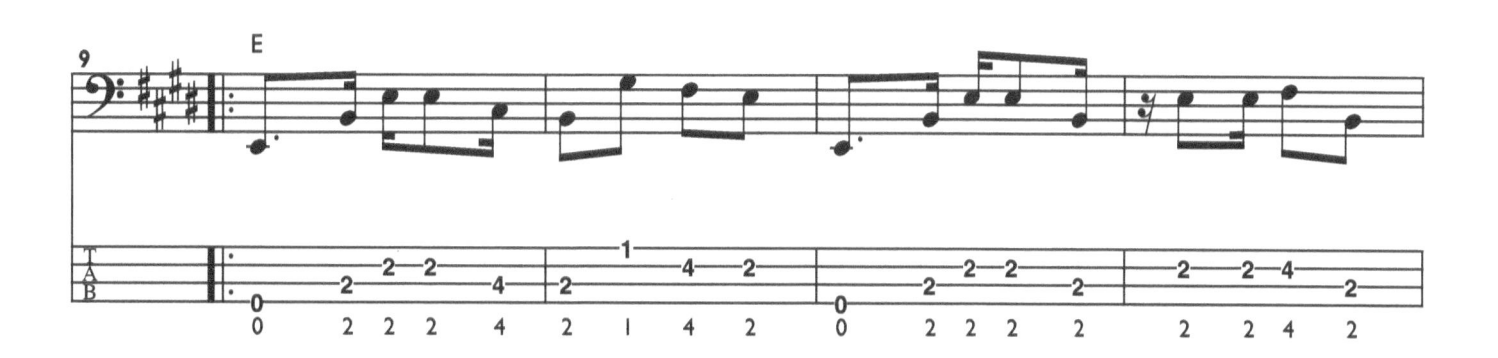

(Continued on next page)

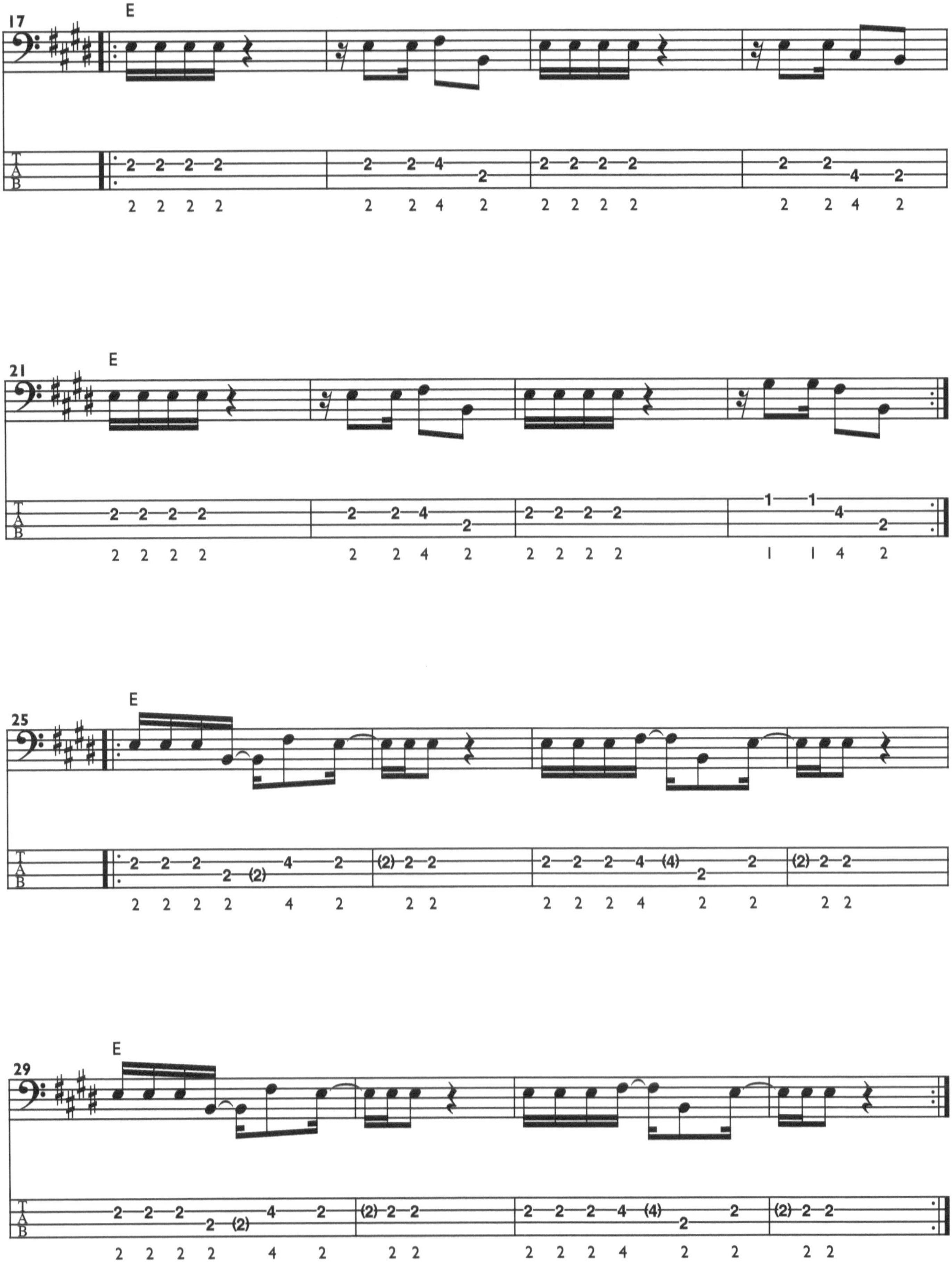
17
E
21
E
25
E
29
E

Chapter 7: Country Music

A Brief History of Country Music

The style of music we call country was first documented in the early 20th century as folk music from the Appalachian mountains. It was derived from a combination of Celtic music, gospel music, traditional music from the British Isles, and the various musical styles brought to the U.S. by other immigrant groups. This musical mix combined with the unique collection of instruments brought from the various cultures (guitar, banjo, mandolin, dulcimer, and violin or fiddle) to create a uniquely American musical form that was commonly referred to at the time as "hillbilly music." As recording and radio technology began to create a wider audience, the related style called "cowboy" music, which developed in the Southwestern U.S., also became popular and the two styles were marketed together as country and western. Over the years, the name has been shortened to country and now includes an even wider variety of styles.

Starting in the 1920s, live country music performances (often known as "barn dance" shows) began to be broadcast on the radio. The most important of these country music radio shows (and also the longest-running radio show in history) was The Grand Ole Opry in Nashville, TN. The Opry became an incubator for country music stars, and through it, artists like Patsy Cline, Johnny Cash, and Loretta Lynn became household names. In the 1930s, as the Opry's popularity increased, many careers were built on its weekly broadcasts. One of the more unique styles heard was the Texas swing style played by Bob Wills and His Texas Playboys. This style combines elements from country, cowboy, jazz, and even Hawaiian music, creating a truly singular sound. For bassists, it is interesting to study the Texas swing bass style, which includes country style "2 beat," jazz style swing feel and walking bass, and even some Mexican-influenced rhythms. Wills was one of the first country bandleaders to use electric guitars, including the electric steel guitar, and helped to usher in the sound of modern country music.

In the 1950s, country music went through a renaissance thanks to the artistry of a number of musicians and producers in Nashville. Guitarist and producer Chet Atkins and others created a new, more sophisticated style of country, which became known as the Nashville sound. This period created countless country hits and stars. It also solidified Nashville's place as the capital of country music, as well as one of the three centers of the U.S. music business, along with New York and Los Angeles. The influence of Nashville's many talented musicians and producers continue to make it a magnet for performing and composing talent, and as more and more talented musicians of all styles arrive in Nashville, its musical character and influence continue to grow along with the ever-expanding umbrella of country music.

Country music is a style that seldom features the bass line and instead relies on the steady time-keeping accompaniment of the bassist. As in the blues, country bass playing sounds deceptively simple. In fact, there is a commonly repeated truism among country bass players that "there's no money above the 5th fret." This humorous reference to keeping the bass part low and simple is based on several important elements of country bass playing: careful ensemble work, emphasis on the low register, and a clear, strong statement of time and harmonic structure. Country music has had many great bassists, but among the most important is the legendary double bassist Bob Moore. Moore, as a member of the so-called "Nashville A-Team," has played on more than 17,000 sessions and with countless country greats. In addition to his vast contributions to country music and bass playing, Moore performed with orchestras, pop stars, and jazz artists, and led the Bob Moore Orchestra. He can be heard on recordings by Chet Atkins, Elvis Presley, Bob Dylan, Roy Orbison, and thousands of other artists. His beautiful sound, perfect time feel, and simple, yet sophisticated bass lines are the essence of what makes great bass playing in any style.

Since the 1950s, the sound of country music has included electric guitars and electric bass. Today's country bands, while still sometimes using the double bass, almost inevitable include an electric bassist. There are many fine bassists performing in country music today, including Dave Pomeroy, Glenn Worf, and Michael Rhodes, who have performed and recorded with a veritable "who's who" of country and pop stars.

Suggested Listening
- Amos Garren (Bill Monroe and His Blue Grass Boys)
- Marshall Grant (Johnny Cash)
- Herbert "Lum" York (Hank Williams)
- Leon Rausch (Bob Wills and His Texas Playboys)

Bluegrass in the Style of Amos Garren (with Bill Monroe and His Blue Grass Boys)

Country music began as what was called "hillbilly" music. Part of this "all acoustic" country music has been kept alive as bluegrass. Bluegrass is a style that has produced a tremendous number of virtuoso stars over the years. Musicians like mandolin player and band leader Bill Monroe, and the duo of Lester Flatt and Earl Scruggs, all helped create the modern bluegrass style that a new generation of musicians like Ricky Skaggs and Alison Krauss are continuing today.

Bill Monroe and His Blue Grass Boys exemplified the bluegrass style, and the band's first bass player was Amos Garren. Following is a bass line in his style.

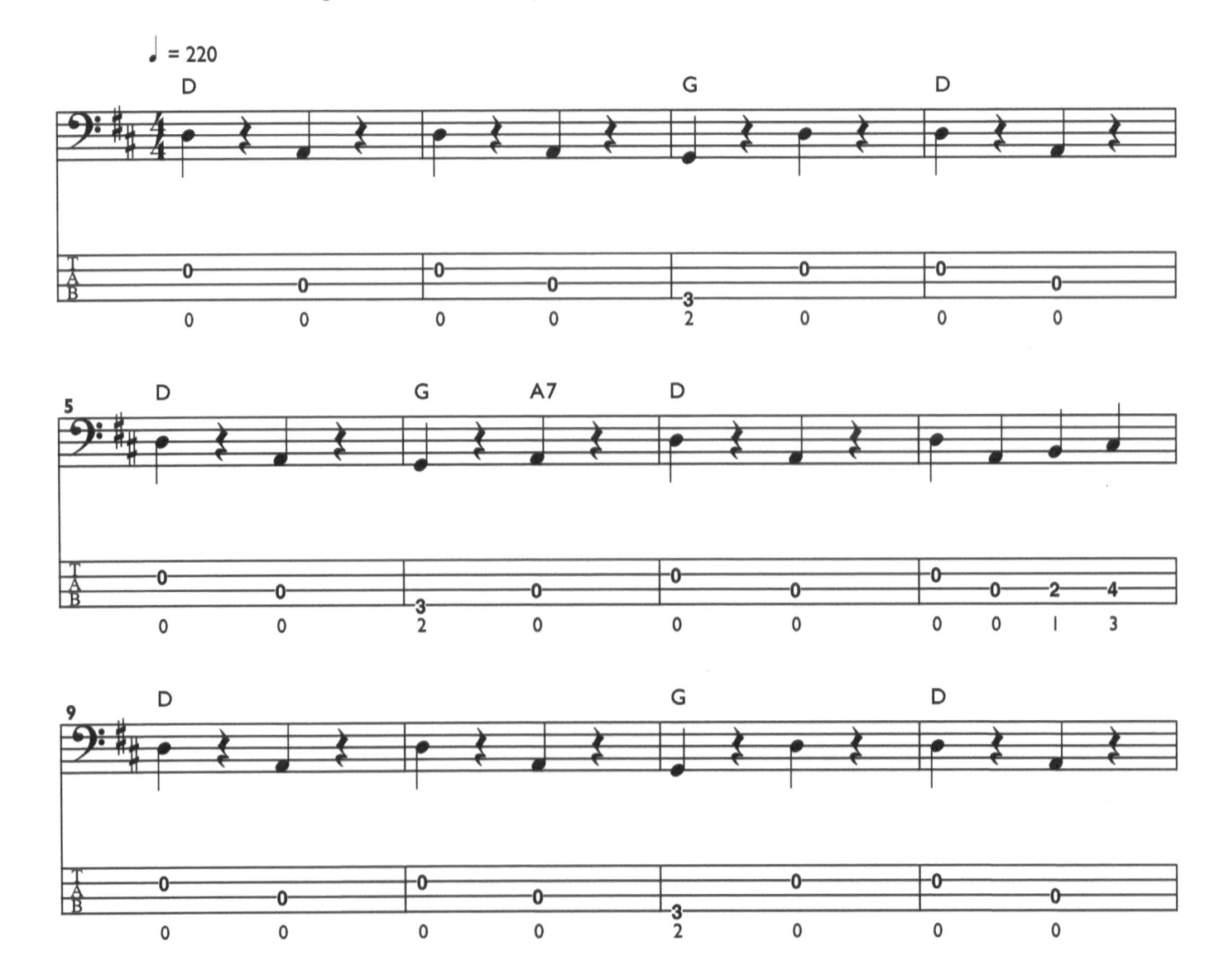

117

Country Waltz

The country waltz, typified by the 3/4 time signature, was popularized in barn dances (see page 115) and is a staple of the country music style. Bill Monroe and His Blue Grass Boys played several country waltzes. Below is an example of a country waltz bass line.

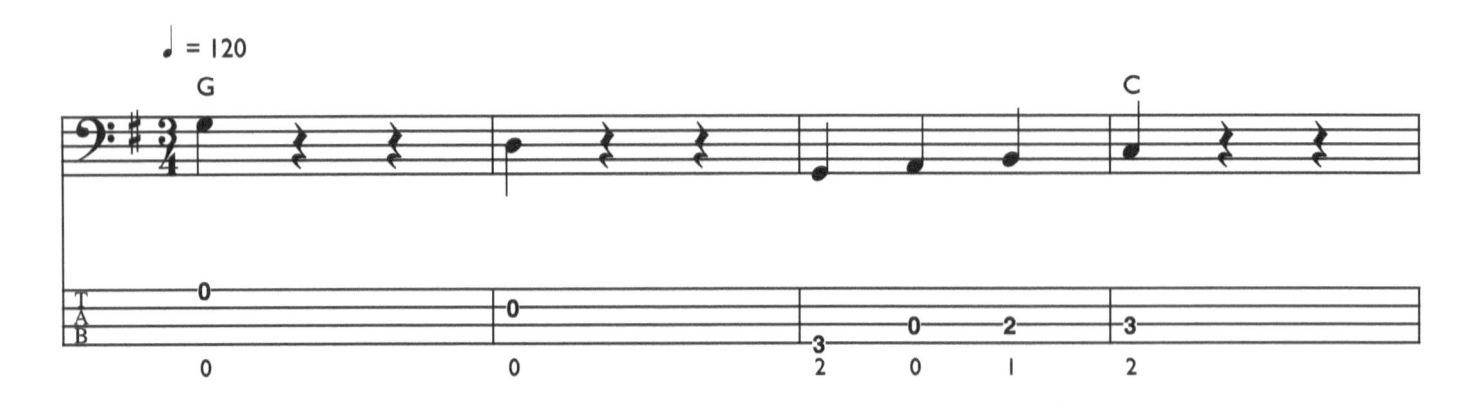

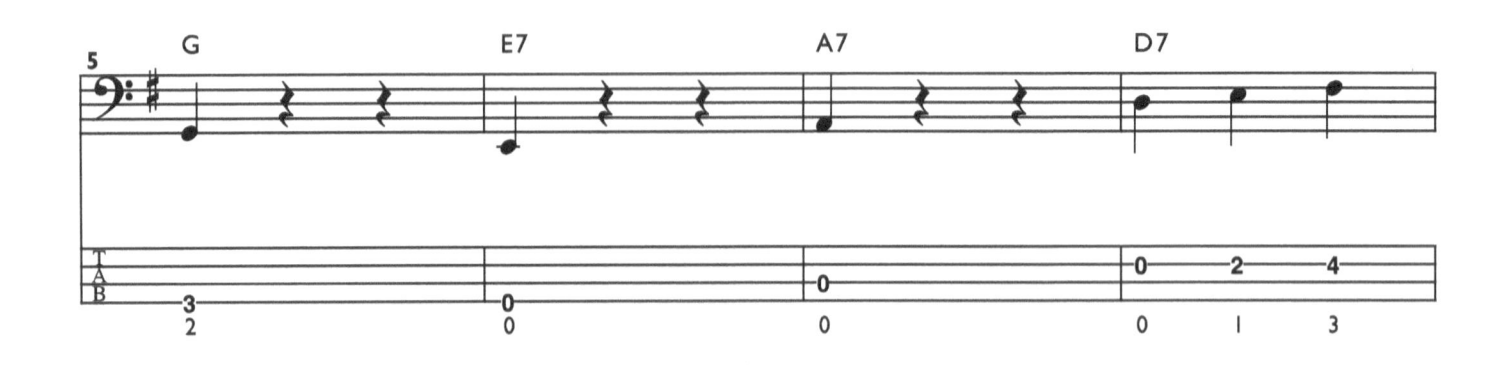

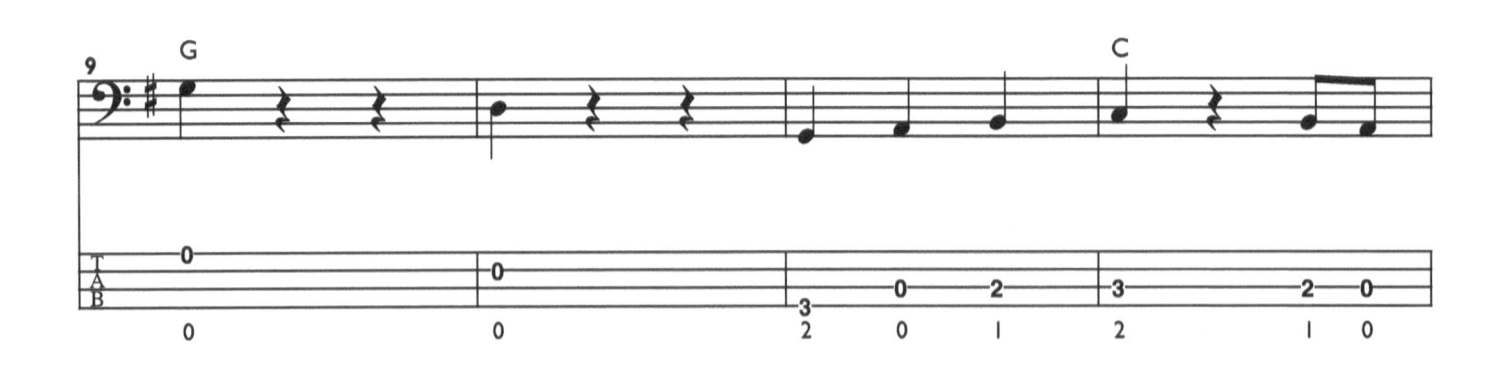

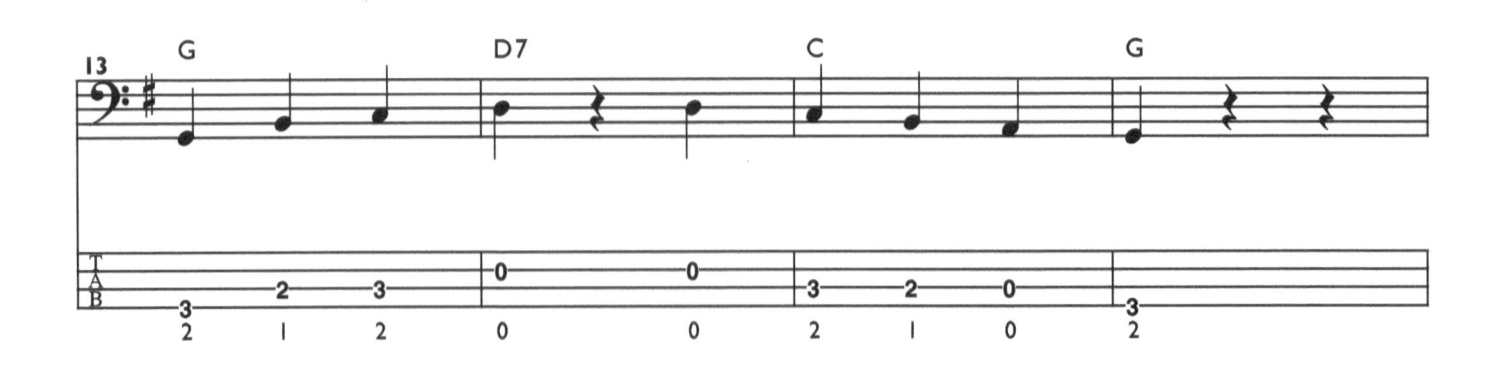

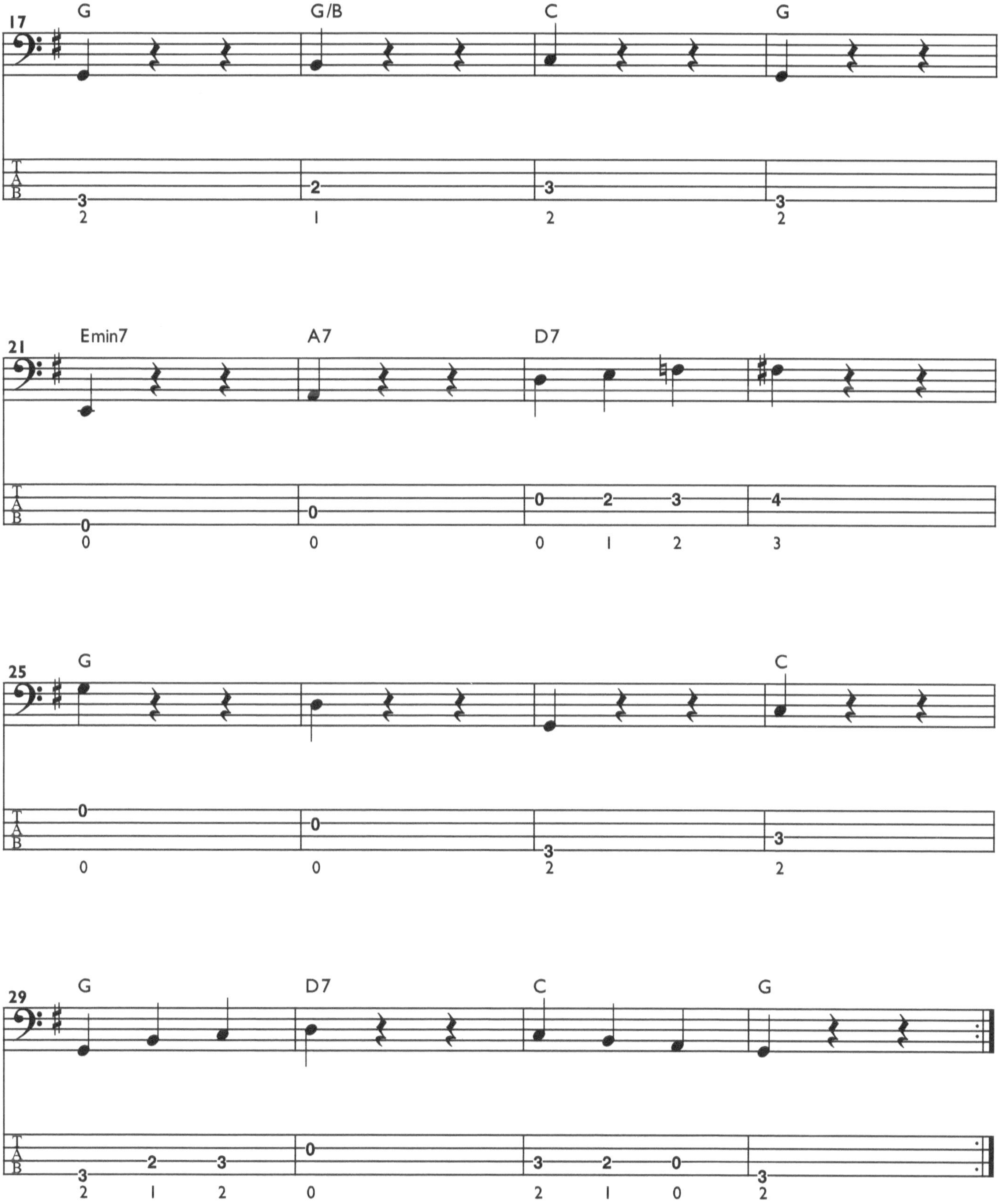
17
G
G/B
C
G
21
Emin7
A7
D7
25
G
C
29
G
D7
C
G

In the Style of Marshall Grant (with Johnny Cash)

Johnny Cash put his own unique stamp on the country music style. His trio, The Tennessee Three, was known for a simple but effective rhythmic style of bass and guitar playing that they called the "boom chick-a-boom." Double bassist Marshall Grant played the "boom" on beats 1 and 3, and Luther Perkins answered on the guitar with the "chick-a" on beats 2 and 4. Here's a typical bass part in that style.

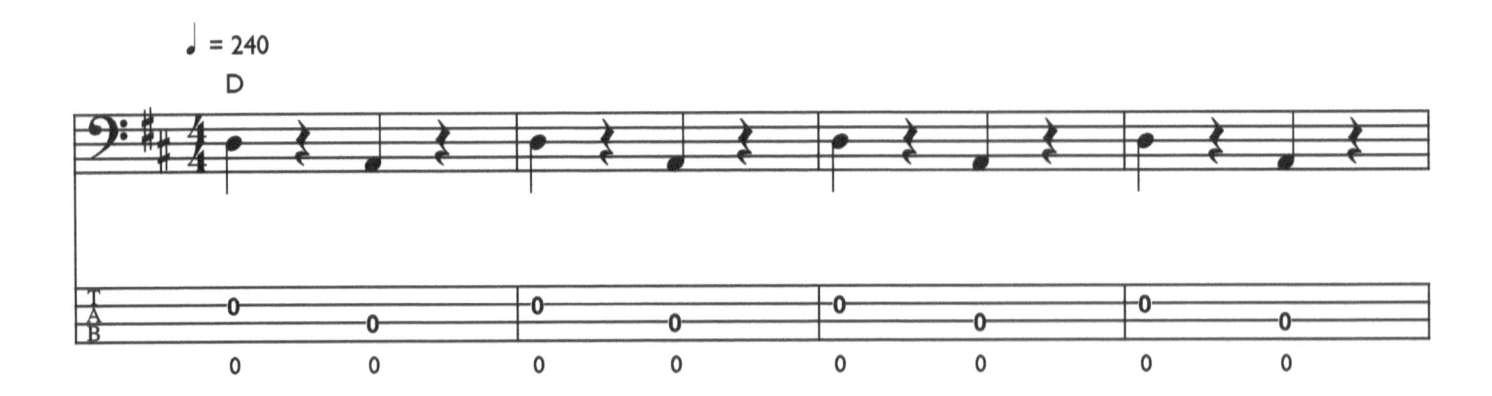

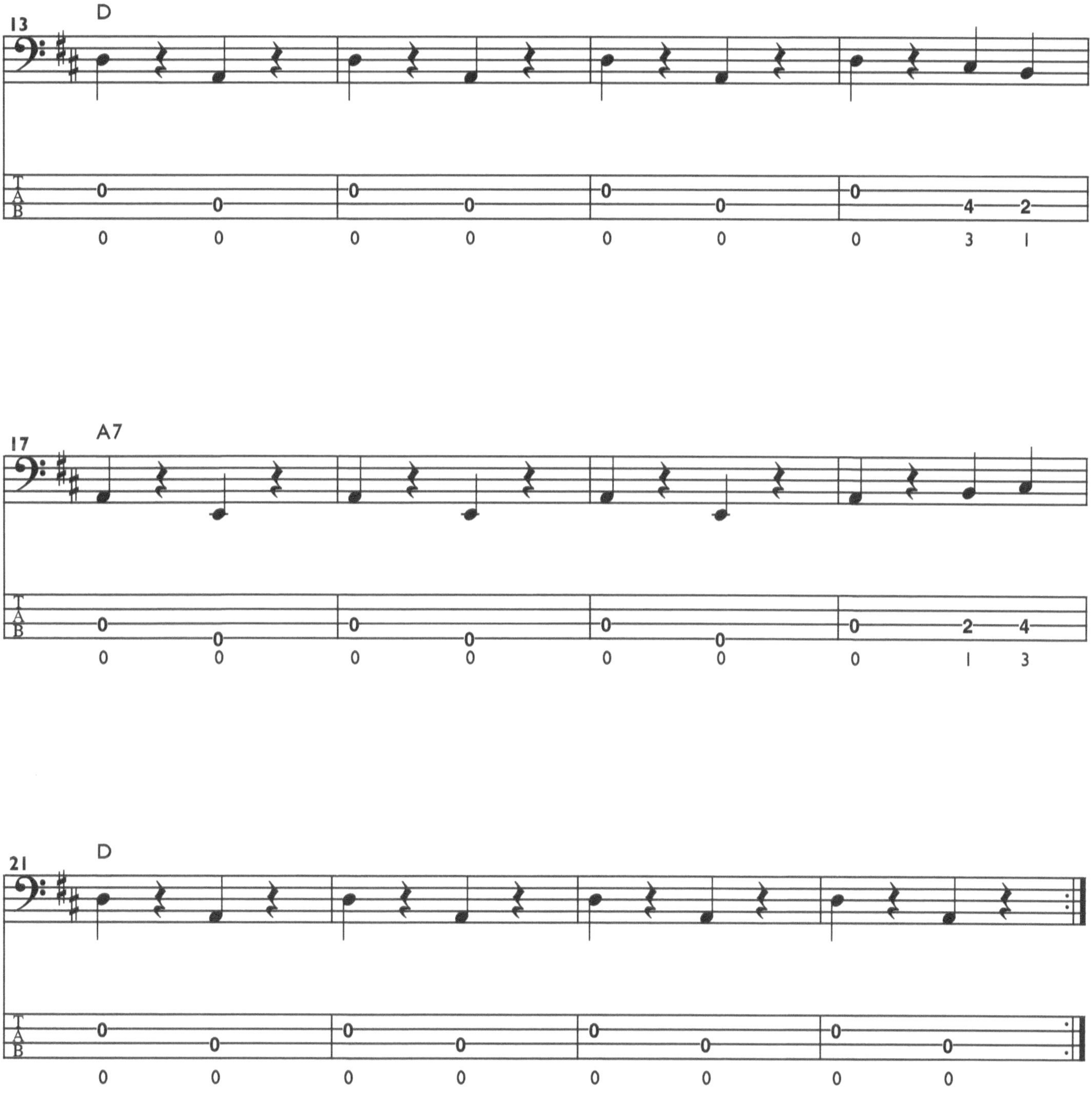
13
D
17
A7
21
D

In the Style of Herbert "Lum" York (with Hank Williams)

Hank Williams' influence on country music cannot be overstated. With his unique style of singing and playing, he was a true innovator of the style. Williams' bassist Herbert "Lum" York played strong and simple bass lines that gave Williams' music the foundation it needed. Following is a typical bass line in York's style.

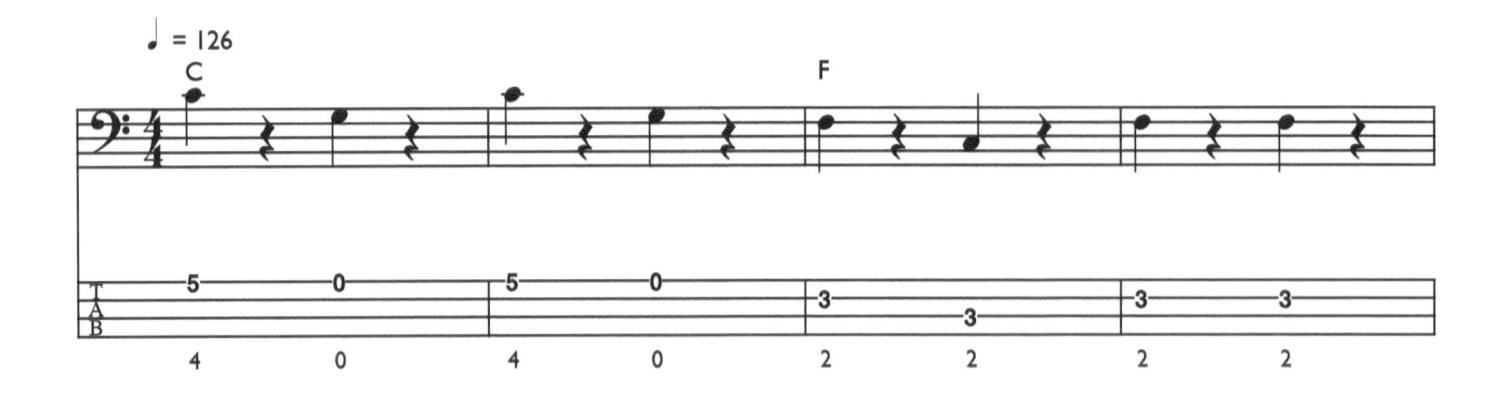

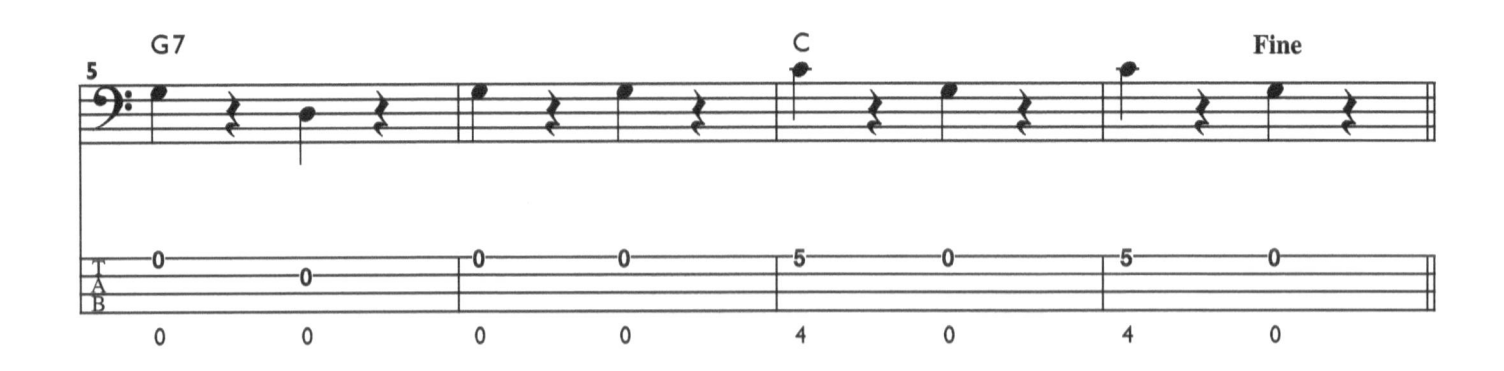

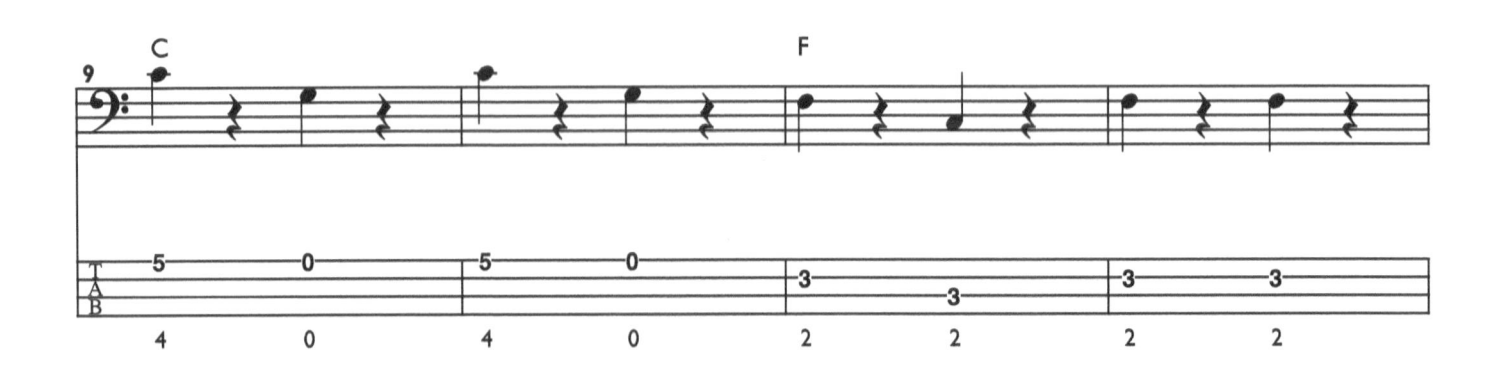

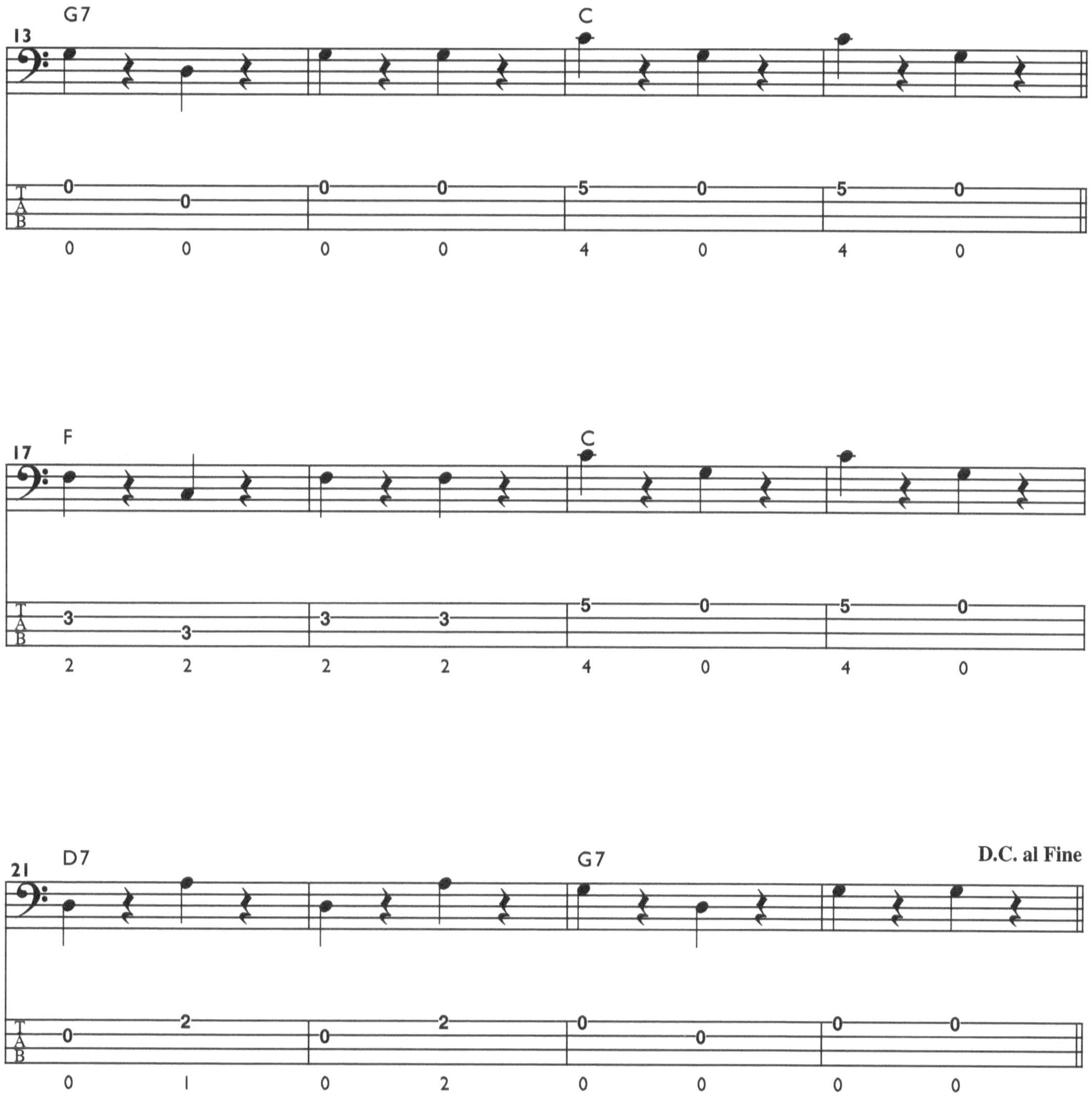
13
G7
C
17
F
C
21
D7
G7
D.C. al Fine

In the Style of Leon Rausch
(with Bob Wills and His Texas Playboys)

The unique Western swing style of Bob Wills and His Texas Playboys had a lasting influence on country and popular music and has been emulated by bands as diverse as Asleep at the Wheel and The Grateful Dead. During Wills' career, the band went through a number of bass players, but Leon Rausch, who was the Playboys' bassist and lead vocalist from 1958 to 1961, exemplified the Western swing bass style that was such an important part of the sound. Following is a bass line in his style.

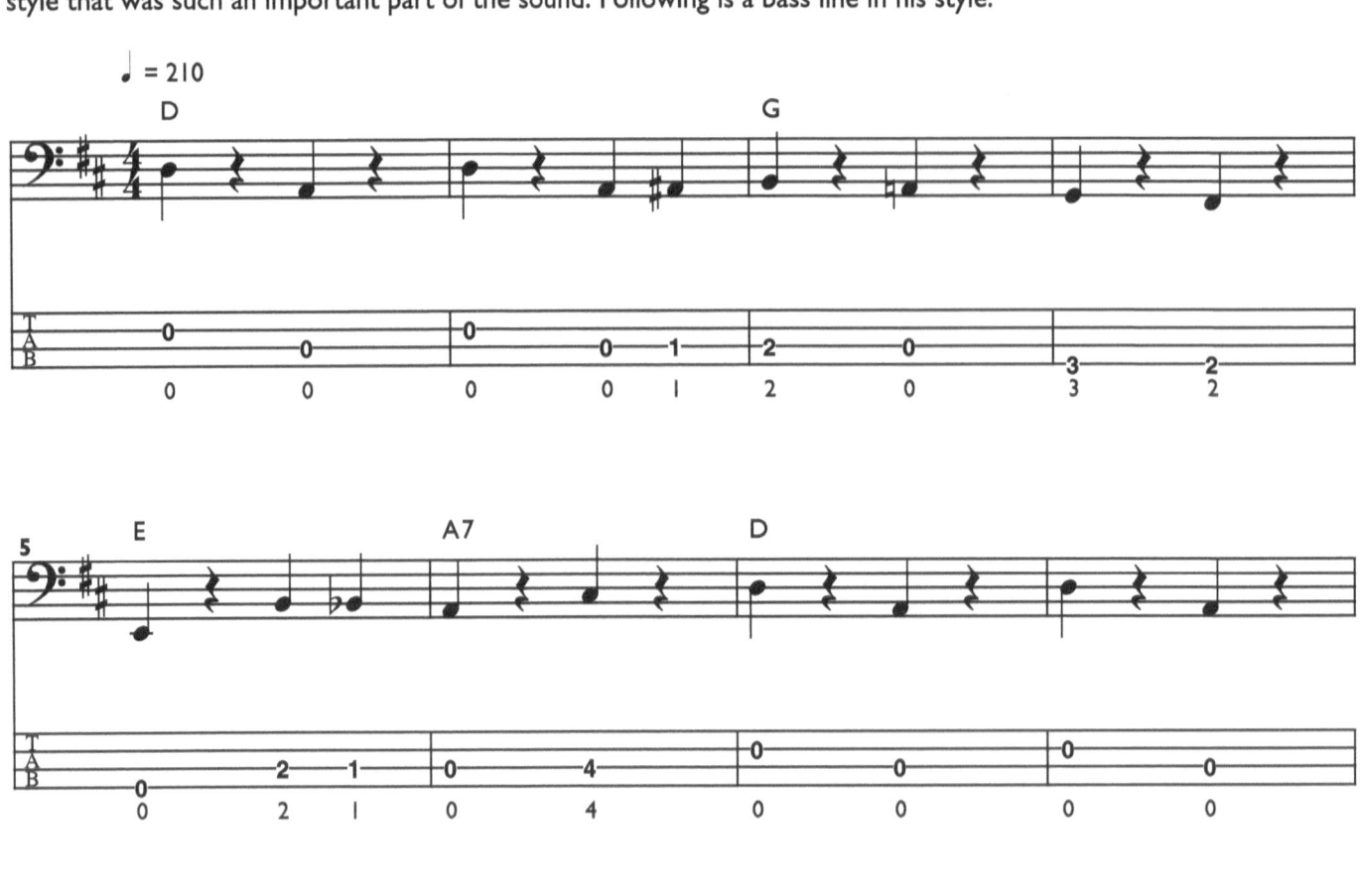

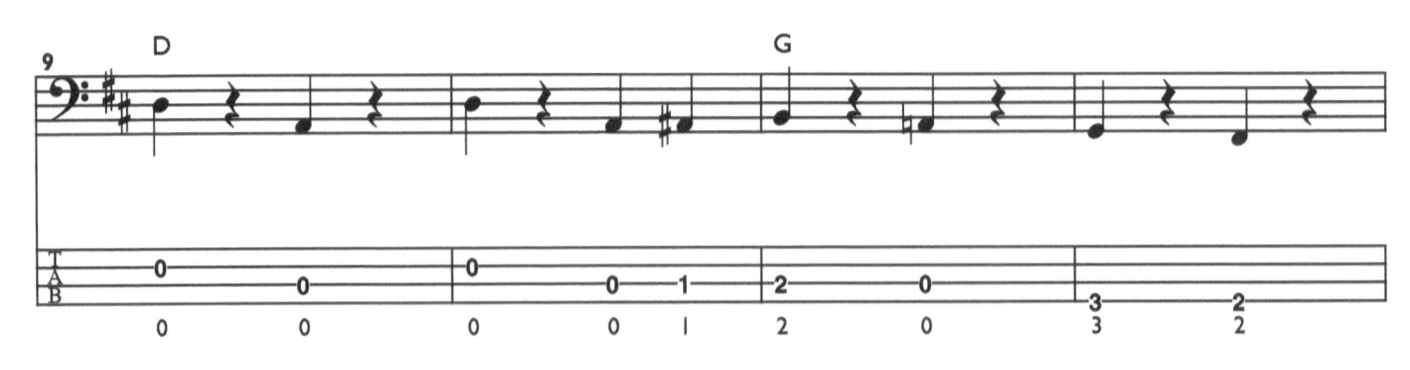

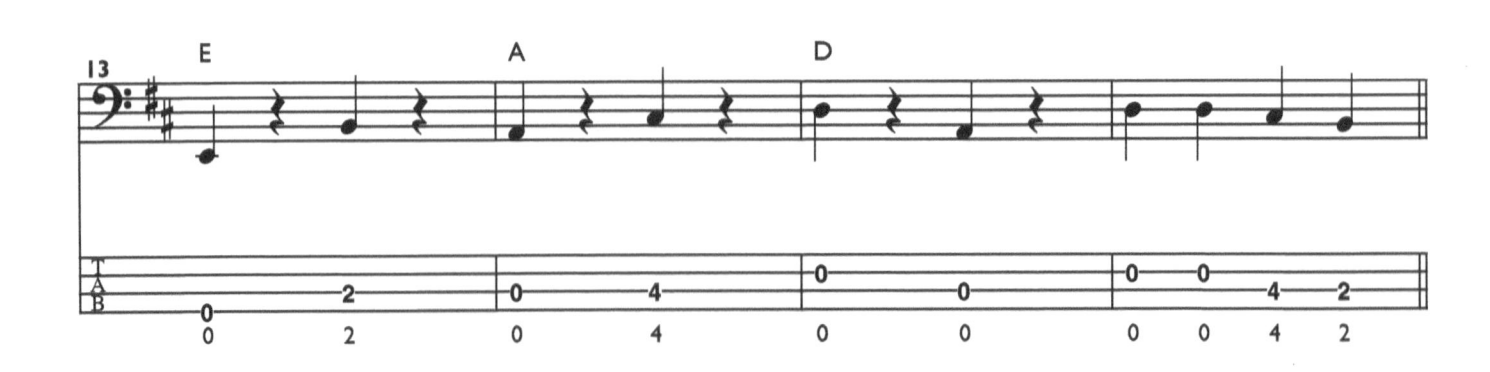

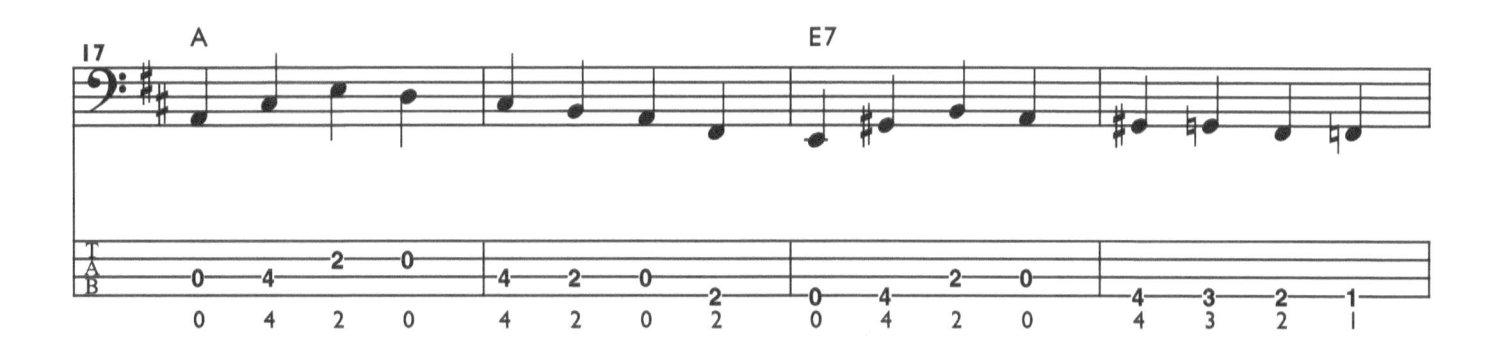

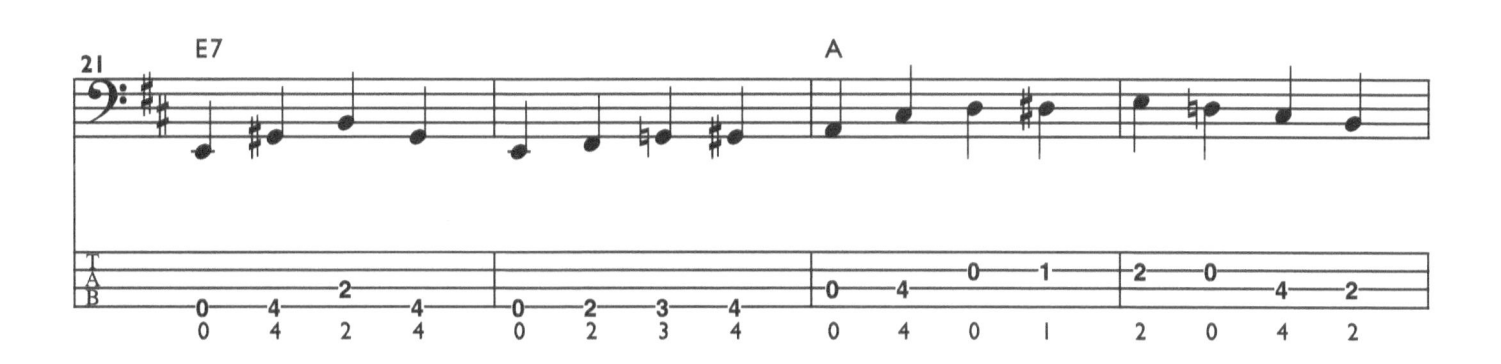

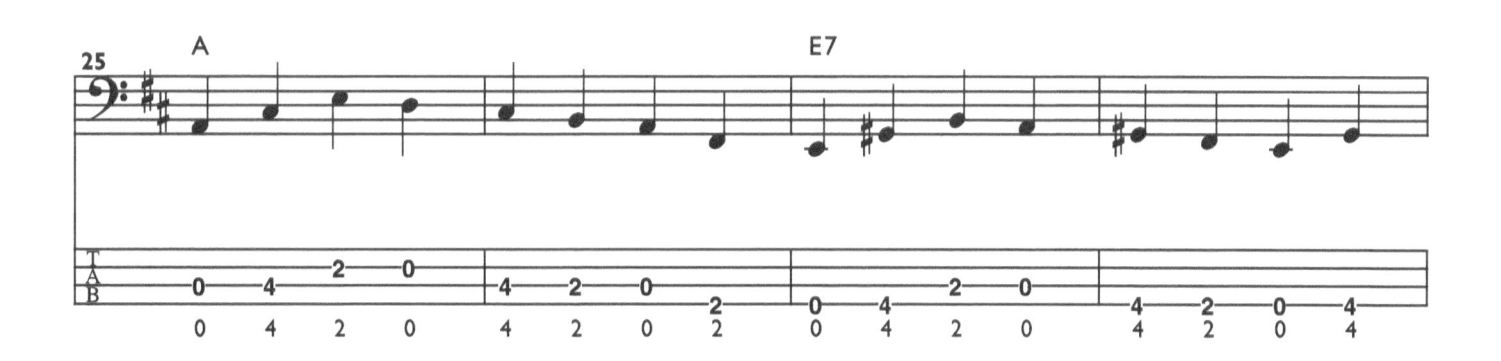

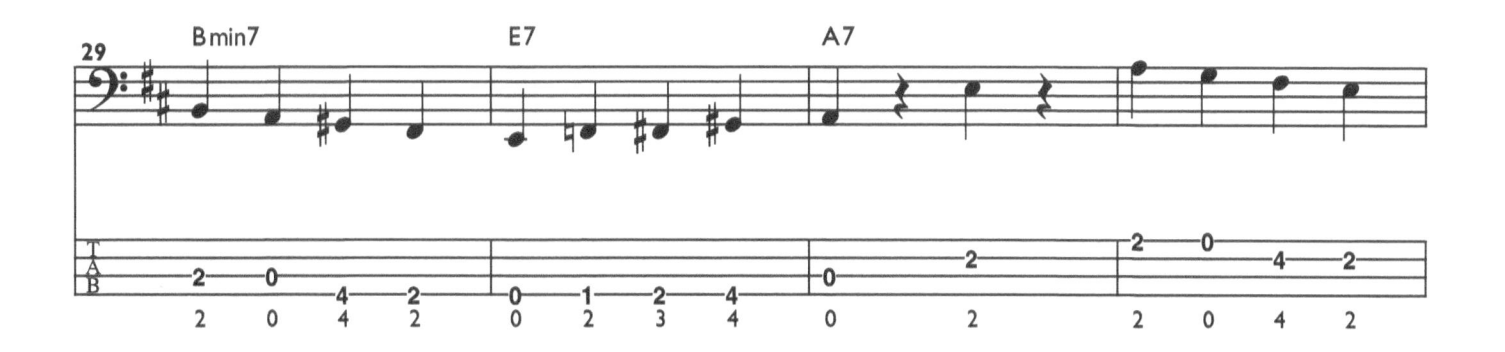

(Continued on next page)

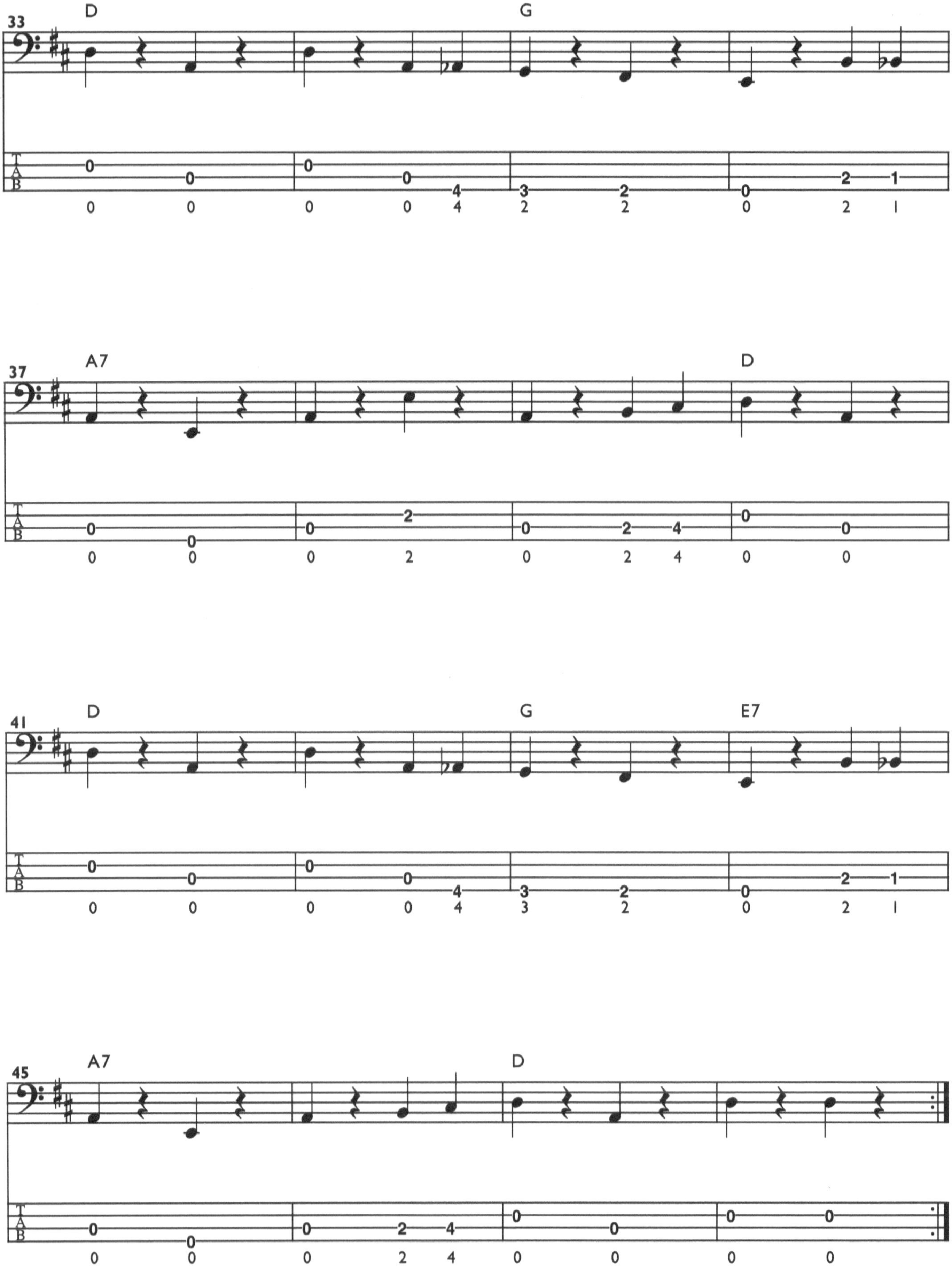
33
D
G
37
A7
D
41
D
G
E7
45
A7
D

Conclusion

By playing through this book, you have experienced a wide variety of musical styles and approaches to bass playing. You have been exposed to many different sounds and techniques, as well as key players in the various styles. However, while every attempt has been made to cover the most important and influential styles and players, it is impossible to cover them all. That's where you come in. Keep your eyes and ears open. Actively seek out new music and musicians. Go out to hear live music at every opportunity. While bass lessons are an enormous aid in learning to play, and books like this are an important part of a well-rounded musical education, there is no substitute for live music. Play at every opportunity, preferably with musicians who are better than you! Teachers, authors, and colleagues can impart a great deal of information, but hearing a great musician play live just once can change your musical life forever. You can read or hear about Jack Bruce or Baikithi Kumalo, or better still, you can listen to their recordings, but hearing them play live is a very different thing. Music is about human communication, and the communication possible in just one note is infinite. A great musician tells us things that can never be expressed with words and that is what compels us to play. So, while it is hoped that this encyclopedia has been, and will be, a welcome addition to your library, let it be a springboard to send you out into the wonderful world of bass playing and music making.